THE NEXT STEP

Next Level Leadership Network exists to discover, strengthen, and serve ministry teams and leaders. The leadership principles and practices delivered by Next Level Leadership Network are Biblically-based and powerfully practical. Each leadership workshop utilizes hands-on learning tools, multimedia presentations and interactive exercises that stimulate learning and application.

The Next Step is published in conjunction with Next Level Leadership Network.

Next Level Leadership Network is honored to be a part of *The Next Step*. We believe our ministry relationship with Bob Sorrell and The Associate, Inc. will enable us to better achieve our God-given mission to serve and equip His leaders and His teams.

Mastering the Mystery of Visionary Leadership is a leadership workshop that introduces the seven steps of ministry planning described in *The Next Step*, as well as going deeper in the first step, "The Captain's Compass." Our network of workshop facilitators can deliver this high impact workshop throughout North America.

If you desire to discover or refresh God's vision for your personal life and ministry life, the principles and processes in this workshop will assist you starting your journey down the seven step plan. We would greatly value the opportunity to serve and assist you in your leadership journey to the next level.

For further information on *Mastering the Mystery of Visionary Leadership* workshops, contact:

Next Level Leadership Network
4200 North Point Parkway
Alpharetta, Georgia 30022-4176

1-888-253-2823
www.nextlevelleadership.com

THE NEXT STEP

A Seven-Step Planning Process to
Help Fulfill Your God-Given Vision

BOB SORRELL

with Patrick Springle

For more information about The Associate's consulting services, contact:
Robert L. Sorrell, President
The Associate, Inc.
7831 Woodlark Cove
Cordova, TN 38018
bsorrell@theassociate.org
www.theassociate.org

Formatted by Anne McLaughlin, Blue Lake Design, Dickinson, Texas
Cover design by John Gilmore, Houston, Texas
Edited by Stan Campbell, Woodridge, Illinois
Photos by Michael Cowey, Houston, Texas
Boot painting by Perfect Design, Friendswood, Texas

TABLE OF CONTENTS

Acknowledgements 8
Foreword 9
Preface 11

INTRODUCTION *The Trail Ahead* 15
   Integrity and Skills 16
   Common Questions 17
   Principles, Practices, and Processes 18
   To Plan or Not to Plan 21
   Managing Change 22
   You Can Expect 24
   What Kinds of Churches Can Use These Principles? . . 26
   Take a Step 27

STEP 1 *The Captain's Compass* 31
   A Vision Is Vicarious 32
   A Vision Has Value 33
   A Vision Has Virtue 33
   The Phases of a Vision 34
   Your Personal Vision 39
   Take a Step 49
   Your Ministry Vision 55
   God's Calling 57
   A Philosophy of Leadership 70
   The Three-Fold Function of the Office of Pastor 72
   The Three-Fold Formula for Orderly
      Programming 78
   The Three-Fold Framework for Operational
      Planning 81
   A Ministry Vision Statement 82
   Take a Step 82

STEP 2 *Look at the Map* 105
   Planning to Plan 105
   Determine Your Ministry Philosophy 109
   The Necessity of Leadership Development 110
   An Atmosphere of Faith 112
   Discernment and Prayer 113
   The Scriptures and Planning 113
   Your Church's Vision Statement 115

A Closer Look 116
The Leadership and Its Structure. 117
The Budget and Its Struggle. 125
The Deacons and Their Service 127
The Administration and Its Stability 128
The Church and Its Size 129
Take a Step 130

STEP 3 *Watch for Obstacles and Opportunities* 167
It's All in How You Look at It 167
Review Leadership Assignments, Job Descriptions,
    and Work Practices 169
Review the Growth History of Your Church 170
Research Your Community's Demographics 171
Examine Space Utilization 172
Take a Step 173

STEP 4 *Get Your Equipment Ready* 207
Strategy and Structure 207
Develop a Leadership Position Manual 210
Develop a Leadership Accountability Structure. 211
When to Hire Staff 212
Develop a Communication System 215
Take a Step 217

STEP 5 *Plot Your Course* 235
The Three-Fold Framework for Operational
    Planning 235
The Ministry Plan 237
The Master Calendar 241
The Financial Plan. 241
Where the Rubber Meets the Road 242
Finalize Your Plan 243
Prepare Your Presentation 244
In Summary 246
Take a Step 247

STEP 6 *Look Over the Next Hill* 267
Building a Team for the Future 267
The Long-Range Ministry Plan 268
Project Strategic Growth. 269
Project Space Requirements 269
New Construction. 270
The Long-Range Financial Plan. 271
Presenting the Long-Range Plan to the Church 271
Take a Step 272

STEP 7 *Get on the Trail* 297
    The Leader's Personality and the Process
        of Change 297
    Common Responses to Change 298
    Stay on Track: The Habit of Planning 300
    Issues and Answers. 301
    Affirmation and Celebration 306
    Take a Step. 307

Resources from The Associate, Inc. 312
About the Author 315

ACKNOWLEDGEMENTS

I want to thank Pat Springle and Baxter Press for bringing this work to a reality. Pat's godly character has been an inspiration to me personally, and his gifting has brought both order and creativity to some concepts not easily presented outside a seminar setting.

My life and many of my thought processes have been profoundly influenced by Dr. Adrian Rogers. Most of what I have learned about the Word of God has been through his preaching. The application of business and leadership principles from a biblical perspective has been refined during my 27 years of lay and staff association with this great man of God. To have had this relationship is indeed a gift from God.

The great staff and lay team at Bellevue Baptist Church have contributed in many ways to my life and ministry. I was called by God from their midst when I was a layman, and the benefits of my association with them cannot be measured this side of heaven.

Dr. Stephen Olford is one of my heroes. I am greatly enjoying my service and ministry with Olford Ministries International while continuing to learn from a man so mightily used by God for so many years.

Thank you, Bobby Lewis, for your significant help over the past months, and thank you, Gina Smith, for the screening and coordinating so many details.

Finally, to my family, I want to say a profound "Thank you" for your patience and encouragement. This past year has required much travel, many seminars, and several associations with some great churches in proving the principles in this book. We did well in protecting our time, but it was still a sacrifice. Thank you, Buna, for 41 wonderful years of marriage. You are a joy! Thank you, LeAnn, for being all that I could ever want in a daughter. Thank you, Mark, being a man of God and for loving my daughter. Thank you, Joshua and Joseph, for making our family complete. You're the greatest! Thank all of you for loving our Lord Jesus.

FOREWORD

During my years as a pastor, I have noticed that many of the problems churches encounter are rooted in difficulties with management, not doctrine or morality. A clouded vision, poor delegation, and faulty communication create confusion between the pastor and his people. Satan, the enemy of our souls and of God's purposes in the church, delights in the confusion and conflict brought about by poor management.

One of the most powerful metaphors about the church is that it is "the body of Christ." The human body is wonderfully organized in order to function properly. The same is true of God's church. Sometimes I want to smile when I hear someone say that he doesn't "believe in the organized church." I wonder what kind he believes in . . . a disorganized church? The apostle Paul instructed the church in Corinth that everything is to "be done decently and in order" (I Corinthians 14:40). And when Jesus performed the miracle of feeding 5000 with a lad's lunch, he had them sit in groups of 50. Even in the middle of a miracle, Jesus wanted things organized and managed properly.

The principles and processes in this book are both simple and profound. They are clearly explained, and they are illustrated so that every church can implement them. They focus first on the Lord Himself and the vision He gives the pastor for his flock. Out of the riches of that vision, God directs the pastor to gather important information and garner the support of key leaders to make the vision a reality by the power of God's Spirit. The planning process you will find in these pages is not dry at all. It is full of the richness of an intimate relationship with God and His leading as we trust Him to give us wisdom to set clear goals, equip the saints for the work of service, and take the steps of faith to accomplish His purposes.

I'm pleased to recommend this book because of the content, but I'm even more eager to recommend it because of the character of its author. My friend Bob Sorrell is a uniquely gifted man and is remarkably able to teach management skills. The principles in these pages are not just theory to Bob. He practices them diligently. God has graced him with uncommon wisdom, and he has the ability to provide insightful and practical suggestions at each stage of the planning journey.

It has been my privilege to serve with Bob at Bellevue for some 20 years. During that time when Bob was my associate, our church experienced explosive and healthy growth—a remarkable combination.

Perhaps the best affirmation of a man's gifting is the lasting fruit of his ministry, and Bob's impact on our church continues to be seen day after day. He laid the tracks on which our ministry continues to run, and our body is still growing and happy as we follow Christ together. Of course, to God be the glory, but I would be remiss if I did not recognize the powerful leadership and clear planning principles Bob Sorrell has provided for our ministry.

Adrian Rogers, Senior Pastor
Bellevue Baptist Church
Memphis, Tennessee

PREFACE

I welcome the request of my good friend, the Reverend Bob Sorrell, to write this brief preface to his book, The Next Step. I do so for two reasons. First, I highly esteem my brother for his life and accomplishments as Associate Pastor for twenty years to Dr. Adrian Rogers at Bellevue Baptist Church, Cordova, Tennessee. Second, this book is the fulfillment of the hope that I have treasured for years that someone who had proved himself in ministry would write out the lessons learned for the guidance and enrichment of others.

It is my conviction that a course on pastoral administration should be a "must" in all our pastoral training in the seminaries of our land; but I have yet to see a published work on the subject.

The seven steps delineated in this book follow a sequence that enables the senior pastor to give himself more fully " to prayer and to the ministry of the Word" (Acts 6:4) by organizing his leadership to effectively carry on the programs of the church. The principles here outlined can be applied to any size church and the many denominations that make up the body of Christ.

My main contribution in this preface, however, is to highlight the office and ministry of the associate pastor because of the leadership perspective that it offers. You will notice that this book is offered by The Associate, Inc.! I like that! No leader, pastor, or CEO can function to the fullest without a loyal and competent associate. Even if the associate is a volunteer layman, a senior pastor, under God, must have his Joshua, as Moses did; his John, as Jesus did; his Timothy, as Paul did.

In Philippians 3:20, Paul the apostle refers to Timothy as "a man my equal" or "an equal soul." By choosing to use this Greek word, Paul makes clear to the saints at Philippi that whatever Timothy had to say or do—during his mission to that local church —reflected with accuracy Paul's heart and mind. This is what an ASSOCIATE is all about. He is a person who sees the vision, shares the passion, and serves the mission of his pastor, and then faithfully "fleshes" this out to the leaders and members of the body. Every thinking member of the local church will ask, at one time or another, "What is THE NEXT STEP?" The true associate is the voice that affirms the pastors direction and confidently states can confidently states, "This is the way; walk in it."

I pray that this workbook will be greatly used to the glory of God. Thank you, Bob, for a job well done!

Stephen F. Olford, Founder and Senior Lecturer,
The Stephen Olford Center for Biblical Preaching
Memphis, Tennessee

STEP 1 *The Captain's Compass*

- Your Personal Vision
- Your Ministry Vision

STEP 2 *Look at the Map*
- Your Plan for Planning
- Ministry Review
- Planning Team Evaluation

STEP 3 *Watch for Obstacles and Opportunities*
- Task Summaries
- Job Descriptions
- Historical Growth Statistics—Bible Study
- Historical Growth Statistics—General Church Criteria
- Community Demographics
- Obstacles and Opportunities
- Space Utilization

STEP 4 *Get Your Equipment Ready*
- Ministry Flow Chart
- Organizational Chart
- Communication System

STEP 5 *Plot Your Course*
- Ministry Leader Planning Worksheet
- The Ministry Plan
- The Master Calendar
- The Financial Plan
- Communication Plan

STEP 6 *Look Over the Next Hill*
- Long-Range Ministry Plan
- Growth and Capacity Analysis
- Growth Projections
- General Church Criteria
- Building Plan Schedule and Expenditures
- Long-Range Financial Plan

STEP 7 *Get on the Trail*
- Monthly Planning Worksheet

THE TRAIL AHEAD

The phone rang, and a pastor I had met at a conference a few weeks earlier poured out his frustrations to me. After a few minutes, he exclaimed, "Bob, I'm about to pull my hair out—and I don't have much left to spare!" As we talked, I learned that he had been at his church for about two-and-a-half years. During that time, the church had almost doubled in size, from 325 to almost 600. He was grateful for God's blessings, but he felt more exasperation than joy. He tried to frame it as positively as possible. This man of God certainly is not a whiner. He told me, "We've seen some wonderful things happen at our church. God has blessed us. I've enjoyed preparing my sermons, and they are well-received. We have changed our music from only traditional hymns to a blend of hymns and contemporary music, and many young families have joined our church. Our youth program is doing really well. Bible study is growing, and we have a lot of people who have attended our classes on spiritual gifts."

The strained, tired tone of his voice, however, didn't match his words about growth and blessing. Hoping to draw him out, I remarked, "It sounds like you are right where God wants you to be."

He shot back, "I sure hope not! I've never been so frustrated in all my life. The more our ministry grows, the more conflict we experience. The people who were 100 percent for me at the beginning now are dragging their feet. And some are doing more than that. They are accusing me of all kinds of things. My associate was here when the previous pastor left. We got along wonderfully well . . . until lately. I've asked him to help with the administrative load because of all the growth, but he said he doesn't feel called to that part of the ministry. I'm working harder than ever, and the joy has gone out of the ministry for me." He paused for a moment, then asked, "Bob, will you help me figure out what's going on at my church? I really need some help."

"I'm working harder than ever, and the joy has gone out of the ministry for me."

This dear brother is like many others I've talked to over the past 20 years: They have a genuine calling and passion for serving Christ, but for some reason they are bogged down. It has been my great privilege and joy to help these men, to give them some insights about vision and planning, and to watch them step out of the mire and onto the firm ground of purpose and fulfillment.

INTEGRITY AND SKILLS

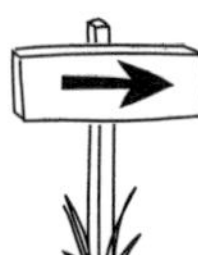

Planning is far more than a fill-in-the-blanks simple process. It must be rooted in a genuine vision, the kind that comes only from God Himself, and one that sustains us through the dry and difficult times that inevitably come to all spiritual leaders.

I had the privilege of serving as the Executive/Associate Pastor at Bellevue Baptist Church in Memphis under Dr. Adrian Rogers for 21 years. God used him and my lay and staff associates during those great years to shape my perspectives and sharpen my own vision. I was known there for helping to develop our planning systems, but planning is far more than a fill-in-the-blanks simple process. It must be rooted in a genuine vision, the kind that comes only from God Himself, and one that sustains us through the dry and difficult times that inevitably come to all spiritual leaders. Our planning processes, then, are more about God than they are about us. As we understand His heart and follow His ways, we will accomplish His purposes. We will get excited about the right things, foremost among them, the advancement of the Kingdom of God instead of our own success and prestige. And we will stand strong for those things that God cares about: reaching the lost, upholding the Word of God, and seeing God produce righteous people in a sinful generation. Good planning keeps us focused on the things that really matter and prevents us from getting stuck spending too much time on other things.

We learn a lot by looking at the life and leadership of King David. He was an incredible leader of men. He inspired his "Mighty Men" (II Samuel 23:8) with his words and his deeds, and they followed him anywhere. I believe the source of his strength was in those many lonely hours he tended sheep as a boy. There, he touched the heart of God, and he gained God's perspective on his life. When the time was right, God thrust David into the crucible of service, and the young man was ready. His courage to fight Goliath, then Saul's armies, then other armies was honed in time alone with God. Another psalmist recounted David's exploits in Psalm 78. At the end of that psalm, he explained the dual nature of David's powerful leadership:

"He chose David His servant
and took him from the sheep pens;

from tending the sheep He brought him
to be the shepherd of His people Jacob,
of Israel His inheritance.
And David shepherded them with
integrity of heart;
with skillful hands he led them" (Psalm 78:71-72).

Integrity of heart and skillful hands: Those are the chief requirements of spiritual leaders. One without the other is not enough. Christian history is littered with the tragic stories of men who were skillful in gathering thousands of men and women to follow them, but the absence of integrity led them to self-indulgence and ruin. On the other hand, we seldom hear much about the good-natured people who have personal integrity but haven't honed the skills necessary for leadership. Their stories are lost in the abyss of small visions and less-than-effective service. My heart's desire is that those who read this book will come away with a strong passion for Christ and skills to help them be the best spiritual leaders they can possibly be. Not just one. Both. Integrity of heart and skillful hands.

In my years at Bellevue and as I have traveled across the country assisting pastors and their leadership plan more effectively, I have noticed that a few questions surface time and time again. Many pastors struggle with issues such as clarifying their call, finding a ministry pattern that maximizes their strengths, delegating well, handling finances, and scheduling events and programs. Some of the most common questions I hear are:

— "We grew a lot for a while, but we've plateaued at about 500. What will get us unstuck?"
— "My staff member and I argue about things all the time, and I'm afraid that tension is spilling over to other leaders in our church. I want to have a terrific team, but we're a long way from that. What can I do to remedy the situation and build unity?"
— "The joy has gone out of my ministry. I feel so much stress: my wife, my kids, my finances, preparing sermons, visiting all the people who want me to come see them, meeting the expectations of my deacons. . . . Will I ever enjoy serving God again?"

Integrity of heart and skillful hands: Those are the chief requirements of spiritual leaders.

My heart's desire is that those who read this book will come away with a strong passion for Christ and skills to help them be the best spiritual leaders they can possibly be.

COMMON QUESTIONS

— "We have grown tremendously over the past five years, and we need a new worship center. How do you build a building without it consuming all your time?"

— "I feel like this is a one-man show. I am doing all I can do, but I seem to fall further behind every day. Can you help me figure out what's wrong?"

— "There's a lot of tension between the deacon body and me. When I came here, they told me they'd handle the running of the church. They wanted me to focus just on preaching. But I don't see that kind of dichotomy in spiritual leadership. I believe God has called me to be the leader of *all* of our church, not just the preaching. How can I resolve this conflict with the deacons?"

— "Our church struggles with money all the time. Some of the lay leaders want to move forward and do some things that will bring in more people, but others don't want to spend a dime unless we're sure we already have it in the bank. What's the right balance between vision and caution?"

— "A lot of young couples have been coming since we started singing choruses instead of hymns, but if we don't change back, we're going to have a revolt among the older members—and they're the ones who write the checks! How can we satisfy the older folks and still reach the younger generation?"

Do any of these questions sound familiar? All of these, and many others, are addressed in this book. I trust God will give you the insight, encouragement, and steps to answer the questions that apply to your situation.

PRINCIPLES, PRACTICES, AND PROCESSES

A pastor called me to ask for help. He was frustrated . . . so frustrated, in fact, that he was thinking about leaving the ministry. Over several years, tension had built up in his church. He explained, "My people just don't want to follow me." As I met with him and with some of his leaders, a clearer picture emerged. It was true that many of the people in his church were reluctant to follow him, but in truth, this pastor wasn't giving them clear direction. They were just as frustrated as he was!

Tremendous tension had grown between the pastor and two groups in the church: the finance committee and the personnel committee. The pastor and the personnel committee saw the need for a new staff member to shoulder the growing burdens of the ministry, but the finance committee said "no" because they didn't have the money in the budget. The pastor tried to argue for them to see his logic and make alterations in the allocations, but the finance committee refused to budge. Unresolved conflict caused hurt feelings and resentment, and the tensions among these groups—and among the individuals—grew. The pastor was caught in the middle of this power struggle, but he failed to communicate a vision strongly and clearly enough, and he failed to assume his God-given role of leadership. In this vacuum, each committee leader had his own agenda. Instead of working together under the direction of the pastor, each one demanded control of the situation.

I met with him and his leaders for a vision-casting exercise to identify where God was at work changing lives. We also exposed some areas where things needed to improve. Open communication helped each person voice his hopes and frustrations, and with this honesty, we could make decisions to move ahead. This exercise also showed us who the *real* leaders were among the men in leadership *positions* in his church. These were the men who had a real following in the church, not just words and ideas. Our discussions provided an honest and objective look at the situation for this pastor, and he took that information to heart. He spent time with God to gain a new sense of vision, and the Lord gave him a fresh sense of purpose.

Almost as soon as this pastor's sense of direction was clarified, his people gladly responded in following him. Tensions on both sides were replaced with thankfulness, zeal, and joy in ministry. His thoughts were transformed from "How can I get out of this mess?" to "How can we enjoy the Lord and serve Him more effectively?" His discouragement was transformed into excitement.

As I have taught this material to pastors across the country, in many denominations and in churches of all sizes, some have asked me, "What is the specific ministry philosophy you are teaching?" These pastors are actually asking, "Are you sure these principles apply to me and my church?"

The insights and steps of implementation found in *The Next Step* are not based on any particular ministry philosophy. These principles are focused on getting your vision from God and implementing sound principles of analysis and planning, so they apply to every denomination, every ministry philosophy, and every size church. We will focus our attention on those churches of 300 to 1500, but these same principles are effective with church plants and mega-churches. We will

In this vacuum, each committee leader had his own agenda. Instead of working together under the direction of the pastor, each one demanded control of the situation.

Tensions on both sides were replaced with thankfulness, zeal, and joy in ministry.

examine both biblical and common-sense principles of planning, we will give examples of specific practices you can use at your church, and we will outline the clear processes of getting from where you are to where God wants you and your church to go in the future.

Some of you are naturally gifted in planning. Out of the strengths of your personality, training, and experience, you have developed the skills of analysis, planning, and implementation. For you, I trust God will use these pages to encourage you and give you some tools and techniques to use with your church leadership so you can "excel still more."

Many pastors, however, know they should plan more effectively but simply don't know how. They didn't learn how to plan in seminary. As pastors, they focus their time and energy on their preparations for preaching, and they let traditional church programming continue the way it has in the past. They give little attention to leadership development with a vision for the future. Some pastors avoid planning because they are afraid a thorough analysis will uncover simmering tensions and create unnecessary conflict among staff or between staff and lay leaders. If you haven't been a good planner, I hope the principles in this book help you get your vision for ministry from God, and then provide clear tracks on which to run. In the end, you will have a clear plan that outlines specific steps toward accomplishing God's purposes for your life and your church.

This book begins with our calling, our vision from God for our own lives and our ministries. Then, we do a careful analysis of our current situation. We can't move forward until we know exactly where we are. From that analysis, we can continue to gather information and resources, and we carefully construct our plan. At that point, the real work of implementation begins, and God will work in and through us to accomplish His will.

There is no exact template for a finished plan. Some of you will want to spell out the details, but others will paint the vision in broader brush strokes. Your plan will probably be between five and twenty pages, including a vision statement, an organizational chart, clear goals for each aspect of your ministry, and a summary schedule and budget for each segment. I encourage you to put this plan in a very attractive format to present to your church. But your plan is not just words on a piece of paper or images on PowerPoint. It is a gripping vision of what God wants to do in and through you, no matter what the obstacles, no matter what the cost, for His glory and honor.

As I have talked to hundreds of pastors from across the country about the planning process, on rare occasions I have sensed reluctance to the use of what they call a "business model for ministry." Their assumption is that this model is inappropriate for the church. My conviction, however, is that all good business principles are biblical principles. These principles are relational in nature, and the Bible is the ultimate authority on relationships. Good planning processes equip people to find common purposes and work together to accomplish them. That is true in business, in the church, in families, and in every other group of people.

A few other pastors have expressed quite different concerns about planning. Some have said, "Planning is limiting God." Others have remarked, "I want to be free to be responsive to God however and whenever He leads." And still others have told me, "I feel straight-jacketed when I plan. I want to feel the Spirit's leading and not be tied to a fixed, rigid plan." That comment certainly sounds spiritual, but I believe it shrouds a lazy approach to seeking God's best. Both the heart and the head are consecrated to God, and both are essential to good planning in order to accomplish His will.

I certainly don't want anybody to be so tied to a man-made plan that he misses out on God's best, but good planning first and foremost puts us in touch with the heart of God and compels us to listen carefully to Him so we will discern and follow His path. We aren't omniscient, so we need to keep our hearts open to God's leading so we can discern the direction He charts for us and make any necessary mid-course corrections.

The criticism of planning for the church is valid if it is only a sterile approach to goal-setting. Our goal, however, is the practical implementation of a God-given vision. Throughout the Scriptures, we see men of God carefully listening to God and to input from others. With careful analysis, they made plans and took bold steps of faith. The list of accomplishments of the men and women of faith in Hebrews 11 is, in many cases, a testimony of the effectiveness of their God-focused planning. Paul's plans for his missionary journeys were based on understanding God's heart to seek and save the lost in every land. At each point, he prayed and sought God's guidance. He had a plan, but he was open to God's leading and often changed course based on the Lord's

Good planning processes equip people to find common purposes and work together to accomplish them. That is true in business, in the church, in families, and in every other group of people.

direction. His experience is a model for you and me as we find the balance of planning and flexibility.

MANAGING CHANGE

Good planning is essential if we are to implement change which accomplishes God's purposes in a way that builds up, instead of frustrating, those who are involved.

Some of us thrive on change; others avoid it at all costs. Most of us, however, acknowledge the necessity of changing direction, methods, programs, and leadership when the situation calls for it. If we see this time of change as a opportunity, we will be energized. If, however, we feel threatened by the confusion and disagreements or lose patience, that process will be very difficult (if we proceed at all). Good planning is essential if we are to implement change which accomplishes God's purposes in a way that builds up, instead of frustrating, those who are involved.

As you begin reading this book, open your heart to the Lord's guidance. Tradition may be a strong part of your church's way of operating, and you may be one of those who is threatened by change, but open your heart to the Spirit of God and let Him guide you. Of course, tradition can be very meaningful and provide continuity and stability to a ministry, but it shouldn't be allowed to limit creativity and vision for the future. Ask the Lord for a fresh perspective of your own life and your church's ministry in your community. At the beginning, be as creative as possible. Then, as your plan slowly develops, you can ask the more pragmatic questions about how this vision can be implemented in your specific situation.

Every organization, including your local church, has a culture. Your culture is defined by your tradition, methodology, theology, and people. Your church has a system for doing business and addressing change. It is impossible to cover all the differences in denominational and organizational polity in a book like this, so the people you choose to assist in the planning process must be knowledgeable about how your organization works, what forms are negotiable and what forms are non-negotiable. Your team of planners must be ready and willing to work with your unique organizational heritage in mind.

Let me offer some practical helps for leading and implementing change in your church. We will look at each of these in more detail later in this book, but for now, I want you to have a taste of our operating principles.

Leading the Process of Change

1. Know yourself. Discern what your spiritual gifts are and what they are not. Identify your passions in ministry and be able to articulate them. Understand your personality type and be aware of how your "style" is perceived by others. Be ready to communicate your vision with clarity and passion.

2. Know your people. Have an objective understanding of your church's groups, personalities, gifts, passion for ministry, resources and opportunities.

3. Make prayer and the constant seeking of God's will a priority in your life and in the life of the church you serve.

4. Share your vision with key leaders who are the opinion-makers and influencers in the church. Don't surprise your leaders by communicating new directions and plans in a congregational meeting without their understanding and input. You need them as allies.

5. Always keep in mind that your church has a history, and with history comes tradition. That tradition can be an asset to be used effectively or a liability which hinders progress. Your perspective will make a tremendous difference.

6. The planning process involves defining your vision, gathering information, implementing your plan, and making any necessary adjustments. Follow-up and follow-through are usually the toughest parts of accomplishing any plan. Be tenacious.

7. Don't threaten your people with change. Instead, expand their vision and provide attractive options that will substitute for the old ways they value. If people perceive they will lose a tradition dear to them, they will probably dig in their heels and resist you. Give them attractive new concepts, programs, and expectations which they can call their own.

8. Anticipate questions of why and how. Don't expect or demand people to follow you blindly. Value people who

ask hard questions, are thorough, and want to understand your heart and your reasoning for implementing change.

9. Be flexible. Timing is everything. Be willing to adjust your expectations and schedule as you see how your leadership responds to your ideas. Give them time to get on board.

10. Trust the Holy Spirit in others. Be open to new ideas and ministry from God's family, especially those on the planning team or those who have proven their trustworthiness and wisdom in recent years.

11. Choose your battles wisely. Some of the things churches fight over have no eternal value. Don't compromise truth, but while remaining relevant, be flexible with methodology.

12. When you come up against people resistant to change, build a wall of love around them, then follow your God-given vision. Love people into change. You can't afford to be perceived as a bully.

YOU CAN EXPECT . . .

At the end of this planning process, you will have three documents that comprise your plan:

— a ministry plan, which specifies the programs you will conduct;
— a financial plan, which includes your plan for providing resources as well as your budget for how you will spend them; and
— a master calendar, on which you will schedule events for maximum effectiveness.

Along the way, you will be involved in analysis of your leadership team, the effectiveness of your current programs, and how all your resources are being utilized. Research and reflection are essential preparation to be sure your plan is both bold and reasonable. After you prepare your yearly plan, I invite you to think about your long-range plans (see Step 6). Looking five to ten years into the future will give you insight, courage, and perspective about the decisions you need to make today.

Church planning is a dynamic spiritual exercise for you and your leadership team, not just a dry, fill-in-the-blank process to fill up pages in a planning notebook. If we are not in touch with God and if we don't trust His wisdom and capture His heart, then we will have missed the God-dimension of ministry. Our vision, as we will see in Step 1, comes from Him and is entirely about His glory. Church planning addresses issues concerning people and buildings and events, but it is focused on Christ and emanates from the vision He instills in us by His Spirit and through His Word.

The planning process can stimulate deep, rich communication among leaders. In some cases, planning provides the opportunity for our hearts to be communicated more clearly than any other way. In this process, we find out what excites and motivates each other. We find we are alike in our passion for Christ, but very different in how that passion may be expressed. If we work together toward a common goal, those differences become a powerful, positive force which shapes the body of Christ. Let the Lord bring people together during this process. As you patiently ask questions, listen intently, and ask follow-up questions to find out what's really in their hearts and minds. And use this time to see the Lord at work in each person. Affirm everyone for their desire to serve and honor Christ. I trust your team will grow stronger as a result of the rich conversations you enjoy as you plan. As Paul wrote to Timothy, "Now the purpose of the commandment is love from a pure heart, from a good conscience, and from unfeigned faith" (I Timothy 1:5). As God encourages each member of your team during the planning process, I hope you all experience love, from God and from each other, because your hearts are encouraged and purified, your consciences are strengthened by the integrity of your mission, and your faith is built as you trust God for more than ever before.

A term we often hear when we talk about pastors is that this man or that man is "burned out." We sometimes equate this term with overwork, thinking that burn-out is the product of doing too much, but I believe this is an inaccurate assessment. Burnout is primarily an emotional and spiritual problem, not the result of too much work. When a person is suffering through each day with a clouded purpose and conflicts over his leadership, the emotional and spiritual toll saps his energy and enthusiasm for his work. He feels physically exhausted. Some of us try to resolve this frustration by working harder and longer to earn others' approval, but no matter how much we work, we feel emotionally and spiritually dry, and we burn out. The solution is not just to schedule our time more efficiently (though that may help to some degree). Instead, we need a fresh word from God about who we are and about what He has called us to do. The solution

If we are not in touch with God and if we don't trust His wisdom and capture His heart, then we will have missed the God-dimension of ministry.

In this process, we find out what excites and motivates each other. We find we are alike in our passion for Christ, but very different in how that passion may be expressed.

The solution for burnout, then, is to experience the presence and purpose of God, allowing His power to accomplish His purposes.

for burnout, then, is to experience the presence and purpose of God, allowing His power to accomplish His purposes.

You may be opening this book because you have a specific question about a particular need in your ministry. Or you may be reading this book because your church is growing so fast that you need some help so you can keep up with God's pace of progress. Or perhaps you may be reading this book as a last resort. You may feel burned out. Your wife and kids are tired of you working so hard and coming home physically and emotionally exhausted, and you need some hope and help if you are to stay in God's service. Whatever your specific situation, this book offers:

— encouragement to hear God's clear call,
— principles to set reachable goals,
— administrative processes,
— principles of selection, delegation, and oversight,
— ideas to help you create a team spirit,
— specific practices to gather and process information,
— exercises with examples on virtually every topic, and
— the hope of genuine fulfillment as you see God work in your own life, your family, and your church.

Each chapter of this book describes and illustrates planning principles so you can accomplish what God has for you and your church. At the end of each chapter, you will find worksheets and exercises that will help you apply the principles in that chapter. In most cases, you will use these worksheets with your planning team, but some of them can also be used by your staff and ministry leaders to help them plan on a monthly or yearly basis. Each chapter includes some core exercises that you will need to work on before you go to the next one. In some chapters, a few additional exercises are included. You can use those if you have time or if you think they will help clarify your direction.

WHAT KIND OF CHURCHES CAN USE THESE PRINCIPLES?

What kinds? All sizes and in every state of health and growth. The concepts and processes in this book are not targeted for a particular type of church at all. They are designed to equip every pastor of every church—no matter what denomination, no matter how large or small the church may be.

These principles will help all kinds of churches:

— Bi-vocational churches can learn to build solid leadership so they can grow.
— Small churches can develop strategies to mobilize laity.
— Small churches can gain a genuine vision for growth and develop clear steps to fulfill that vision.
— Medium-sized churches which are stagnant or in transitional environments will gain new perspectives and skills.
— Medium-sized, growing churches need help in keeping up with the growth.
— Large churches which have plateaued can find new vision.
— Large churches that are seeing great growth will learn how to get their arms around all God is doing.
— Mega-churches that attract a lot of people but have a soft infrastructure can get the most out of their momentum and have a greater impact on individuals and their community.
— And every church and every pastor need a fresh sense of God's grace and purpose.

I hope God will nourish your soul and refine your skills as a leader as you work through these seven steps.

Using the following exercise, take a few minutes to pray and think about your needs and expectations before you begin the steps.

TAKE A STEP

BEFORE YOU BEGIN . . .

Before you go any farther, reflect on these questions and express your heart to the Lord.

1. What is the specific reason you wanted to read this book?

2. What are some of the questions you want answered?

3. Seek God about your hopes for what He will do in you and in your church as you work through the seven steps.

Dear Father, I hope . . .

STEP 1 *The Captain's Compass*
- **Your Personal Vision**
- **Your Ministry Vision**

STEP 2 *Look at the Map*
- Your Plan for Planning
- Ministry Review
- Planning Team Evaluation

STEP 3 *Watch for Obstacles and Opportunities*
- Task Summaries
- Job Descriptions
- Historical Growth Statistics—Bible Study
- Historical Growth Statistics—General Church Criteria
- Community Demographics
- Obstacles and Opportunities
- Space Utilization

STEP 4 *Get Your Equipment Ready*
- Ministry Flow Chart
- Organizational Chart
- Communication System

STEP 5 *Plot Your Course*
- Ministry Leader Planning Worksheet
- The Ministry Plan
- The Master Calendar
- The Financial Plan
- Communication Plan

STEP 6 *Look Over the Next Hill*
- Long-Range Ministry Plan
- Growth and Capacity Analysis
- Growth Projections
- General Church Criteria
- Building Plan Schedule and Expenditures
- Long-Range Financial Plan

STEP 7 *Get on the Trail*
- Monthly Planning Worksheet

STEP 1

THE CAPTAIN'S COMPASS

Frustrated. Exhausted. Ready to quit. Over the last 20 years, I have talked to many pastors who genuinely enjoyed serving God, but I have also talked to many whose passion for Christ has eroded over the years due to stress and struggle. It may sound simplistic, but I believe there are two kinds of pastors: those whose ministry continually overflows from a rich, personal experience of God's great grace, and those for whom ministry has become a heavy burden instead of a joy. One group is energized by challenges; the other is threatened and defeated by them. One serves because they want to; the other serves because they feel they have to.

The first step in our planning process has nothing to do with facilities, childcare, finances, or organizational charts, but it has everything to do with our hearts as children of God. Each of us needs a *personal vision* of who we are in Christ, apart from our performance and apart from the criticisms or acclaim of men. From that foundation, we can build a strong *ministry vision* that is consistent with our abilities and spiritual gifts. This dual vision is operative whether we are serving a start-up church or a mega-church, whether we are asked to speak at pastors' conferences or if nobody knows our names. If we don't have these two elements rooted strongly in our hearts, we may produce a beautiful plan, but our motivation may be to prove ourselves instead of a pure desire to serve the Lord Jesus.

Let's be careful not to cheapen the meaning of the term "vision." It is not just a fleeting feeling. It is a *word from God* and a *work of God*. It is God's message to us, a special manifestation of God's will and purpose in and through leaders He has chosen. We must look deeply into His Word to understand the truth and the significance of a vision. It is the foundation of everything else we will discuss.

I believe there are two kinds of pastors: those whose ministry continually overflows from a rich, personal experience of God's great grace, and those for whom ministry has become a heavy burden instead of a joy

Let's be careful not to cheapen the meaning of the term "vision." It is not just a fleeting feeling. It is a word from God and a work of God.

A VISION IS VICARIOUS

Before we address the pastor's personal vision, I want to share some principles about visions in general. A genuine vision is vicarious, which means it comes from outside us, and specifically, it comes from God. The word "vicarious" has two related meanings. One is "substitutionary, or taking the place of another," like the vicarious death of Christ to pay for our sins. He took our place. The word also means "delegated." That's the sense we mean it here. Visions do not originate from us; they are delegated to us by God. Their origin and substance come from Him. Let's see why this is important.

A true vision is delegated to us by God.

I've known people who had a burning desire to have power and status. This desire to dominate may function well in the business world (though I have real doubts even about that), but this is not a God-given vision. Through the prophet Jeremiah, God made a scathing pronouncement:

> "And do you seek great things for yourself? Do not seek them . . ." (Jeremiah 45:5).

If a vision is centered on promoting prestige or advancing careers, it is not God's vision. A vision that is delegated by God is one that is centered on Christ . . . to accomplish His purposes . . . according to His ways . . . for His glory.

A true vision is not just a copy of someone else's success.

We can certainly learn from others, and we can benefit by being around those who are genuinely following God, but ultimately, we need to hear His voice ourselves. If we only copy somebody else, we may not be able to stand as strong as we need to stand when difficulties arise. Know this: Copying without confirmation means coping without confidence.

A true vision is given by God to us individually.

Those who hear the Lord's unmistakable voice can return to Him day after day to draw on His wisdom, strength, and encouragement. When our hearts are focused on bringing Jesus honor, the Spirit equips us to accomplish His tasks. That's what I want, and unless I miss my guess, that's what you want, too.

This is the difference between drinking from a cistern and drinking from a well. The cistern is a reservoir of water that

If a vision is centered on promoting prestige or advancing careers, it is not God's vision

Copying without confirmation means coping without confidence.

has no means of replenishing itself, so the water can become stale and foul-tasting. But the well draws from deep, underground aquifers with a limitless supply of fresh and refreshing water.

In my own life, I have recognized the utter necessity of drawing from the deep well of Christ day after day. As a Christian businessman and layman, I got very much involved in ministry, and I had to get my encouragement and strength from God to stay focused. Then, when God called me into the vocational ministry at Bellevue, my desire to hear from Him greatly intensified. During these years, I had to come back time after time to the heart of God, to draw from that deep well of His grace. For me, then, as well as for any man of God today, this first requirement of spiritual leadership is a genuine heart for God, which is totally independent from successes or failures, or the praise or criticisms of others. And that's what keeps us going in the ministry year after year.

This first requirement of spiritual leadership is a genuine heart for God, which is totally independent from successes or failures, or the praise or criticisms of others.

A VISION HAS VALUE

We are dominated by the visions God gives us. God's calling, as His child and as His servant, becomes our highest and deepest motivation for all we do. This domination, however, is not oppressive. Instead, it invigorates us, and everything we do is tied to that vision. Our minds are sharper and our hearts are more full of joy as we watch God work to unfold His gracious plan in our lives.

Those who are dominated by a self-serving purpose are motivated by comparison and fear. Their thoughts are of success, and they want to win to prove themselves. Those who are dominated by God's vision are just as dedicated, but for the right reason: to honor Christ. But no, they aren't intense all the time. They know when and how to relax, and they don't take themselves so seriously. A vision rooted in the purpose of God and the grace of God is a wonderful thing to experience. We "no longer live for ourselves," as Paul wrote to the Corinthians, "but for Him who died for them and rose again."

A VISION HAS VIRTUE

When we get a glimpse of what God wants to do, we are deeply and supremely dedicated to His vision for our lives and ministries. We realize it is a course set by God for us individually. Our faith is multiplied, and our passion for Christ and His Kingdom consumes us. Our prayers take on focus and direction because they are directed and energized by His voice, His heart, and His purposes.

Those with a "have to" motivation grumble about any kind of sacrifice they are asked to make, but those gripped by

Our prayers take on focus and direction because they are directed and energized by His voice, His heart, and His purposes.

a vision of what God wants to do in and through them make glad sacrifices.

<table><tr><td>

THE PHASES OF A VISION

</td><td>

As we look in this passage of Scripture and as we analyze how God works in us, we can see three distinct phases in the granting and the fulfillment of a vision: the vision received, rendered, and realized. This follows the pattern in Paul's letter to the Romans. He wrote:

</td></tr></table>

> "For of Him and through Him and to Him are all things, to whom be glory forever. Amen" (Romans 11:36).

— "Of Him" shows the origin of the vision. We receive it from God.
— "Through Him" demonstrates the source of power to accomplish the vision.
— "To Him" is the object of our motivation, to glorify the Lord Jesus and Him alone.

Let's look at these three phases:

Phase 1: The Vision Received: The Purpose of God

As we seek God's face and trust Him to direct us, we wait for Him to give us a clear sense of His calling. This calling is not primarily to a title, or even to a position, but to Christ and His purpose. Our personal calling is more "being" than "doing," and God's purpose takes sovereign precedent over any position in leadership. If we are in tune with the Suffering Servant Savior, we won't be enamored with the trappings of power. Instead, like our Lord, we will yearn to see the lost saved, the hurting comforted, and the confused led to peace and purpose.

The source of the vision is God, and the subject is the purpose of God. He doesn't call us in order to elevate us in the eyes of man. He calls us to fulfill His own divine purpose. Paul wrote to the Corinthians:

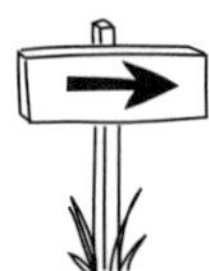

The source of the vision is God, and the subject is the purpose of God.

> "For you see your calling, brethren, that not many wise according to the flesh, not many mighty, not many noble, are called. But God has chosen the foolish things of the world to put to shame the wise, and God has chosen the weak things of the world to put to shame the things which are mighty; and the base things of the world and the things which are

despised God has chosen, and the things which are not, to bring to nothing the things that are, that no flesh should glory in His presence. But of Him you are in Christ Jesus, who became for us wisdom from God—and righteousness and sanctification and redemption—that, as it is written, 'He who glories, let him glory in the Lord' " (I Cor 1:26-31).

The "vision received" is humbly discerning the will of God and being sensitive to the direction He chooses to lead you. That vision is not just a thought or a dream or a feeling. It has spiritual substance. It is getting in on what God is up to!

Phase 2: The Vision Rendered: The Power of God

The vision received has to do with the purpose of God; the vision rendered taps into the power of God. When an artist renders a painting, he gives expression to his vision of the portrait, still life, or scene. In the same way, when our vision is rendered, God's power finds expression in the big and small, in great programs and in individual moments of service. The power of God is revealed through abilities and accomplishments beyond our natural capabilities.

The vision received is vertical communication between God and you as you discern the leading and calling of God. The vision rendered is horizontal communication, upholding the Word of Truth that transforms lives. This horizontal communication finds its expression in the various leadership roles in the pastorate. Your communication with people is only successful, though, when they accept your role as leader and when they find their appropriate place in fulfilling that God-given vision. Proverbs 29:18 says:

The vision rendered is horizontal communication, upholding the Word of Truth that transforms lives.

> "Where there is no vision, the people perish; but he who keeps the law, happy is he" (Proverbs 29:18).

The New King James Version says: "Where there is no revelation, the people cast off restraint," that is, where there is no prophetic vision, the people wander like sheep without a shepherd. They become people without form or focus.

If leaders don't lead, followers can't follow. We find that principle throughout the Scriptures when people did "what is right in their own eyes." Judges 21:25 says:

> "In those days there was no king in Israel; everyone did what was right in his own eyes" (Judges 21:25).

Everything rises on *focused* leadership, and everything falls on *fractured* leadership.

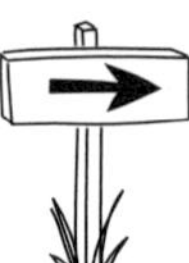

Fractured leadership causes confusion, discouragement, and division. This can occur when one person is going in different directions or when several leaders confuse people by giving conflicting messages,

There is a common saying that "Everything rises or falls on leadership." It is more accurate to say: Everything rises on *focused* leadership, and everything falls on *fractured* leadership. I've seen and heard about some tragic church splits and terrible bitterness among the family of God. I believe these are caused primarily by a lack of focused leadership. As the vision wanders and wanes, people develop their own agendas and demand their own ways. That's a recipe for disaster.

The second part of Proverbs 29:18 is: "but he who keeps the law, happy is he." People need and want instruction. If people in our churches comprehend that we are leading with a word from the Lord, they will probably follow. If we don't communicate that we are following God's vision and direction, unity is often forfeited and leadership is fractured. If we will only lead with a sense of God's direction, people will follow. Fractured leadership causes confusion, discouragement, and division. This can occur when one person is going in different directions or when several leaders confuse people by giving conflicting messages,

God's call includes both adventure and adversity. Even when we hear God's clear voice and follow His direction with passionate commitment, that path isn't necessarily smooth. One of the causes of confusion and discouragement is that some of us have unrealistic expectations of what God's calling means. We think it is primarily a calling to assure personal success in every venture, and we are surprised and disheartened when we encounter difficulties. The Scriptures give us several rich examples of what God's call might include:

— Abraham was called to be the father of a great nation (Genesis 12), but he was childless for years.
— Joseph had a vision of leadership (Genesis 37), but was sold into slavery by his brothers and then languished in prison until God's timing was right.
— Gideon was called to lead an army, but God chose to decrease the size of his force so God would get more glory from the victory (Judges 6).
— David was called to unify Israel and Judah, but he had to fight many battles and suffer much heartache before he fulfilled God's call (II Samuel 5).
— Jeremiah faithfully spoke God's message, even when few if any would listen, and he was persecuted for his faithfulness to God (Jeremiah 37-38).

— Paul's obedience to God's call established many churches, but it often led to him being beaten, flogged, and jailed (II Corinthians 11:21-33).
— The Lord Jesus did the Father's will, but that led Him to temptation in the wilderness, to conflicts with those who opposed Him, and ultimately to the cross.

We are not called to be successful, just obedient to the One who calls us. If He gives us success, we are thrilled. If not, we learn to find joy and contentment in the knowledge that we are His and that He is pleased with our faithful service. Obedience, though, is not an option. I am reminded of the Coast Guard motto: "We don't have to come back, but we do have to go out." In the same way, we don't know what the future holds, but we are called to be obedient to take steps of faith into that future.

As we take steps to fulfill God's calling in our lives, we can expect several things to occur. The character, Christian, in John Bunyan's classic book, *Pilgrim's Progress*, followed God's path. Along the way he encountered blessings and curses, people who spoke truth and people who spoke lies, situations that brought peace and comfort and calamities that tested him to the breaking point. Following Christ is a joy every day, though some days are not without a struggle. Those who are passionate about changing the world for God's sake desperately need God's great power to accomplish His will. In his excellent book, *Spiritual Leadership,* J. Oswald Sanders noted, "The real qualities of leadership are to be found in those who are willing to suffer for the sake of objectives great enough to demand their wholehearted obedience."[1]

Phase 3: The Vision Realized: The Providence of God

Remember Romans 11:36: "For of Him and through Him and to Him are all things, to whom be glory forever. Amen." We now look at the object of our motivation: to glorify God by our faithfulness as the vision takes shape.

God doesn't call perfect people, just those who need His grace. He doesn't call powerful people, just those who will depend on His strength. He doesn't call know-it-alls, just those who trust that He knows all. God has given us principles that help us lead and manage His flock, and as we

We are not called to be successful, just obedient to the One who calls us. If He gives us success, we are thrilled. If not, we learn to find joy and contentment in the knowledge that we are His and that He is pleased with our faithful service.

We now look at the object of our motivation: to glorify God by our faithfulness as the vision takes shape.

1 J. Oswald Sanders, *Spiritual Leadership,* (Moody Press, Chicago, IL, 1967) p.17.

follow these principles, He is gracious to allow us the privilege of seeing Him change lives—including ours.

As we trust God to accomplish His purposes, the power of His Spirit is unleashed. Lives are changed, and God is honored. In fact, the one thing people will say is: "God is at work here." No one will be able to explain the changes in individuals, families, and the community apart from the work of the Spirit of God. And maybe even more significant, those in leadership will recognize this fact, too. Instead of taking the credit, they will reflect the attitude of the servant in Jesus' parable: "I am only a servant doing what my Master commanded me." And with that, we are content.[2]

An Example: Eleazar, Abraham's Servant

A wonderful biblical example of a vision received, rendered, and realized is found in Genesis 24. God "spoke" to Abraham about a wife for Isaac, a wife who was to come from the land of his family (verse 7). If the woman would not return with Abraham's servant, Eleazar, then the servant was released from his oath to find a wife for Isaac—but under no circumstance was Isaac to be taken to that land. We see in this a vision received, with specific guidelines for achieving the purpose of God. Eleazar, obedient to his master, traveled to Nahor (Mesopotamia), and at a well outside the city, he prayed for success. The Lord miraculously led him to Rebekah as the chosen bride for Isaac. Eleazar's testimony was, "I, being in the way, the Lord led me. . . ." We see then, the vision rendered according to the power of God through His obedient servant.

Eleazar told the family of Rebekah about Abraham's charge to him, the miracle at the well, and the need to return immediately to his master with Rebekah. He told them, "Do not hinder me, since the Lord has prospered my way." The vision was then realized as Rebekah was brought to Isaac. By the providence of God's hand, "Isaac took Rebekah and she became his wife, and he loved her."

This is a strategic process. God certainly doesn't need a process to accomplish His purposes, but we do. Pastors may try to communicate and conquer before they grasp the challenge of the vision. Why? Because they haven't taken the time to go before the throne of God to ask Him for direction. Oh, they pray and ask for help, but I'm talking about a

> I'm talking about falling on our faces and searching the Word and the heart of God for clear direction—and not getting up until He gives it. That kind of prayer takes both courage and patience.

---

2 *The Servant Principle*, a book by Dr. Rick Ferguson and a workshop sponsored by Next Level Leadership Network, gives insight and encouragement for us to serve passionately and selflessly.

different level of seeking God. I'm talking about falling on our faces and searching the Word and the heart of God for clear direction—and not getting up until He gives it. That kind of prayer takes both courage and patience.

This diagram shows that the pinnacle component of the planning process is the pastor's personal and ministry vision. If that vision is clear and strong, everything else—all the other responsibilities and activities—find meaning. At this point, we will focus on an often-neglected but essential element: the pastor's personal vision.

We have spent some time already describing the necessity of a vision and the phases of a vision. Now I want to break that vision into two distinct areas: personal and ministry. Most pastors can't separate these two. Many of us are so consumed with the pressures of ministry that we think we simply don't have time to reflect on our personal needs, desires, and direction. In fact, many of us feel guilty if we relax at all! We push ourselves day after day, week after week, month after month and year after year . . . until we collapse—or worse, we make a very bad decision that disqualifies us from service.

The average tenure of a pastor is two-and-a-half years. At that point, the stresses of the role or the grumbling of the people are simply too much to bear. Because we are so absorbed in grumbling and bickering, 65 percent of churches are failing. One of the casualties of all this stress is the self-worth of the pastors. Many of us see ourselves as failures, or we are so afraid of being labeled as failures that we are driven to work as hard as we can to prove our value. We need a

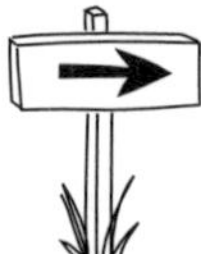

A defeated, driven, depressed, and demanding pastor needs a fresh word from God, not only about himself, but also about his wife and children.

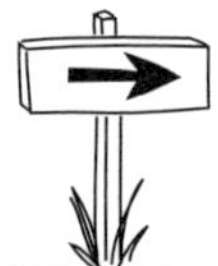

Our first and primary calling is to walk with God in freshness and joy, drawing on His grace and strength, and enjoying all He has given us.

new sense of who we are in Christ so we can rest in God's marvelous love and move ahead under the umbrella of His grace. This is what I mean by "personal vision." A defeated, driven, depressed, and demanding pastor needs a fresh word from God, not only about himself, but also about his wife and children. A penetrating question for some of us is this: Is my immediate family experiencing the joy, love, and life I am prescribing for the family of God?

Recently I talked to a pastor who had lost his personal vision (if, indeed, he ever had one). He had no secure anchor in his life, so he drifted—or more accurately, ran!—back and forth doing everything he could do to please people. The more he tried and the harder he worked, the more dissatisfied everyone became: His wife and children felt abandoned, his leaders lacked direction, his people always wanted more than he could give, and he felt a deep sense of frustration that he was a failure. He needed a fresh perspective on what is important in life, and a fresh look at his own identity. These are the anchors he had been looking for.

I believe we are, first and foremost, children of God with the responsibilities of husband and father, and pastors second. Our first and primary calling is to walk with God in freshness and joy, drawing on His grace and strength, and enjoying all He has given us. One of the most compelling passages in Scripture is in Paul's second letter to the Corinthians. Paul wrote:

> "For the love of Christ constrains us, because we judge thus: that if One died, then all died; and He died for all, that those who live should no longer live for themselves, but for Him who died for them and rose again" (II Corinthians 5:14-15).

Paul's service came out of a full heart of love, the love Christ extended to him and his love for Christ in return. He was compelled (or constrained) by the love of God to serve, not driven to minister so he could prove himself. He makes it clear that his passion to preach the gospel to the world was not so he could pat himself on the back or so people would applaud him. In fact, in his letter to the Galatians, he wrote:

> "For do I now persuade men, or God? Or do I seek to please men? For if I still pleased men, I would not be a servant of Christ" (Galatians 1:10).

Paul's statement echoes Jesus' insight that if we seek the favor of men, we won't receive the favor of God. We must choose between the two. Paul wrote often and eloquently of the need for all believers to have a deep and sincere experience of the love of Christ as the foundation for everything they say and do. Read his prayer in Ephesians 4 to capture the depth of his desire for the people of his day—and you and me—to "know the love of Christ which passes knowledge."

I have a suspicion that Paul, the brightest young star in the Hebrew heavens in his day, struggled with the desire for fame and approval. Out of his struggle (see Philippians 3:1-9), Paul developed a genuine passion for Christ alone. Not Christ and fame, not Christ and security, not Christ and comfort, not Christ and responsive people, not Christ and anything else. Just Christ.

It is so easy, so incredibly easy, for our focus to slip a bit and for us to desire these other things along with Christ. Yet when our hearts become clouded by them, every thought and action is double-minded. Then, instead of serving people, we use them; instead of rejoicing in others' successes, we are threatened by them; instead of enjoying the Lord, our prayers are full of thoughts of success so we can get ahead or stay ahead.

In one of the most startling passages in the Bible, Paul wrote to the Corinthians:

"But I fear, lest somehow, as the serpent deceived Eve by his craftiness, so your minds may be corrupted from the simplicity that is in Christ" (II Corinthians 11:3).

Paul wasn't afraid of much. He walked into cities knowing he may be whipped or stoned for his faith. He endured incredible hardships, and never stopped going from city to city to tell anyone who would listen about the Savior. No, we don't see much fear in him, so when he writes, "But I fear," it catches my attention. What was he afraid of? Suffering? No. Hardship? Not at all. Death? Hardly. But Paul was afraid that you and I would be deceived by the enemy of our souls, and our minds and hearts would be led astray from purity and simplicity of devotion to Christ.

When our hearts are deceived and our motives are mixed, we (even we who tell others about God's love every day) lose the joy of knowing Him. Instead of serving Christ out of a full heart of gratitude, we are driven to:

Then, instead of serving people, we use them; instead of rejoicing in others' successes, we are threatened by them; instead of enjoying the Lord, our prayers are full of thoughts of success so we can get ahead or stay ahead.

When our hearts are deceived and our motives are mixed, we (even we who tell others about God's love every day) lose the joy of knowing Him.

— prove our value to ourselves and others by being successful, and we are threatened by the slightest criticism or others' success;

— please people by agreeing with them even when we disagree, and we change our opinions, words, and behavior to suit them;

— hide from people and avoid risks because we can't stand to be seen as failures; or

— avoid confrontation because being liked is more important than doing what's right.

If these are our methods of dealing with life, problems only crystallize these misguided motivations. Driven people become more driven; people pleasers lose themselves even more in their attempts to win approval; and those who hide crawl even farther back into their caves to avoid conflict.

A young pastor, strong in the Word, told me that God had revolutionized his motivation at a prayer retreat. He was meditating on Colossians 3, and as he read verse 12, God gave him insight he had never had before. It reads:

> "Therefore, as the elect of God, holy and beloved, put on tender mercies, kindness, humbleness of mind, meekness, longsuffering . . ."

He related, "I've read that passage a hundred times before, and I've preached on it several times, too, but that day, God gave me fresh insight. At the time, I was terribly driven to prove myself as a pastor. I wanted—in the worst way I wanted—to be a success. I got up early to go to the hospital to visit people. I studied about 20 hours for my sermon each week and polished it until it was perfect—I hoped. I met with anybody and everybody, and I prayed like crazy. But I was the one who was going crazy! On the outside, I was trying to be the perfect pastor, but on the inside, I was dying. When something went well, like when people loved my sermons, I felt intense pride. But when something failed or somebody didn't appreciate something I'd done, I felt tremendous fear and guilt. That day at the retreat, I read that God had chosen me, loved me, and declared me holy in His sight. It was like a flood of cool water washed over me. I felt so refreshed and free! In the eyes of Almighty God, I was chosen, holy, and loved. What could be more wonderful? What could bring more freedom from being driven to perform? The passage says that our actions of love and service spring

I felt so refreshed and free! In the eyes of Almighty God, I was chosen, holy, and loved. What could be more wonderful? What could bring more freedom from being driven to perform?

from that truth. I'm not sure what clicked that day, but I'll never forget that moment. I ran to a friend and told him what God had shown me. Both of us rejoiced in the Lord. Since then, I've had many other times when I felt pride, fear, and guilt, but that day and that passage have given me a benchmark to get me back where I need to be so I can focus on what I already have instead of trying to earn it. God is good."

We have all read and preached the identity truths in the Scriptures, but perhaps some of us need to be reminded of them again. Paul wrote the Ephesians that we are "chosen, adopted, loved, forgiven, and sealed by the Holy Spirit." Peter reminded us of our lofty status:

> "But you are a chosen generation, a royal priesthood, a holy nation, His own special people, that you may proclaim the praises of Him who has called you out of darkness into His marvelous light" (I Peter 2:9).

On this side of heaven, we will struggle with gaining and maintaining a simple and pure devotion to Christ. We will feel tempted to impress others with our successes—especially if they are talking about theirs! We will feel pressure to say what others want to hear instead of speaking the truth boldly. And we will be tempted to avoid conflict and failure by simply not making waves. It is not sin to be tempted; it is a sin to give in to that temptation. As we saturate our hearts with the fabulous truths of God's Word about our status as beloved children of God, we will be able to say with Paul:

> "But indeed I also count all things loss for the excellence of the knowledge of Christ Jesus my Lord, for whom I have suffered the loss of all things, and count them as rubbish, that I may gain Christ" (Phil 3:8).

The Shorter Version of the Westminster Confession states: "The chief end of man is to glorify God and enjoy Him forever." I ask you, and I look in the mirror at myself, "Are you enjoying the Lord today? Am I?"

"Are you enjoying the Lord today? Am I?"

King David was one of the most powerful, successful, and complicated leaders in our history. He was a man of action, yet he also was a man with a genuine passion for God. He had great goals to unify the tribes into one nation, to conquer invading armies, and bring prosperity to his land. But these were not his chief goals. In Psalm 27:4, David wrote:

"One thing I have desired of the Lord, That will I seek:
That I may dwell in the house of the Lord
All the days of my life,
To behold the beauty of the Lord,
And to inquire in His temple."

And I again ask, "Is the Lord beautiful to you today? Is He delightful to me?" I believe we need a shift in our thinking, and maybe in our believing, of what's really important in life. We need to stop living under the "tyranny of the urgent" and begin to enjoy the Lord and all He has given us. Let me ask a few questions:

— *Why do you do what you do?*
This question reflects on your purpose in life. If we are honest, many of us would have to admit that we are driven by fear of failure, the fear of someone criticizing us, or the desire to take the next step up the ladder of success.

— *What are some things you really enjoy?*
Are you taking time to recharge your own engine with fun, relaxation, and stimulating hobbies or trips with your wife and family? Do you have some friends around whom you can relax and be yourself? We can't run long if we run all the time, and some of us are running internally even when we are in bed each night. We simply can't "turn off." Find some things you enjoy, and make time for them. You and your ministry will be better off if you do.

— *If you could accomplish only three things before you die, what would they be?*
This question focuses on your performance. Your "to do list" may be a mile long, but the problem is that after a while, everything seems to have equal importance—and they all seem urgent! We need a new sense of priority. Isn't it amazing that the Lord Jesus was never in a hurry? But we are. He never felt pressured to do what others demanded of Him, but we do. Take time to reevaluate what you want your life to be, and don't let the urgent crowd out the important.

— *Where do you see yourself and your family ten years from now?*
No, we don't know exactly what the future holds for us, but we can dream and plan and trust God to lead us. Put ministry aside for a moment and consider your own devel-

opment and your family's welfare. What is your wife's dream? Do you even know? What do your children really want for their lives? What can you do to encourage them to fulfill their dreams?

We've all heard from children of pastors who said, "My father was never around when I really needed him. He always found time for the church, but not for me." We are accountable to God for our families before and above our ministries. Many of us spend so much time ministering to others that our wives feel like widows and our children like orphans. Beloved, that ought not to be. I know men who are so focused on their ministries that they don't think about the financial needs, like college and retirement, down the road. When asked about these needs, they have said, "Oh, that's a long time from now. God will provide." God can, and sometimes does, supply spontaneously, but to expect Him to provide without our involvement can be very presumptuous.

I believe God gave us minds so we can plan ahead, especially to provide for those He has entrusted to us. Think about the future. Make plans. Of course, you'll need to be flexible, but plan ahead to provide for those who depend on you. And value your family more than any ministry God could ever give you. God has called you first to walk with Him in peace and joy, and to be a model of love and strength to your family. From the deep well of your love for God and your family will spring a fountain of love for your church and your community.

The Phantom Pastor

Not long ago, I learned that Fuller Seminary conducted a survey of pastors and asked them in what activities they felt their congregations expected them to be proficient. These pastors listed 76 specific responsibilities, and they felt they were supposed to be experts at all of them!

The measuring stick for these tasks was always the person who was the best in the denomination at that activity. For example, they felt they had to be just as good an evangelist as the one who was asked to speak on evangelism at the pastors' conferences, just as good a preacher, just as good a fund raiser, just as good an administrator, and church planter, and counselor, and minister to youth, and minister to senior adults, and organizer, and joke teller, and husband and father, and neighbor, and on and on and on.

They had created a "phantom pastor" who could do everything the best it could be done. Then they labored

What is your wife's dream? Do you even know? What do your children really want for their lives? What can you do to encourage them to fulfill their dreams?

They had created a "phantom pastor" who could do everything the best it could be done. Then they labored under the incredible pressure of trying to meet that same set of unrealistic expectations.

under the incredible pressure of trying to meet that same set of unrealistic expectations. Comparison, they recognized, could ruin their lives.

Distractions and Disappointments

I'm convinced that many of us are not even aware of all the stress—the distractions and the disappointments— that rob us of the joy of walking with Christ. Let me ask a couple of questions:

— *What are some distractions in your life?*

Many pastors are distracted by the same stresses other people face every day: money, in-laws, children, and sexual struggles. They know their minds should be focused on the things of God and the advancement of His Kingdom, but their thoughts drift to vain hopes or fears: hopes that somehow they'll get what they want, and fears that someone will find out how empty their lives really are.

— *What are some disappointments that have robbed you of joy and energy?*

In addition to distractions, many of us have experienced deep disappointments that stay ungrieved and unresolved, eventually becoming roots of bitterness in our hearts. For some, a difficult childhood still haunts them; for others, it's a broken or strained marriage, or estranged children; or perhaps a failed pastorate is an open wound, even if it happened long ago.

Disappointments are watersheds in our lives. They can either draw us closer to God or push us away from Him, depending on how we view them. If we blame God for not protecting us, we will drift away, but if we are assured that He is still good and faithful, we will cling to Him during the darkest hours.

I want to take plenty of time to dwell on this issue of the pastor's personal vision because we skip over it far too quickly to focus on ministry issues. We need to stop and take stock of what's going on in our hearts and in our families, instead of being constantly consumed with the mental gymnastics required to address the ever-present church needs.

If we enjoy the Lord and experience a rich relationship with Him and with our families, we will minister in that strength, and it will make a difference—a big difference.

If we enjoy the Lord and experience a rich relationship with Him and with our families, we will minister in that strength, and it will make a difference—a big difference.

Being Authentic

Being a pastor is a tough job. The demands on our time, energies, and abilities are enormous. We often respond to this stress by becoming two people: one for show, and one for home. However, we have no record of Jesus trying to impress anyone. We have no indication that He was anything less than completely authentic all day every day. Certainly, He was more relaxed with His closest followers, but He never tried to be someone He was not. In the same way, you and I need to be authentic people, to take off our masks and be real with those around us. I'm not advocating that we "air our dirty laundry" to everybody, but we can admit some of our faults and acknowledge that we are human after all. Several years ago, I met with a telephone receptionist at our church who had a problem. After she told me about her difficulty, I related a similar situation in my own life and how God dealt with me. To my amazement, she replied, "Brother Sorrell, I never knew you had any problems! You seem to have it all together." Pastors can erect a facade of "having it all together," often without even being aware it is happening.

We can still lead with vigor and conviction, even if we admit we don't have all the gifts and need help in some areas. Honesty is a mark of our integrity, and that honesty comes from our secure position as loved, forgiven, children of the King.

A personal vision is not the result of one time of prayer or an hour of reflection. It is chiseled out of the marble of life by a lifetime of regular attention to the Word of God. In Isaiah 22, the prophet describes Jerusalem as "the Valley of Vision." Jerusalem is 2500 feet above the Mediterranean and 3800 feet above the Dead Sea, but it is surrounded by hills, so it is actually in a valley. Jerusalem is the lightning rod of biblical prophecy and history, as well as the focal point for Christ's earthly ministry. It was in the Temple in this city where God chose to dwell in the Holy of Holies, and it was outside her walls that our Savior was sacrificed for us.

I believe we can draw a parallel between the role of Jerusalem in history and the role of the pastor in his local church. Both the city and the pastor are in elevated positions and have the privilege and responsibility of being the centerpoint of God's calling to proclaim the truth to others, but both are surrounded by mountains, in one case, literally, and in the other case, figuratively.

I believe "the Valley of Vision" for pastors is unhurried time of prayer, meditation on God's Word, and reflection on God's calling for his ministry.

Mountaintop experiences may excite us and elevate our souls, but what happens day after day in the valley and in the pastor's heart determines the value and effectiveness of ministry. The daily devotional life of the pastor keeps his heart pure and responsive to Christ, and his daily attention to the purposes and plans God has entrusted to him are the measure of his effectiveness. I believe "the Valley of Vision" for pastors is unhurried time of prayer, meditation on God's Word, and reflection on God's calling for his ministry. It is a time when the man of God seeks the presence of God for insight, affirmation, and direction. It is in these times of exercising the spiritual disciplines that his personal vision is sharpened and strengthened as he touches—and is touched by—the heart of God.

A Personal Vision Statement

Take time to pray, ponder, and pen your own personal vision statement, one that is based on your relationship with Christ, apart from success or failure in your role in the church. Reflect on the passages of Scripture in this chapter, as well as others the Lord brings to mind from your own study. Meditate on the rich truth you find, and let God's Spirit draw those insights deep into your heart. Some of us will want to fast or take a prayer retreat to find solitude. Don't rush this stage. It may be the most significant part of the entire planning process because it shapes your motivation for everything else you do.

Some people have written broad personal vision statements such as:

— "That my heart and actions would reflect the grace of God."
— "To know the love of Christ that surpasses knowledge."
— "To honor the One who bought me."
— "To experience all that God has for me as His beloved child."
— "That my heart would be completely His."

These statements are a good start, but they need to be broadened and deepened. As a part of your personal vision statement, it is wise to consider what kind of influence you want to have on your family. One pastor said he wanted to treat his wife and children with such consistent love that they will be completely assured of his love for them.

And think about what it will take for you to stay on the cutting edge spiritually, not just to read books about God, but to know Him intimately and trust Him more as your love for

Him grows stronger. That kind of powerful relationship requires time, attention, and effort. It demands that we make decisions to use our time to pursue God instead of doing other, more convenient things.

Your personal vision statement, then, may include those three things: your commitment to honor Christ above all else, your commitment to be a powerfully positive example for your family, and your commitment to pursue a deep, rich relationship with Christ. This statement, then, provides great encouragement for you to grow personally, practically, and professionally.

Your personal vision statement, then, may include those three things: your commitment to honor Christ above all else, your commitment to be a powerfully positive example for your family, and your commitment to pursue a deep, rich relationship with Christ.

TAKE A STEP

Before we go any farther in Step 1, I want to stop so you can reflect on your identity and calling as God's child. Don't rush this time. Let the Scriptures speak clearly to you, and let the Spirit of God refresh you deeply.

YOUR PERSONAL VISION

— *Who?:* This exercise is primarily for the pastor, but each staff member and lay leader will also benefit from this reflection.

— *Why?:* To be refreshed in your primary calling as a dearly beloved child of God.

— *How?:* A careful articulation of your personal vision is an important part of the planning process, so don't rush it. Find time to be alone, preferably away from phones and any other distractions so you can fully concentrate on the Lord and listen to His Word.

— *Then what?:* As you soak up the truth of your identity and are refreshed by God's great grace and strength, you will be ready to focus on the next topic, your ministry vision.

YOUR PERSONAL VISION

This exercise is designed to help you reflect on your own life and God's calling you to Himself. Our sense of security in that relationship gives us strength, joy, and perspective on everything that happens to us.

1.   Ask God to open your heart and mind as you begin. Mediate on the prayer in Colossians 1:9-14.

2.   The Bible calls each of us to a deep, strong, intimate relationship with God. Paraphrase these passages and write your insights about each one of them:

— II Corinthians 5:14-15

— Galatians 1:10

— Philippians 3:1-9

— II Corinthians 11:3

— Colossians 3:12-17

— I Peter 2:9

— Psalm 27:4

— Other passages God brings to mind

3. When our personal vision is clear and strong, we feel secure, and we are compelled by the love of Christ instead of being driven to prove ourselves. Reflect on these questions:

    — How would a clear personal vision affect:

        your motivations?

your hopes and fears?

your priorities?

your relationship with your family?

4. Now that you have reflected on your motivations and priorities, summarize your thoughts: Why do you do what you do?

5. What are some things you really enjoy (hobbies, sports, time with friends, etc.)?

6. If you could accomplish only three things before you die, what would they be?

7. Where do you see yourself and your family ten years from now?

8. Write your own personal vision statement, one which reflects your commitments to respond to the grace of God instead of selfish ambition, to helping your family grow strong in faith, and your ever-deepening love for the Lord.

We have examined our personal visions, and I trust God refreshed your heart through His Word and His Spirit, and by the encouragement of people who have affirmed you throughout your life. Now we want to turn to our ministry vision. Jeremiah wrote of his time:

> "How lonely sits the city
> That was full of people!
> How like a widow is she,
> Who was great among the nations!
> The princess among the provinces
> Has become a slave!" (Lamentations 1:1)

In Jeremiah's day, Jerusalem had been a great city, but no more. This once grand city lay in ruins. Greatness, for Jerusalem as well as for pastors and churches, provides no assurances for tomorrow. The destruction Jeremiah saw in Jerusalem was similar to the rubble of bombed cites in modern wars, but Jerusalem's physical destruction was intensified by the spiritual and emotional trauma of the people. Jerusalem, the jewel of God's grace and favor, was shattered. The markets were empty. The animals were gone. The young men were not to be found. The synagogues were empty of both people and priests. The golden utensils of the Temple were in the hands of pagans. No longer was the sweet savor of incense rising to the Lord. Instead, the stench of the smoldering Temple—and worse, the stench of the people's disobedience—filled the air. Nebuchadnezzar, the pagan king, served as the hand of God's judgment against the sins of the priests and the people.

Today, cities need not be destroyed for our people to be sheep without a shepherd. Too often today, a great man, a great church, a great people, or even a great nation is brought down by God's judgment. In some cases, God acts overtly to overturn sin, but many times, He simply withdraws His hand of protection and lets the consequences of sin run their course.

Jerusalem fell because God removed His protection. In the next chapter in Lamentations, we find that:

> "The Lord has spurned His altar" (Lamentations 2:7).

The Lord's presence had been rejected by willful disobedience of the people. God had adopted the Jews as His special people, and He had made precious and magnificent

YOUR MINISTRY VISION

Today, cities need not be destroyed for our people to be sheep without a shepherd. Too often today, a great man, a great church, a great people, or even a great nation is brought down by God's judgment.

When the presence of the Lord is removed, purpose, power, and providence are sacrificed.

promises to the nation of Israel, but the people chose to go their own way. They forfeited their incredible position of being favored by the God of the Universe, and they no longer sought God's guidance. Jeremiah identified a major result of their disobedience:

"And her prophets find no vision from the Lord" (Lamentations 2:9).

When the presence of the Lord is removed, purpose, power, and providence are sacrificed. The *purpose* of Jerusalem (and God's people) was inherent in the vision God gave to the prophets. The *power* of God rested in the faithfulness of the priests and the people. The *providence* of God was to be the outworking of the vision by faith and practice.

The leaders of the ancient city of Jerusalem desperately needed the presence of God, or they would be destroyed. It is the same today in your church . . . and in mine. The clarity and strength of your ministry vision shapes not only your own zeal and boldness; it also affects each person around you. J. Oswald Sanders observed this principle:

"Those who have most powerfully and permanently influenced their generation have been the "seers"— men who have seen more and farther than others. Men of faith, for faith is vision. This was true of the prophets or seers of the Old Testament times. Moses, one of the greatest leaders of all time, 'endured as seeing him who is invisible.' His faith imparted vision. Elisha's servant saw with great vividness the vastness of the encircling army. Elisha saw the invincible environing host of heaven who were invisible to his servant. His faith imparted vision."[3]

Without a strong, clear personal vision, a ministry vision often produces drivenness instead of joy, guilt instead of gladness, and conflict instead of contentment.

Your *ministry* vision is not the beginning point. The vision for how God uses you to advance His Kingdom is an outgrowth of your *personal* vision. Without a strong, clear personal vision, a ministry vision often produces drivenness instead of joy, guilt instead of gladness, and conflict instead of contentment. Your ministry vision is not the same as your church's vision statement. We'll get to that later, but for now, we want to focus on you personally, your gifts and skills, and

3 Sanders, Op. Cit. p. 48.

your calling to serve God no matter where He leads you. The exercises at the end of this Step are designed to help you create a profile of how God has uniquely shaped you to serve Him and advance His Kingdom, particularly at your present church, but wherever He may lead you in the future. Your ministry vision is an understanding of your gifts, talents, and passion that captures your heart and compels your actions no matter where you serve.

Experience and Expression

Your personal vision is centered in your *experience* of Christ; your ministry vision is about the *expression* of all you are in Him. First and foremost, we are called to radical commitment. Jesus told His followers:

> "If anyone desires to come after Me, let him deny himself, take up his cross, and follow Me. For whoever desires to save his life will lose it, and whoever loses his life for My sake will find it" (Matt 16:24-25).

Let's look at the elements of this invitation. Jesus makes no assumptions. He says, "If anyone desires to come after Me. . . ." He doesn't take it for granted that you and I will become disciples after we see the price tag. He wants us to weigh the costs and the benefits carefully, and make an informed decision. Jesus instructs us to "deny" ourselves. In this context, this means to get rid of our selfishness, not our identity. (Some have misinterpreted this verse to mean that we give up our identities, but the "self" in the New Testament is the sinful self, not one's identity in Christ.) We identify our selfish patterns of thought, attitudes, and behaviors, and we choose to repent. We call the desire for prominence "sin," and we choose humility. We call the desire to control others "pride," and we choose instead to love and serve. "Taking up our cross" means to obey Him in the big things and the little ones, to value what He values, and to follow His example of servanthood. Our service, then, is built on the solid foundation of our radical experience of the love of God and our radical commitment to honor Him in all we say and do.

No matter how clearly our strategies are outlined, no matter how finely tuned our organizations might be, nothing can take the place of the indisputable calling of God to serve. Much has been written over the generations about this

Your personal vision is centered in your *experience* of Christ; your ministry vision is about the *expression* of all you are in Him.

Our service, then, is built on the solid foundation of our radical experience of the love of God and our radical commitment to honor Him in all we say and do.

GOD'S CALLING

calling, and believers have had widely varied experiences, from ecstatic to rational, from biblical to existential. I believe God can call a man in any way He chooses, and I'm not going to suggest that there is any "right" way, but I believe the chief way that God communicates and confirms His heart to us in our day is through His Word. As our hearts are gripped with the message of the gospel and the incredible privilege of taking that gospel to a lost and dying world, we will be open to God's leading. He obviously doesn't lead all believers into the pastorate, (and it may be true that there are quite a few men in the pulpit this week who have gotten there by a route other than responding to God's call), but however we discern the calling of God, it should point to a clear understanding of God's purpose for us, and that understanding must come from the counsel of the Word of God and the Spirit of God.

Our calling to the ministry is to follow the example of Jesus, to serve the Father faithfully, through success and failure, through acclaim and rejection, through others' faith and faithlessness, through joy and suffering.

Some pastors might say that God has called them to lead great and magnificent congregations. Their ministry visions are of huge numbers and great power. Could this be selfish desire rather than a God-inspired direction? God calls us to serve Him faithfully no matter what the cost, no matter what the success or failure. Paul wrote, "Moreover, it is required in stewards that one be found faithful" (I Cor 4:2). Not successful; just faithful. Our calling to the ministry is to follow the example of Jesus, to serve the Father faithfully, through success and failure, through acclaim and rejection, through others' faith and faithlessness, through joy and suffering. My friend, God has not called you and me to be successful, but to be servants. When we respond to His call in humility and faith, He will choose the path for us that brings Him the most glory. The psalmist Asaph wrote that God is ultimately the One who promotes or humbles us:

> "For promotion comes neither from the East
> Nor from the West, nor from the South.
> But God is the judge;
> He puts down one and sets up another" (Psalm 75:6-7).

Certainly, all of us want to be successful, but if we believe our calling is to be a success, we will try to use God instead of loving and serving Him, and we will compete with His other servants instead of supporting them. Too often we refer casually to God's calling, but it would serve us well to ask God to refine and refresh our sense of spiritual direction.

The calling of God is not just the public part where people see our efforts and applaud our work. It also includes the many hours of diligent preparation and prayer, the times of desolation in the hospital with a grieving person, and the sometimes boring responsibilities of administration. Ministry is both direct and indirect. The direct portion of ministry is preaching, teaching, personal evangelism, visitation, and discipling. The indirect part is not as glamorous, but it is just as essential: planning, preparation, and prayer.

A pastor's perception of his calling may be too limited: It may begin and end with himself. When this is the case, he thinks only about his own preaching, his own evangelism, and his own planning. He has forgotten about, or perhaps he has never seen an example of, the joy of multiplying himself into the lives of others. One of the main purposes of pastoral leadership, and indeed, the one that creates the broadest base for growth, is leadership development. Raising up laborers, equipping them to serve effectively, and shepherding them so they stay on track is a high calling for pastors.

At the point God gives us a clear vision of how He wants to use us, we are excited about what comes next. As those initial impressions gel into a direction and then into concrete plans, the vision comes alive. If these budding concepts, however, fail to lead to legitimate steps of implementation, the vision can be lost. Great thoughts, clear visions, and genuine enthusiasm are wasted if they are not converted to realistic concepts and a systematic plan to accomplish those visions. A vision without systematic steps of implementation is nothing more than a dream . . . and in fact, may even be a nightmare!

Great thoughts, clear visions, and genuine enthusiasm are wasted if they are not converted to realistic concepts and a systematic plan to accomplish those visions. A vision without systematic steps of implementation is nothing more than a dream . . . and in fact, may even be a nightmare!

Three Areas of Leadership

A pastor enjoys three areas of leadership: public, personal, and practical. All three are woven together in his ministry of service, and they form a tapestry of his ministry vision. His public ministry is how most people see him, preaching on Sunday morning, leading worship, or speaking at various meetings. He gains his insight and inspiration from the Word of God, and his task is to "accurately handle the Word of truth."

The pastor's personal ministry consists of his counseling, discipling, mentoring, and encouragement of those in his care. No matter how large the church becomes, the pastor will continue to be involved in person-to-person ministry. Others will also be involved, but he sets the example of caring for others "as a nursing mother cherishes her own children" (I Thessalonians 2:7).

His practical ministry is one of administration and planning. He is involved in selecting, training, placing, and overseeing leaders for every ministry in the church. In smaller churches where the pastor is the only staff member, all of his leaders are lay people. As the ministry grows and staff are added, the pastor's role evolves, too. He still is the chief vision-caster and leader, but others are also involved in "equipping the saints for the work of service." Most of our applications in these pages are focused on the pastor's practical ministry, but our practical ministry is most effective if it functions in concert with strong personal and public roles.

Stages of Leadership

Another aspect of the ministry vision is to understand the stages of leadership. As a ministry grows, the pastor's role changes accordingly. The larger the church becomes, the more he is involved in leadership development and administration.

In smaller churches, the pastor does the grass roots ministry of preaching, teaching, evangelism, discipleship, and organizational necessities. As the leadership base expands, he is still the example of grass roots ministry, but he is no longer the only one doing it. To broaden the leadership base, he is actively engaged in selecting, equipping, and directing others. Still later, the pastor's role evolves to create a culture where many people are actively engaged in evangelism and personal ministry, and many leaders are involved in developing still more leaders. The three stages of leadership, then are:

Stage 1: The Pastor Does the Ministry.

A church planter or pastor of a small church must necessarily be a "jack-of-all-trades." He is in charge of preaching, counseling, raising money, visiting the sick, and doing all the planning and administration. This style of leadership needs to gradually change as more people join the church. If a pastor in this stage insists on doing all the work himself, the growth of his congregation will be stifled, even in burgeoning bedroom communities.

Stage 2: The Pastor Equips Others.

Pastors who learn to equip others experience fulfillment—and perhaps a measure of frustration when those we train fail to serve well—in leadership development. Many feel comfortable equipping leaders in just one or two areas of ministry, like small groups or teaching classes, and are adept at imparting vision, direction and motivation to those particular church leaders. But an increased willingness to equip leaders across the whole spectrum of the church will enhance its growth. Churches led by equippers often grow to considerable size.

Stage 3: The Pastor Develops a Culture of Equippers Which Multiplies Leadership.

Some pastors move beyond equipping a select group of leaders to create an environment in which leadership development flourishes in every corner of church life. These pastors are unthreatened by church members who have great gifts and abilities, and they attract men and women who are mature spiritually and who have their own sense of ministry vision which is consistent with the pastor's vision. In this stage, many leaders in the church are involved in planning, selecting, motivating, delegating, and resolving conflict. The benefits of this approach are enormous. There is no limit to the growth potential where this kind of leadership provides ample opportunities for gifted and able people to serve the Lord.

Your gifting and skills may fit better in one of these stages than another, but most of us will need to develop skills in all three stages in order to become the effective servant leaders God wants us to be. As your ministry grows, you will be thrust into new challenges and opportunities, and in these, you will develop new skills. Your growth and development will broaden your ministry vision, and you will develop a God-inspired confidence to serve in new ways and with greater resources of experience and skills.

These pastors are unthreatened by church members who have great gifts and abilities, and they attract men and women who are mature spiritually and who have their own sense of ministry vision which is consistent with the pastor's vision.

Serve According to Your Gifting

In the past two decades, the biblical teaching on spiritual gifts has been communicated more broadly and clearly than perhaps in any time in church history. Most pastors can readily tell others what their gifts are, and many churches use inventories to help new members find places of service in the church family. Most pastors, too, can give a detailed explanation of why they believe the sign gifts are—or aren't—operative today. Teaching about gifts isn't lacking today, but too often, pastors don't take their gifts into account as they select their staff and design their leadership structures. Instead, they use the same old organizational charts without taking their own gifts into consideration.

For example, one pastor very definitely has the gift of exhortation. After he meets with individuals and small groups, they often come away with a renewed zeal for

He realized he needed to make some changes, first to take advantage of those times to encourage and exhort others; second, to weave some of those times into his plan and his schedule; and third, to find others who were gifted in administration to shoulder that part of his burden.

following Christ, and sometimes a new sense of how their sin saddens God and limits their effectiveness. This brother, however, found himself bogged down in administrative details, and he often said "no" to opportunities to "charge up the troops" because he was so overwhelmed with administrative details. As we talked, he realized that saying "no" to these opportunities demotivated him, and his people missed out on the encouragement of his exhortation. He found himself bogged down in an area where he wasn't gifted, and consequently, he sometimes turned down the privilege of using his great gift to minister to others. He realized he needed to make some changes, first to take advantage of those times to encourage and exhort others; second, to weave some of those times into his plan and his schedule; and third, to find others who were gifted in administration to shoulder that part of his burden.

To be frank, this pastor caught some flak for making this very reasonable change in his direction. There were those in his church who thought he ought to buckle down and do the administrative trivia. That work, they felt, demonstrated a servant's heart. But we fail to serve when we fail to serve to the best of our ability, and the best he could do for Christ and His Kingdom was to shift his responsibilities so he could use his gifts more fully. After a while, those who benefited from his encouragement won over most of the detractors.

Most people serving in churches today have been placed in responsibilities primarily or solely because a slot needed to be filled, not because the leadership identified their spiritual gifts. For example, there is a crying need for childcare volunteers in almost every church I've visited. Far too often, the coordinator of this ministry begs and pleads for help, and after a while, enough people sign up to fill the slots. The coordinator may say something like, "You aren't going to let those dear children down, are you? If you don't help, I just don't know what we'll do." Guilt trips are effective in the short-run, but they have very negative long-term consequences.

If a person is using his spiritual gift, he will feel energized by serving. If not, as is the case for many of these childcare volunteers, his service will drain him, leaving him frustrated or disinterested. Of course, there is a balance between finding the perfect fit to use your gifts and being willing to serve in any way at any time. This is the heart of a servant who appreciates what Christ has done for him, but sometimes leaders are better off not filling a vacancy than filling it with the wrong person.

Spiritual gifts inventories come in many different varieties. Some measure experience, and some measure desire. The ones which measure experience are designed for believers who have "been in the trenches" of ministry and who have tasted both fulfillment and disappointment as they have served. The ones based on desire are for relatively young Christians, like high school students. These focus on areas of service which may seem attractive or interesting to them, whether they have had experience in those areas or not. Obviously, the experience-based inventories are much more accurate and useful for those in leadership positions in churches.

Some spiritual gifts inventories include all the gifts listed in the four passages of Scripture (found in Romans 12, I Corinthians 12, Ephesians 4, and I Peter 4); some include only a portion of the list; and some add a few new ones. Whichever list you use, I believe it is important to measure both desire and experience. If you only measure experience, most of us will have self-fulfilling inventories because we will give high marks to the activities we are already doing. It is important, then, to also identify the activities that give us the most joy, even if our current responsibilities don't allow much time to be involved in them. For example, most pastors will rank high in pastoring and teaching because much of their time is focused on these ministries. They may, however, have a latent, unused gift of mercy, giving, or something else that has atrophied for lack of use.

Pastors need to come to grips with the reality that God has gifted them in certain areas, but their people probably expect them to be experts in every area of ministry. Such high and unrealistic expectations put a terrific burden on a pastor's shoulders unless and until he is objective with himself and his leaders about his limitations. This gives him the opportunity to make choices, to focus his attention on his areas of strengths and gifting, and to find resources for those areas in which he is not as strong. Everybody, the pastor as well as members of his church, will benefit from an accurate assessment and good planning in this area.

A pastor may serve in an aspect of ministry with great ease and great anointing, but it is also possible to serve in an area with great anointing, yet with great difficulty. He may have clear direction and the power of God's Spirit, but that service may be outside his gifting. Effectiveness, then, is not dependent only on spiritual gifts. God's anointing and calling may lead him to serve in a way that challenges him greatly. If,

This gives him the opportunity to make choices, to focus his attention on his areas of strengths and gifting, and to find resources for those areas in which he is not as strong.

however, both the joy and the anointing of the Spirit are absent, he needs to reassess the Lord's will in that area.

I've known pastors who had an obvious gift in pastoral ministries. These men were energized by comforting those who were sick or grieving, and they enjoyed counseling troubled people. Quite often, these men neglected sermon preparation because their time was consumed by pastoring their flocks, but this decision had very negative consequences in their overall ministry. Dr. Adrian Rogers has said to pastors, "Your people will forgive you for almost anything except boring them to death on Sunday morning." No matter what a pastor's spiritual gifting, his primary responsibility is to accurately and passionately proclaim the Word of God from the pulpit.

God's calling supersedes gifting, and if He has called us to serve in some capacity, we are to obey even if it doesn't match what we consider to be our spiritual gifting.

Identifying our spiritual gifts helps us prioritize our time and efforts, but it is not the answer to all things. God's calling supersedes gifting, and if He has called us to serve in some capacity, we are to obey even if it doesn't match what we consider to be our spiritual gifting. In our obedience, God develops our sense of dependence on Him and builds new strengths into us. Those who are not open to God's leading apart from their perception of their gifting miss the excitement of seeing God work in fresh and unusual ways.

At the end of this chapter, we have included a spiritual gifts inventory for you to use. Even if you have done similar exercises in the past, take time to do this one. Consider not only your experience, but also your sense of fulfillment as you fill it out.

The Power of Personality

For millennia, philosophers have sought to understand why people respond the way they do to life's varied situations. Most of these divide human personality (or temperament) into four quadrants, two which are people-oriented, and two which are task-oriented; two with direct communication styles, and two with indirect styles. I've seen several personality inventories, and they are all useful because they encourage us to reflect on how God has constructed us. If we understand our behavioral tendencies, we can anticipate how we will respond in given situations. Perhaps the most important use of these tests is that they open doors for discussion between spouses, staff, co-workers, teams, and friends.

Any ministry vision is shaped to some degree by the person's temperament. Some of us are strong and bold. We are quick to see opportunities and take action, but we may not communicate the process of change well enough for those who are more reflective. Some of us are very reflective and patient. We work well with those who need depth and understanding, but we aren't usually bold in our decision-making. Some of us are very detailed and meticulous. We are great at doing research for a plan, but we are often timid or unsure about implementing it. And some of us are wonderful at making people feel comfortable, but we aren't quite sure where we're taking them.

On a staff or ministry team, understanding personalities can make or break the working relationships. One error pastors often make is selecting staff and lay leaders who are just like themselves. This leaves the leadership team unbalanced and less effective. I encourage pastors to hire staff and select lay leaders with complementary gifts and personality so they will create a balanced, well-rounded leadership team.

I encourage pastors to hire staff and select lay leaders with complementary gifts and personality so they will create a balanced, well-rounded leadership team.

Another common mistake is for each person to devalue, and even to despise, the way others think and communicate. The sensitive people accuse the bold ones of not caring, and the visionaries accuse the more reflective people of being disloyal because they don't jump on board immediately. Identifying and discussing differences can smooth the way for better communication and more unity on any team. Each person can learn to acknowledge the differences and appreciate the unique contribution of all the others.

Under the leading of the Holy Spirit, our personalities are refined over time. Our strengths become more pronounced, and our weaknesses become less of a hindrance because we learn to be bold or patient, to be more thorough or to take action, as the case may require. At the end of this chapter, take some time to fill out the temperament inventory. Use it as a conversation starter with your spouse, and use it with those who work closely with you to promote greater understanding and effectiveness as you serve together.

"Killer Skills"

Some people in business or in the church find themselves in roles in which they are skilled but are not fulfilling to them. Instead of building their confidence and generating enthusiasm, these jobs sap their strength and demotivate them. These are called "killer skills."

James is an associate pastor in a large church who graduated at the top of his seminary class. He was, and is, an extraordinary teacher. He distills complex theological

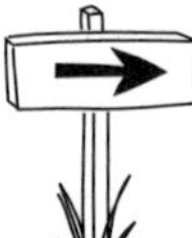

arguments into understandable bites for others to understand. Soon after he arrived at his church, however, the office had computer problems. The secretary's system crashed, and she thought she had lost her database. James told her, "I was on a network like this not long ago. Let me see if I can fix it." And he did. He saved the database, and he saved the church a lot of time and money because of his skills. They all felt good about James' contribution. A few days later, another staff member had computer problems. Guess who he called. Yes, it was James. Again, he fixed the problem, much to the delight of the entire staff. Before long, the staff counted on James for any and all computer questions. They asked him to research a new program to handle the church finances, and they asked him to upgrade the entire system. He enjoyed it for a while, but after about six months he said, "I didn't come here to be a computer whiz. I came to teach. I want to be a servant. I haven't complained about spending almost three-fourths of my time on the church's computers, but I'm wondering if I need to move on, you know, look for another church."

The senior pastor of the church was well aware that James was spending most of his time on the computer system, but he thought he enjoyed it. After all, James certainly was gifted in understanding and implementing the systems they needed.

Ironically, our ministry vision can be short-circuited by a valuable skill we possess. This doesn't happen very often, but when it occurs, it is confusing and makes the person question his calling.

The Three-year Rule

Some pastors have told me that they have questioned their calling. As I ask a few questions, I often find that many of them have been at their church for about three years. Marriages go through a transition period after about a year. At that time, the honeymoon is long over, and each person looks at the other and wonders, "Why in the world did I marry that person?" Pastors and churches go through much the same experience. At the beginning, both the new pastor and the congregation are often willing to try a few different things, and the people are hopeful that the new pastor will be better than the previous one. After about three years, however, the grace that was first extended by the congregation, and especially the leaders, is withdrawn. Now, failure is not winked at, and change again becomes a threat to the old guard. Some in the congregation want the pastor to go in one direction, while others insist he take them in another.

Suspicions and accusations threaten the pastor's role and weaken his resolve.

The three-years point is the time that determines whether a pastor has established credibility and earned trust—or not. Paul admonished people, "Follow me as I follow Christ." Similarly, as we model integrity and skills in leadership, those in our flocks realize we are worthy of their trust, and they are willing to follow us as we follow our Savior. After three years, the congregation has begun to take on the personality and attitude of the pastor. If we are optimistic, our people will be full of faith, too. If we are somber and morose, seemingly more at home at an undertakers' convention, our people will probably reflect the same demeanor. It is rare to find a healthy and strong congregation without a stable, faithful, optimistic pastor. After three years, the church is—for better or worse—very much a reflection of the pastor.

Before reaching this pivotal, three-year juncture, a pastor needs to clarify his ministry vision, and he needs to stick with what he does best. If he doubts himself and tries to be what others want, he will know he is not being authentic, and he'll probably not please them anyway. He needs to remain strong in the Lord, listen patiently, and communicate vision and passion for the ministry God has called him to.

Created and Crafted

As I meet with pastors across the country, I find some with hearts like lions, boldly trusting God for great things. But I also find pastors who doubt themselves. Their doubt clouds their thinking and undermines their leadership. Some of us need a fresh reminder that we have been created by God Himself and equipped by Him to fulfill His purposes. In Psalm 139, David gave us this insight:

> "For You formed my inward parts;
> You covered me in my mother's womb.
> I will praise You, for
> I am fearfully and wonderfully made;
> Marvelous are Your works,
> And that my soul knows very well.
> My frame was not hidden from You,
> When I was made in secret,
> And skillfully wrought in the lowest parts of the
> earth" (Psalm 139:13-15).

After about three years, however, the grace that was first extended by the congregation, and especially the leaders, is withdrawn. Now, failure is not winked at, and change again becomes a threat to the old guard.

It is an incredible thing to realize that God, in His infinite wisdom and sovereignty, carefully constructed each one of us. Yes, we make jokes about our baldness or long noses or whatever, but this passage tells us that we have been created by God Himself. Our DNA is God's doing, but there is an even greater code than the genetic code. Our ability to think, to feel, to choose, and to relate to others are characteristics of God Himself, given to each of us when we were created in His likeness. Even the fact that God created us with a desire to know Him is His work in us. Have you thanked God for His wisdom in creating you? That would be a proper response to the truth in this passage of Scripture.

God has given us the raw materials of our DNA and our abilities. It is up to us to walk with Him in such a way that these are crafted into a vessel suitable for His use and which brings Him glory. Leadership is a blend of natural and spiritual qualities. Both come from the open hand of God and are gifts to us. We find our deepest fulfillment and our highest achievement when both our natural abilities and our spiritual abilities are under the Lordship of Christ. We trust in His direction, not our own; we draw on His power, not our own efforts; and we find contentment in seeing Him honored, whether we receive praise or not.

How does this happen? By presentation and transformation.

— *By presentation:* Offer yourself to God so that your motivations and your actions will be changed, so that you honor God in all you think, say, and do. Paul wrote:

"I beseech you therefore, brethren, by the mercies of God, that you present your bodies a living sacrifice, holy, acceptable to God, which is your reasonable service. And do not be conformed to this world, but be transformed by the renewing of your mind, that you may prove what is that good and acceptable and perfect will of God" (Romans 12:1-2).

— *By transformation:* Let your natural abilities be energized and used by God so they become supernatural abilities. Paul also wrote:

". . . till we all come to the unity of the faith and the knowledge of the Son of God, to a perfect man, to the measure of the stature of the fullness of Christ" (Ephesians 4:13).

"Perfect" in this verse means "mature, whole, achieving the end for which we have been created." God wants to use every aspect of our lives for His honor and glory. He will transform our natural abilities into instruments of His grace, and He will give us new abilities to accomplish His purposes.

Identify Your Strengths and Admit Your Weaknesses

Each of us has been gifted by God, but far too many of us get bogged down in doing things we aren't good at doing. In fact, we spend so much time and energy on those things, we neglect the things we do really well.

If we can admit where we are weak, we can make the necessary adjustments. Instead of being driven by "the tyranny of the urgent," we will learn to live according to "the priority of the important." Ruthless objectivity gives us the motivation to change. This adjustment is called "ego-alteration." The question is: Are we too proud to admit we need help? If we are, we will be stuck spending too much time on things we don't excel in doing. We will be frustrated and burned out, and we'll rob someone else of the joy of working in their strengths. Admitting our weaknesses is a first step in finding others to support us, strengthen us, and extend our ministries of teaching, shepherding, and administration. We often despise our weaknesses and try to hide them, but God uses them to keep us dependent on Him. They are valuable in shaping our lives and building our faith. As we build our leadership teams, we need to look for people who are secure enough to be objective about their weaknesses.

In most cases, we have the choice to select those we will lead, either as staff or as lay leaders. They, in turn, will be the ones who extend the ministry to others in every sphere of the church and the community. Selecting well is incredibly important! We need, however, to look below the surface and discern the hearts of those we may select. Some look good on the surface, but their goals are self-centered. Others, though, are hidden treasures, waiting to be discovered. J. Oswald Sanders gave us this insight about selecting leadership from the life of Christ:

> "Eyes that look are common. Eyes that see are rare. The pharisees looked at Peter and saw only a poor unlettered fisherman, totally insignificant, not worthy

He will transform our natural abilities into instruments of His grace, and He will give us new abilities to accomplish His purposes.

Ruthless objectivity gives us the motivation to change. This adjustment is called "ego-alteration."

We need, however, to look below the surface and discern the hearts of those we may select. Some look good on the surface, but their goals are self-centered. Others, though, are hidden treasures, waiting to be discovered.

of a second look. Jesus saw Peter and discovered the prophet and preacher, saint and leader of the unique band of men who turned the world upside down."[4]

If we select well, delegation is usually received well, and the purposes of God are more readily accomplished. We will focus some attention on selection and delegation later, but for now, realize that a significant task in leadership is to recruit, select, train, and place people who have a heart for God and want His will above all else. A team like this can be used by God to accomplish incredible things!

A PHILOSOPHY OF LEADERSHIP

But all of these sink or swim based on the quality of pastoral leadership which is founded on a steadfast commitment to the Lordship of Christ and the inerrant, infallible Word of God.

Some have asked me which ministry philosophy this book teaches. My answer is that it is more a philosophy of leadership and a planning model than a ministry philosophy. If the pastor has a clear vision for himself and his church, this material will help him plan effectively. A few years ago, the Meta Church model was used in many churches across the country. Recently, the seeker-sensitive model at Willow Creek has gained popularity, and many churches are implementing Natural Church Development. Another popular philosophy of ministry has been developed by Pastor Rick Warren at Saddleback Church in California. Some churches have strong small group ministries, and some are strong in Sunday morning Bible study. A few have only worship on Sunday morning with no classes for Bible instruction. Proponents of all of these will tell you, "This is what really works!" Actually, I believe that many different ministry philosophies can work well as long as they include the powerful preaching and teaching of God's Word, the building of the community of believers, and outreach to the lost. But all of these sink or swim based on the quality of pastoral leadership which is founded on a steadfast commitment to the Lordship of Christ and the inerrant, infallible Word of God.

Many of the conflicts and tensions between the pastor and lay leaders in the church stems from an inadequate understanding of the biblical role of the pastor. Some deacon bodies assert that they are responsible for "running the church," while their pastor is relegated to "spiritual" ministries such as preaching and pastoral care. All of those involved, the pastor and his leadership, need to understand that every aspect of "running the church" is spiritual, from

4 Sanders, Op. Cit. p. 50.

preaching to accounting, from pastoral counseling to setting up a meeting room, from sharing the gospel to balancing the checkbook. Every element of the church serves the function of honoring Christ and advancing the Kingdom of God, and the pastor's role encompasses all of these. A proper understanding of this role is essential, and it will go a long way toward resolving conflict and "turf battles" between leaders.

The local church is the most unique institution of this, or any, age. It is more than an institution, and indeed, more than an organization. It is an organism. It is an organism because it is full of life, both in practice and in promise. Still further, its life has a supernatural quality in response to its Head, Jesus Christ. The church at large is the Body of Christ made up of repentant individuals who have each confessed their sins and accepted the sovereign Christ as their Lord and Savior.

The local church is that family of believers who have voluntarily joined together in a community to worship and serve the Lord. The spiritual leader, shepherd, or pastor of the local body is subservient to Christ. That pastor has the responsibility to preach the Word of God, to lead and minister to the membership. The members are responsible to support and encourage their God-called pastor as he leads in the power of the Holy Spirit. All the while, under his leadership, church members are to discover their spiritual gifts, find a place of effective service, and demonstrate the love of Christ to each other and the world. In short, the church family is to exhibit the life, joy, health, and strength of Christ.

How is the local church to function in order to promote these characteristics? With Christ as its head and the pastor as its spiritual leader, the church must organize itself in a way that energizes the body. This is the challenge of any organization: Does it energize or fractionalize? The organizational structure may be sound, but its potential can be flawed by poor leadership and management. Failure or success is most often caused by the influence of people, not organizational systems.

My 20 years in industry and management proved that clear objectives, effective practices, and focused teams are mandatory for organizational success. This is just as true for the organism of the local church body of believers as it is for business or non-profit organizations. In fact, it is exponentially more important because a believer's service is voluntary, and because each person is at a different level of spiritual maturity. God has allowed me to observe and

This is the challenge of any organization: Does it energize or fractionalize?

experience this dynamic from three unique perspectives over the past 40 years. These are:

1. lay leadership in the local church (from the pioneer to the mega size);
2. multiple management responsibilities in the corporate sector; and
3. hands-on ministry and management as associate pastor of the 27,000 member Bellevue Baptist Church.

THE THREE-FOLD FUNCTION OF THE OFFICE OF THE PASTOR

Several years ago my pastor, Dr. Adrian Rogers, preached a sermon on the role, responsibility, and reward of the pastor based on this passage from I Peter:

"The elders who are among you I exhort, I who am a fellow elder and a witness of the sufferings of Christ, and also a partaker of the glory that will be revealed: Shepherd the flock of God which is among you, serving as overseers, not by constraint but willingly, not for monetary gain but eagerly; nor as being lords over those entrusted to you, but being examples to the flock; and when the Chief Shepherd appears, you will receive the crown of glory that does not fade away" (I Peter 5:1-4).

Dr. Rogers' message explained the role of a good and faithful pastor, to whom the Chief Shepherd will present the crown of glory as his reward. He identified the responsibility of the pastor as categorized by the different terms "elder," "shepherd," and "overseer." These were presented not as different offices in the church, but instead, as different functions of the pastor himself. In the days and weeks after Dr. Rogers' sermon, I realized this was a summary of the basic responsibilities of the pastor, and a crown of glory from the Chief Shepherd was promised because of his faithfulness to these specific areas of ministry. Further reflection brought me to the conclusion that these functions of the office of the pastor should provide the basis for the extension of the ministry throughout the entire church. It became quite apparent that these three roles of the pastor's responsibility could be seen as categories of servant leadership for all who are an extension of the pastor (staff, deacons, lay leaders, and even the people in the pews.) As these three functions are developed, the pastor leads, selects, equips, and develops leadership for service and ministry to and through the church family.

I realized this was a summary of the basic responsibilities of the pastor, and a crown of glory from the Chief Shepherd was promised because of his faithfulness to these specific areas of ministry.

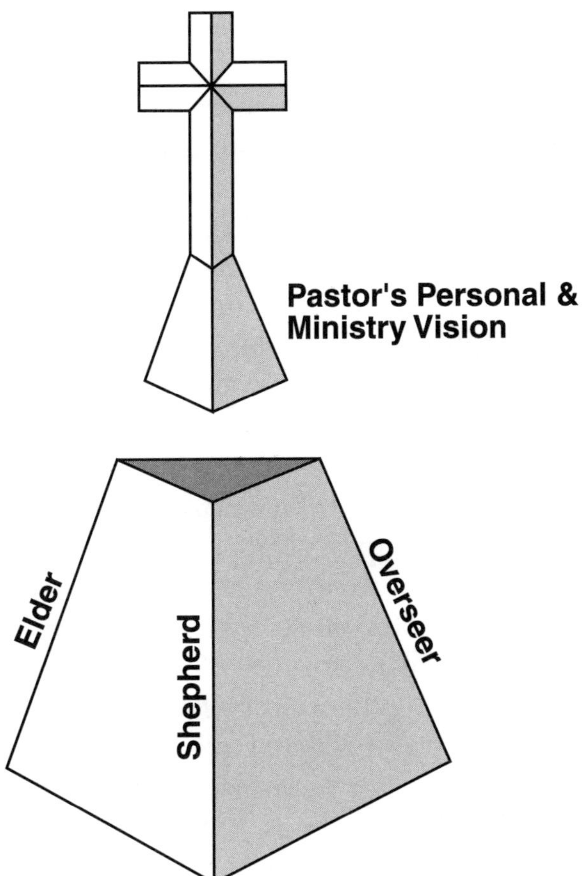

Let's look at these functions:

— *Elder* refers to the person's maturity in the Scripture and in leadership;
— *Shepherd* deals with the care-giving ministry to the church at large and to the individual; and
— *Overseer* refers to management or oversight of the various needs of the church.

Let's look at the first of these functions of the office of the pastor.

As Elder

Elder, from the Greek word *presbuteros*, means "a person of maturity, wise and proven" (I Peter 5:1). These characteristics will be found only in a man saturated with Scripture. The accurate handling of the Word of God must be the primary calling of the pastor. How it is loved, taught, presented, and embraced by the people are matters of foremost importance. The Word of God is the foundation for the pastor's

motivation and methods as he fulfills his calling in every aspect of ministry.

The pastor is to be a man of godly wisdom. True wisdom comes from God, so the pastor needs an intimate knowledge of God and the ways of God. The role of elder also requires that he has proven himself in the ministry, and the character of Christ has molded his life and solidified his integrity. Every area of his life is a testimony to his flock.

John Mott was the leader of one of the greatest missionary movements of all time. Beginning in 1888, the Student Volunteer Movement sent over 30,000 men and women to distant lands to spread the gospel. Mott was a dynamic leader and a captivating speaker. He commented on the effects of leadership: "A leader is a man who knows the road, who can keep ahead, and who can pull others after him." As an elder, the pastor must listen intently to God to know the road. Then, as he takes steps of faith, he steps out in front of his people, taking them by the hand to help them follow him.

The position of elder is mentioned other places in the New Testament. For example, Luke records, "From Miletus he [Paul] sent to Ephesus and called for the elders of the church" (Acts 20:17). And in I Timothy 5:17 Paul instructs, "Let the elders who rule well be counted worthy of double honor, especially those who labor in the word and doctrine."

Some denominations establish the office of the elder for a spiritual leader other than the senior pastor of the church. Some churches include the pastor as one of several elders of the church, no more influential than the others, but with additional preaching responsibility. In some churches, the ordained staff members are an extension of the pastor and have the functions of elders, though they have full ministerial responsibilities as well. The members of the staff are responsible to the senior pastor, who has spiritual authority over them.

I believe that God has called the pastor to be the spiritual leader of a local body of believers. In this role, he is the leading elder, and his vision and integrity shape the methods and ministry of that church. Field Marshall Bernard L. Montgomery, who led the British troops in Europe during World War II, knew a thing or two about leadership. He commented, "Leadership is the capacity and will to rally men and women to a common purpose, and the character which inspires confidence." As an elder, the pastor must exemplify these qualities, too: the capacity and will to rally people to God's purposes, and the character to inspire confidence in them.

As Shepherd

The second function of the pastor is noted in I Peter 5:2, as Peter gives the charge, "Shepherd the flock of God which is among you." The word "shepherd" is derived from the Greek word, *poimen*. Different forms of the word are "pastor" or "shepherd." It means "to feed, to protect, to guide, and to pray for the flock of God." Luke recorded Paul's farewell address to the Ephesian elders in which he instructed them:

> "Therefore, take heed to yourselves and to all the flock, among which the Holy Spirit has made you overseers, to shepherd the church of God which He purchased with His own blood" (Acts 20:28).

This function of the pastor provides the opportunity to express the love of Christ in regard to the spiritual, emotional, and physical needs of the flock. Many pastors have the gift of mercy, and they utilize that gift as they tend to the hurts, illnesses, and sorrowful times of their people. Other than sharing the good news of Jesus Christ, this is the greatest opportunity to show the love of Christ to men and women throughout the community. Indeed, this is a high calling of the church, but it often takes second billing to the more formal programs of Sunday worship, Bible study, and other various organized ministries of the church. This responsibility of the pastor to gently care for his flock places a huge demand upon his time. Caring and counseling must constantly be balanced with preparation, preaching, and administrative responsibilities.

This function of the pastor provides the opportunity to express the love of Christ in regard to the spiritual, emotional, and physical needs of the flock.

As Overseer

The title of "bishop," or "overseer," is another of the terms that is often applied to a leader in the church other than the senior pastor. This term derives its meaning from the Greek word, *episkopos*, which means "one who exercises oversight." The original word comes from two words–*epi* which means "over" and *scopus* which means "to see." As is the case in Acts 20:28, the word *bishop* is used in tandem with the word *shepherd*. Referring to the bishop or overseer, Acts 20:28 says, "among which the Holy Spirit has made you overseers." We will examine the various administrative responsibilities that are consistent with the word *overseer* a little later. As overseer, the pastor or his representative is responsible for the organizational and administrative functions of the church. He also has a sense of responsibility for

As overseer, the pastor or his representative is responsible for the organizational and administrative functions of the church. He also has a sense of responsibility for the spiritual oversight of each person in the flock.

the spiritual oversight of each person in the flock. That responsibility is made clear in the following verses from the writer to the Hebrews:

> "Remember those who rule over you, who have spoken the word of God to you, whose faith follow, considering the outcome of their conduct" (Hebrews 13:7).

In this passage, spiritual leadership is exemplified by the Word preached, faith exhibited, and conduct demonstrated. This attractive and powerful pattern of leadership compels people to follow gladly, as Peter described, "nor as being lords over those entrusted to you, but being examples to the flock."

A second passage gives more light on leading and following:

> "Obey those who rule over you, and submit yourselves, for they watch out for your souls, as those who must give account. Let them do it with joy and not with grief, for that would be unprofitable for you" (Hebrews 13:17).

Hebrews 13:7 gave the admonition to remember and respect leaders. Verse 17 added an the instruction to take action: to obey and submit to leaders.

In these verses, to "rule" also means to lead. Dictatorship is not proposed in these passages at all. Pastors have a clear mandate to lead with a blend of grace and strength. Church members are admonished to allow the pastor to lead, and they are to follow. The Scriptures teach a clear spiritual paradigm of leadership of the pastor and the willingness of the people to follow. This emphatically validates the spiritual authority of the pastor, and the resulting burdens or joys will be, in some measure, the product of the body's acceptance of this biblical principle. Some of us have been "burned" by harsh, authoritarian leaders in the past, and therefore, we may have difficulty with the concept of anyone "ruling" their churches. We are not advocating harshness at all. Biblical leadership, as we have seen in Paul's letter to the Thessalonians, is like "a nursing mother tenderly caring for her children."

Biblical leadership, as we have seen in Paul's letter to the Thessalonians, is like "a nursing mother tenderly caring for her children."

Spiritual Leadership, Authority, and Discernment

In Ecclesiastes we read:

"A three-fold cord is not easily broken" (Ecclesiastes 4:12).

This verse is true of strong relationships, and it also applies to the three essential elements of a pastor's role: spiritual leadership, authority, and discernment. They function best when they are woven together into a strong bond of leadership. Let's look at these.

The spiritual *leadership* of the pastor is a term that encompasses great and varied responsibility, including the three areas we have discussed–as elder, shepherd, and overseer. It would be an oversimplification to expect the varied responsibilities of the pastor to fall neatly into only these three areas. In practice, they interact and overlap with other responsibilities. However, they are foundational for an understanding of the division of ministry for the pastor, as well as the delegation of his responsibilities for the care of and ministry to his flock.

A pastor's spiritual leadership, though, would be neutralized without spiritual *authority.* In the pastor rests the privilege, the responsibility, and the authority to make decisions that shape the ministry of the church. Without this authority, he wanders aimlessly, or he has to follow the lead of someone else. Divided authority threatens to weaken individual hearts, friendships, and churches. Authority, of course, is not a license for being authoritarian. Leaders are admonished over and over again in Scripture to listen to wise counsel. Ultimately, however, the pastor must assume the mantle of leadership.

Spiritual authority needs clear direction, guidance, and wisdom. Spiritual *discernment* is the wisdom of God which is foundational to anointed spiritual authority and leadership. The pastor needs to draw deeply from the heart of God and the will of God. George Truett had unusual insight into the discernment needed by spiritual leaders. He wrote:

"The man of God must have insight into things spiritual. He must be able to see the mountains filled with the horses and chariots of fire; he must be able to interpret that which is written by the finger of God upon the walls of conscience; he must be able to

Spiritual *discernment* is the wisdom of God which is foundational to anointed spiritual authority and leadership.

translate the signs of the times into terms of their spiritual meaning; he must be able to draw aside, now and then, the curtain of things material and let mortals glimpse the spiritual glories which crown the mercy seat of God. The man of God must declare the pattern that was shown him on the mount; he must utter the vision granted to him upon the isle of revelation. . . . None of these things can he do without spiritual insight."[5]

The pastor's functions as elder, shepherd, and overseer find expression in specific elements of planning and programming. We now turn our attention to these elements.

THREE-FOLD FORMULA FOR ORDERLY PROGRAMMING

These three functions, in conjunction with the word "rule," which means "to govern, preside, or lead," extend the responsibility of the pastor to three basic tracks upon which the church program and ministry are developed. These tracks are: (1) preaching and teaching, (2) pastoring and caring, and (3) overseeing and administrating.

Preaching and Teaching

The role of elder requires the mature spiritual leader to teach and preach the Word of God to the flock. This, of course, finds its highest expression in the pulpit ministry. Organized Bible study allows the elder function to be practiced and extended to smaller fellowship groups.

The great leaders of churches are those who have loved and lived the Word of God. No matter how strong a pastor may be in other areas of leadership, his spiritual power will be compromised without a genuine and zealous love for the Scripture. This is true in preaching, in practice, and in programming. Therefore, the first track to be considered in developing the program for the ministry of the church is related to the Word of God. Those functions that relate specifically to the Scripture, its preaching, its teaching, and its practical application, must be organized, developed, and enhanced by a focused ministry team. This is usually seen in Sunday school or Bible study classes, small groups, men's and women's ministries, or other organizations of the church where the Word of God forms the basis of gathering, teaching, and fellowship. While various divisions exist within this

Those functions that relate specifically to the Scripture, its preaching, its teaching, and its practical application, must be organized, developed, and enhanced by a focused ministry team.

---

5 Powhattan James, *George W. Truett,* p. 266, cited in Sanders, p. 48.

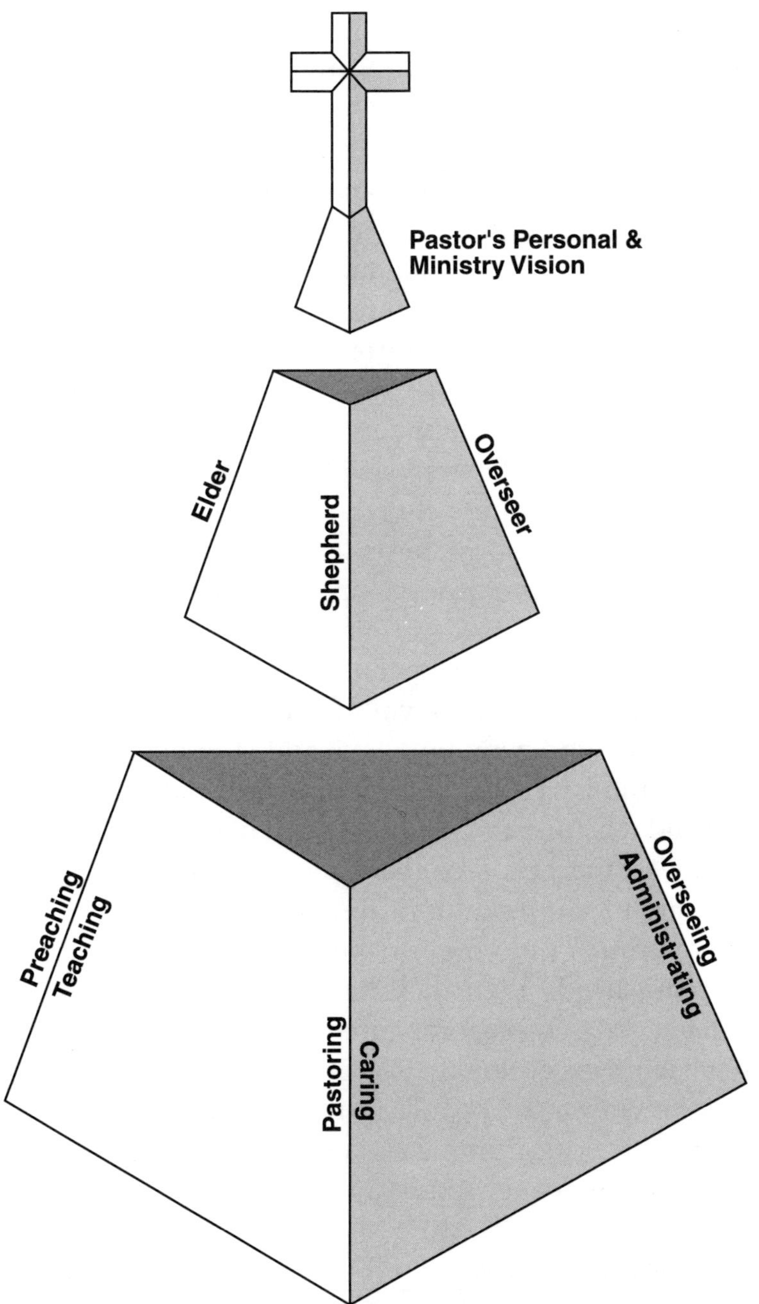

category of ministry (long-term, short-term, specific training, and general application), this function can best be carried out by those whose primary responsibilities are to extend the ministry of the pastor in the study and application of God's Word. The edification of the saints is certainly enhanced more by the fellowship around the Word of God than mere social gatherings.

The preaching/teaching ministry is the primary track for the organization of the church. To extend the pastor's vision and role in this area, select Bible study teachers, associate pastors, group leaders, and others in your church who can "accurately handle the Word of truth."

Pastoring and Caring

The elder role of the pastor can be so demanding that the shepherd role may suffer from lack of attention. While the pressures of time are understandable, they can seriously hinder the pastor's efforts to care for the church family. If the members of the flock do not receive timely attention during illness or sorrow, then in large measure, leadership has failed the individual and his family.

The pastor and leadership need to periodically review the state of this ministry of the church to determine its strengths and weaknesses. As the pastor extends his function through his staff, deacons, and leadership, he must constantly be aware of the pastoral needs of his entire flock, to "even the least of these." The "little people" are often the greatest prayer warriors, the most loyal of the pastor's supporters, and the people who genuinely love and support the church. Care-giving ministry must have comparable attention to the worship and teaching track, or the Word of God will not find application in the needs of these dear saints. Most pastors devote a significant amount of time to this ministry, but no matter how much time they spend in giving care, there are always more needs than they have time to meet. Build a strong team to give pastoral care. Find the highest caliber ministers with exceptional relational skills to provide the very best attention for people in need. Assigning less than the best to this critical ministry is relegating God's beloved saints to an even deeper sense of neglect and sorrow.

Overseeing and Administrating

The third track for orderly programming is often mistakenly exempted from the formula altogether. The organized administration or overseeing of the church requires very specialized attention, to the same extent as the other two tracks. The other two tracks, however, often absorb the energies of leadership because they are the more traditional areas of responsibility. In fact, administration is often relegated to untrained, and sometimes calloused, leaders who know how to "crunch the numbers" but don't have the pastor's heart for each segment of the ministry of the church. Consequently, they don't see administration as a ministry, but as cold and spiritless "business of the church." Financial decisions are based purely on numbers instead of being guided and balanced by

Build a strong team to give pastoral care. Find the highest caliber ministers with exceptional relational skills to provide the very best attention for people in need.

vision and compassion, and church business meetings often prove to be a "two-hour ride through Ulcer Gulch." Fellowship is fractured because focus is lost. The momentum of ministry is given over to the management—or mismanagement—of money. The administrative function, which is intended to be a strong foundation and the launching platform for vibrant church life, is reduced to power plays.

This ministry track presents one of the greatest challenges to a pastor. Whether or not he is gifted in this area is somewhat moot because of the time required for his more public ministry. Even an administratively gifted pastor will not have the time for the research, follow-up, and team building required, which will broaden as his church grows. The pastor may have difficulty in discerning the administrative capability of his leadership, or on the other hand, some of his leaders may intimidate him. It is wonderful, though, when the pastor can give spiritual leadership that balances the God-given abilities of his selected laymen without stifling their potential, and it is marvelous when gifted laymen submit lovingly to the pastor's leadership. Strong relationships, coupled with a comprehensive process of administering the ministries of church, enhances the overall fellowship or "koinonia" of the church family. The pastor's three-fold function is relevant to your vision of your ministry whether you are beginning a church plant, pastoring a mega-church, or growing through the stages in between. These three functions and programming elements shape our concept of our calling. I encourage you to focus on those areas that are your strengths, and learn to choose qualified staff members to offset your weaknesses. In that way, each function will receive the attention it deserves, and you will find more fulfillment, energy, and passion for Christ and His Kingdom.

The three elements of programming must be carefully planned and coordinated to ensure maximum effectiveness. Let's examine the ingredients and processes of good planning.

It is wonderful, though, when the pastor can give spiritual leadership that balances the God-given abilities of his selected laymen without stifling their potential, and it is marvelous when gifted laymen submit lovingly to the pastor's leadership.

THE THREE-FOLD FRAMEWORK FOR OPERATIONAL PLANNING

As we have seen, the pastor's God-given function finds expression in the three tracks of programming. These programming tracks are then outlined and implemented by a clear framework of operational planning, consisting of three crucial elements: a ministry plan, a financial plan, and a master calendar. The vision of the pastor, and by extension, each ministry leader, determines the programs in the Ministry Plan. The implementation of this plan requires resources, and the Financial Plan outlines how the funding will be provided to accomplish God's vision for the church. As elements of the program are identified and prioritized, each event, meeting, and class is entered on the Master Calendar to ensure that space is provided and other resources are available to make each activity a success.

The interworking of these three elements of planning forms the foundation for the vision to be accomplished. We will address each of these elements of operational planning in more detail in Step 5.

A MINISTRY VISION STATEMENT

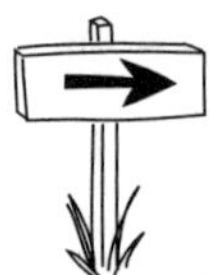

It is important for each of us to be able to clearly articulate the vision in which God has called us to serve.

In the second part of this chapter, we have seen how a ministry vision springs from a pastor's personal vision. We have looked at how the pastor's spiritual gifts and personality shape how he serves, and we have examined the three-fold function of the role of a pastor to give us clarity about that godly calling. It is important for each of us to be able to clearly articulate the vision in which God has called us to serve. The exercise at the end of this Step will help you identify and clarify your ministry vision.

TAKE A STEP

Each of the exercises in this Step are for individuals, primarily for the pastor, but very useful for each person on the leadership team. After each person on the team completes them, take time to share what you learned about yourselves.

This core exercise is:

— Your Ministry Vision

Additional exercises are:

— Spiritual Gifts Inventory, and
— Temperament Inventory.

Note: The inventory included in this book is one we have used in our ministry at Bellevue Baptist Church. In my consulting with pastors, I use a more extensive inventory, the DISC Profile, to reveal a person's behavioral tendencies and to build teams of individuals with complementing strengths. The resource section in the back of this book gives directions about how you can order copies of the DISC Profile.

YOUR MINISTRY VISION

— *Who?:* The pastor, though each ministry leader can benefit from this exercise, too.

— *Why?:* To clarify and refine God's call to serve Him.

— *How?:* Like you did for the Personal Vision exercise, find a time when you won't be hurried and a place where you won't be distracted. Begin by asking the Holy Spirit to open your heart to hear and understand what He wants to speak to you. As you go through this exercise, it is much more important that you pay attention to the Lord than it is that you write in all the blank spaces. Listen intently, and be encouraged.

— *Then what?:* Your ministry vision will renew your passion for ministry, and it will serve as the plumbline for all of your planning.

YOUR MINISTRY VISION

Your personal vision statement answered the question: "Who does God want me to be?" The ministry vision statement answers the question: "What does God want me to do?"

1. Describe a time when God gave you specific direction for your life's calling. How did He communicate His heart and His will to you (through His Word, conviction and confidence in prayer, a wise brother, etc.)?

2. What are your strengths in ministering to others? In other words, how do you see God working through you most powerfully and most often?

3. How does your God-given personality make you a more effective minister?

4. As a pastor, how does God use you in the functions of:

    — elder?

— shepherd?

— overseer?

5. Of the tasks for which you are currently responsible, list those you enjoy the most, from most fulfilling to those that are neutral. What does this list tell you?

6. Now list the tasks you dislike, from the least fulfilling to those that are neutral. What does this list tell you?

7. Take some time to reflect on passages of Scripture that God has used throughout your life to define your ministry vision. List them here and write a short summary of the message from God to you in each one.

8. No matter where you go, no matter how much success or failure you experience, what has God called you to do? Write your own clear ministry vision here:

SPIRITUAL GIFTS INVENTORY

— *Who?:* The pastor, the planning team, and every person in the ministry can benefit from this exercise.

— *Why?:* To identify those abilities that God has entrusted to you so you can focus your energies and maximize your effectiveness.

— *How?:* Follow the instructions in this inventory.

— *Then what?:* This exercise may simply confirm what you already know about how God typically uses you, but it may show that too much of your time is being spent in areas where you are not gifted. If that is the case, some adjustments need to be made in the selection and delegation of responsibilities.

SPIRITUAL GIFTS INVENTORY

The New Testament teaches that every believer has been given at least one spiritual gift, a God-given ability to serve God and minister to others. These gifts shape our roles in the body of Christ, and we need to operate within our gifts so we can make wise decisions about how to use our time and talents. Certainly, all believers are called to minister in virtually all these areas (such as evangelism, giving, and serving), but spiritual gifting gives the servant extra passion and extraordinary ability in that particular service.

Four New Testament passages give us lists and descriptions of spiritual gifts (Romans 12, I Corinthians 12, Ephesians 4, and I Peter 4). Different beliefs and traditions limit or expand the list based on any number of criteria. For our purposes, we will use a list of 15 gifts which include support gifts, service gifts, and a limited number of the sign gifts.

Respond to each of the following statements with one of these three options:

2   Definitely true: You have seen God at work in this area.
1   Sometimes true: There may be a desire, but little experience in this area.
0   Definitely not true: This is not an area of interest or effectiveness.

Mature believers should indicate their answers according to actual *experience;* young believers don't have as much experience, so they need to indicate their *desires and interests* in each aspect of ministry.

____ 1. I enjoy sharing the gospel with unbelievers.

____ 2. I show genuine concern for the well-being and growth of young believers.

____ 3. I am able to explain biblical truth in ways people understand.

____ 4. I enjoy organizing the efforts of other believers.

____ 5. I can effectively encourage people to handle difficult problems.

____ 6. I believe God's promises and trust God to fulfill them.

____ 7. I manage money well and enjoy giving to meet the needs of others.

____ 8. I enjoy helping visitors feel at home at our church.

____ 9. I enjoy studying the Scriptures and going deep into God's truth.

____ 10. I enjoy being an example for others to follow.

____ 11. I look for ways to help those who are disadvantaged.

___ 12. I enjoy performing tasks that free our leaders to focus on their ministries.

___ 13. Other people often ask for my advice on difficult matters in their lives.

___ 14. I can see through situations and determine the right and wrong in them.

___ 15. God uses me to heal people emotionally and physically.

___ 16. I go where there are unbelievers so I can talk to them about Christ.

___ 17. I long to see Christians grow in their faith, and I actively help them.

___ 18. When I teach people, they report that their lives are changed by God.

___ 19. I orchestrate God's work so it is done in an orderly and efficient way.

___ 20. I listen carefully to people before I share God's truth with them.

___ 21. My prayers are full of hope that God will work, even in the most difficult situations.

___ 22. I give generously, trusting God to meet my needs so I can continue giving.

___ 23. I enjoy receiving guests into our home.

___ 24. People ask me to explain difficult biblical issues to them.

___ 25. I thrive on being responsible for others and motivating them to accomplish God's purposes.

___ 26. I enjoy visiting people in hospitals, jails, and retirement homes.

___ 27. I prefer following and helping instead of leading.

___ 28. I try to understand people and carefully apply biblical solutions to their problems.

___ 29. I can readily detect hidden motives in conversations with people.

___ 30. I look for evidence of God's miraculous activity in others' lives.

___ 31. I use almost every opportunity to tell people about Christ.

___ 32. I am patient with those who are slow to grow in their faith.

___ 33. I love to teach God's Word to anyone who will listen.

___ 34. I can break large projects into bite-sized tasks for people so the job gets done.

___ 35. I regularly point people to God and His Word as the solution to their problems.

___ 36. I am annoyed when people trust their own abilities, their organizations, or anything else besides God for wisdom and power.

___ 37. I enjoy making money so I can give even more.

___ 38. I look for ways to make people feel comfortable and welcome at church and in our home.

___ 39. I enjoy studying the Scriptures so much that I lose track of time.

___ 40. I am often asked to lead a group of people to accomplish particular tasks.

___ 41. I enjoy serving other people whether or not they appreciate my efforts.

___ 42. I am glad to pitch in and serve in any way I can.

___ 43. I can find the central question in a discussion more quickly than most people.

___ 44. I can detect a person's character even if he's trying to hide it.

___ 45. When I pray, God accomplishes miracles in situations and individuals' lives.

___ 46. I often see people respond to the gospel.

___ 47. I am happy for people to share their problems with me so I can help them.

___ 48. People make better decisions after listening to me teach God's Word.

___ 49. I have the ability to envision the total scope of a project and organize the work so it is accomplished efficiently.

___ 50. I often encourage and strengthen those who are discouraged or tempted.

___ 51. My heroes are men of great faith, like Noah, Abraham, Elijah, and Paul.

___ 52. I enjoy meeting the financial needs of others.

___ 53. It doesn't bother me to have people in our home when things are not completely clean and in order.

___ 54. People come to me for in-depth information about biblical and practical matters of life and faith.

___ 55. People look to me for direction.

___ 56. I enjoy being personally involved in helping hurting and lonely people.

___ 57. I am one of the first to volunteer to help around the church.

___ 58. I am able to help disagreeable people agree.

___ 59. People ask me to help them understand the underlying motives and goals of other people.

___ 60. I am compelled to pray that God will work in fresh, new, incredible ways to overcome seemingly insurmountable problems.

___ 61. I love being with unbelievers to build relationships with them.

___ 62. I enjoy leading a group of people as they grow in Christ.

___ 63. I enjoy preparation and presentation of God's Word.

___ 64. I enjoy helping people develop goals and plans to accomplish God's purposes.

___ 65. I trust God to lead me to people so He can use me to encourage, comfort, and strengthen them.

___ 66. The faith of other people grows as they are exposed to my trust that God will fulfill His promises.

___ 67. When I hear about a need, I often determine to meet it myself out of the resources God has given me.

___ 68. I enjoy having people in our home for Bible study and fellowship.

___ 69. I enjoy doing research on difficult passages of Scripture.

___ 70. I feel fulfilled when I help others take greater responsibility in ministry.

___ 71. I feel deep compassion for those who suffer, and I am moved to help them.

___ 72. I prefer short-term projects which have a definite goal.

___ 73. People often comment that my advice is practical and helpful.

___ 74. When I talk to other believers, I can readily see their true spiritual condition.

___ 75. I believe that if we really trust God, we will see the same kinds of miraculous activities of God that we find among the early believers in the Book of Acts.

Scoring

In the right column below, add the total points for each of the five statements that apply to each of the gifts listed. (The totals may range from 10 to 0.)

Gift	Statements	Total
Evangelist	1, 16, 31, 46, 61	_________
Pastor	2, 17, 32, 47, 62	_________
Teacher	3, 18, 33, 48, 63	_________
Administration	4, 19, 34, 49, 64	_________
Exhortation	5, 20, 35, 50, 65	_________
Faith	6, 21, 36, 51, 66	_________
Giving	7, 22, 37, 52, 67	_________
Hospitality	8, 23, 38, 53, 68	_________
Knowledge	9, 24, 39, 54, 69	_________
Leadership	10, 25, 40, 55, 70	_________
Mercy	11, 26, 41, 56, 71	_________
Service	12, 27, 42, 57, 72	_________
Wisdom	13, 28, 43, 58, 73	_________
Discernment	14, 29, 44, 59, 74	_________
Miracles	15, 30, 45, 60, 75	_________

Descriptions of the Gifts:

Evangelist: the desire to share the gospel with unbelievers and an effectiveness in this witness.
Pastor: the ability to help people grow in their faith.
Teacher: the ability to teach God's Word powerfully and clearly so it changes lives.
Administration: the ability to organize God's work effectively.
Exhortation: the ability to encourage, rebuke, admonish, and direct people to follow Christ.
Faith: extraordinary confidence in God and His promises.
Giving: the capability and desire to give to meet the needs of others.
Hospitality: the ability to welcome people and make them feel at home.
Knowledge: the ability to analyze the Scriptures and clarify truth for others.

Leadership: the ability to motivate and orchestrate the efforts of others so goals are accomplished and people are encouraged.
Mercy: the ability to relieve suffering of others in a cheerful and selfless way.
Service: the ability to see unmet needs and accomplish tasks to meet these needs.
Wisdom: unusual insight and application of God's Word during difficult situations.
Discernment: the ability to uncover hidden motives and determine if an action is rooted in God, man, or Satan.
Miracles: the ability to pray and see supernatural healing and provisions from the hand of God.

List the three on your scoresheet with the highest scores:

Describe how you have seen God use you in each of these areas:

How does your current ministry responsibility give you opportunities to exercise your gifts?

In what ways does it hinder you?

TEMPERAMENT INVENTORY

— *Who?:* The pastor and each person in the ministry.
— *Why?:* To see how your God-given temperament shapes your motivations, relationships, and work style.
— *How?:* Follow the directions in the inventory.
— *Then what?:* Again, this exercise may simply confirm what you already know about yourself, but it may surface conflicts between you and someone close to you at home or in the church, and it may show you how to fit your style of ministry with your temperament so you are most effective.

TEMPERAMENT INVENTORY

This evaluation is designed to assist you in identifying your temperament or personality strengths and weaknesses as they specifically relate to ministry and service in the local church. It is not designed to put you into a box or a mold, but rather to enable you to understand why you are motivated the way you are and what some of the accompanying weaknesses might naturally be. In turn, you can use this information to assist in finding the ministry or service area that best utilizes your unique strengths.

On the next page, you will find groupings of four unrelated personality characteristics which may or may not describe you as an individual. Each grouping gives either four positive or four negative characteristics. Rank each characteristic in a particular grouping, whether positive or negative from 1 to 4 (one describing you the least and 4 describing you the most) out of these four items.

Keep in mind that the church will not be looking at your answers, but rather using the overall information to highlight areas in which you are especially gifted and motivated. Once your primary areas of ministry strength are identified, we can then use this information to identify specific service opportunities which may be of interest to you.

For each group of characteristics given below, rank each in the group from the one that describes you most (give a "4") to the one that describes you least (give a "1").

Animated _____	Undisciplined _____	Enthusiastic _____
Harmonious _____	Fearful _____	Long-Suffering _____
Precise _____	Moody _____	Dedicated _____
Self-reliant _____	Pushy _____	Convincing _____
Impulsive _____	Liked _____	Forgetful _____
Unwilling _____	Contented _____	Indifferent _____
Hyper-Sensitive _____	Tender _____	Pessimistic _____
Undiplomatic _____	Mover _____	Unyielding _____
Bubbly _____	Disorderly _____	Amusing _____
Amicable _____	Apathetic _____	Constant _____
Detailed _____	Self-Absorbed _____	Devoted _____
Enterprising _____	Overbearing _____	Determined _____
Disorganized _____	Spontaneous _____	Self-promoting _____
Lazy _____	Dry Humor _____	Indecisive _____
Critical _____	Thinker _____	Unforgiving _____
Impatient _____	Productive _____	Proud _____
Inspiring _____	Redundant _____	Congenial _____
Arbitrator _____	Slow _____	Balanced _____
Perservering _____	Solitary _____	Systematic _____
Self-sufficient _____	Impetuous _____	Daring _____
Interfering _____	Encouraging _____	Unpredictable _____
Unenthusiastic _____	Subdued _____	Anxious _____
Self-Conscious _____	Sympathetic _____	Particular _____
Manipulative _____	Tenacious _____	Combative _____

Scoring

Bring totals across from the three columns on the preceding page and write the totals in the spaces below:

Add up all the first lines and place the total score on the first line below. Do the same with the second, third and fourth lines. This will give you a score for each of the temperament types:

_____ Sanguine

_____ Phlegmatic

_____ Melancholy

_____ Choleric

On the following pages, some generalized strengths and weaknesses are listed for each of the temperament types. Look primarily at the temperament types on which you scored the highest and second highest. As always, keep in mind that these are not designed to "stereotype" you or put you into a box but merely to help you understand what may be your strengths and weaknesses as they relate to ministry and service.

Sanguine

This personality is predominantly characterized as being optimistic, extroverted, talkative, energetic, and emotionally expressive.

IN GENERAL
Strengths
- Magnetic personality
- Sees the humor in things
- Pleasant and positive
- Expresses emotions easily
- Lives for today
- Doesn't stay angry for long
- Spontaneous and fun
- Enjoys being around people
- Friendly and outgoing

Weaknesses
- Emotionally changeable
- May be dominant in discussions
- Easily influenced by others
- Prone to lack of discipline
- Not naturally organized
- Lack of follow-through
- More idealistic than practical

IN MINISTRY
Strengths
- Quickly volunteers for service
- Motivates others to get involved
- Enjoys being in front of people
- Contagious enthusiasm for projects
- Easily forgives and asks forgiveness
- Meets new people easily
- Creative in planning activities

Weaknesses
- Volunteers for more than can do
- Doesn't always stay on schedule
- May be self-centered and egotistical
- Easily tempted
- Prone to ministry "burn out"

Phlegmatic

This personality is predominantly characterized as being stable, easy-going, consistent, and quiet.

IN GENERAL
Strengths
- Takes things in stride
- Calm and relaxed
- Often known for dry wit
- Content with life
- Gets along well with others
- Friendly and kind
- Neat and efficient
- Finds effective solutions
- Good mediator

Weaknesses
- Lack of motivation
- Avoids too much work
- May be viewed as a tease
- Self-protective
- Prone to indecisiveness
- Looks for the easy way out
- Tends toward procrastination

IN MINISTRY
Strengths
- Consistent walk with Christ
- Not easily disturbed
- Competent and stable
- Peacemaker
- Stays calm under pressure
- Listens well to others
- Expresses concern for others
- Able to accept trials as well as blessings

Weaknesses
- Keeps true emotions
- Avoids confrontation even when necessary
- Slow to volunteer
- Would rather watch than participate

Melancholy

This personality is predominantly characterized as being sensitive, creative, a thinker, a perfectionist, and self-sacrificing.

IN GENERAL
Strengths
- Emotionally responsive
- High standards of excellence
- Good problem-solving abilities
- Faithful friend
- Dependable
- Knows limitations
- Creative and talented
- Practical and thrifty
- Won't settle for being "average"
- Appreciates the "little things"

Weaknesses
- Prone to mood swings
- Focuses inward instead of outward
- Easily offended or hurt
- Prone to depression and negativism
- Critical and perfectionistic
- Hesitant to make new commitments
- Bothered by insignificant details

IN MINISTRY
Strengths
- Cares deeply about people
- Stays on schedule
- Finishes projects
- Willing to sacrifice for what is important
- In tune to others' needs
- Often gifted in music or creative arts
- Devoted to the cause of Christ
- Good planner and organizer
- Remembers important details

Weaknesses
- Sees potential problems
- Subject to fear and worry
- Difficulty in making new friends
- May be intolerant of others
- May have difficulty forgiving others
- Doesn't enjoy being "up front"

Choleric

This personality is predominantly characterized as being a leader, a doer, and an extrovert.

IN GENERAL
Strengths
- Natural leader
- Makes decisions easily
- Sticks to the job
- Confident and self-reliant
- Excels under pressure
- Organized and "together"
- Thrives on new challenges
- Sets goals and priorities

Weaknesses
- Insists on own way
- Difficulty expressing emotions
- May be insensitive to others
- Uncompassionate
- Loses temper quickly
- Prone to dominate others

IN MINISTRY
Strengths
- Sees the "big picture"
- Quickly motivated to action
- Follows through on projects
- Not easily swayed from goals
- Organized and practical
- Delegates to others
- Accepts leadership responsibilities

Weaknesses
- Difficulty depending on Christ
- May put goals before people
- Subject to bitterness
- May "run over" others' feelings
- Has little need for other people

Temperament Combinations

Most people will find themselves a close combination of two of the personality types. These combinations are discussed below. (It is also possible that an individual be a blend of three or all of the personality types, and distinctions may blur as the weaknesses are brought under the control of the Holy Spirit).

Sanguine-Choleric/Choleric-Sanguine

This individual is extremely outgoing and a natural leader and performer. He seems practically invincable as he not only easily volunteers for projects, but sees them through to their completion. He may have difficulty depending on the Lord as he is naturally self-sufficient. He may at times be insensitive to others because of seeing his own agenda as the most important.

Sanguine-Melancholy/Melancholy-Sanguine

This individual is characterized by emotions. He is either extremely high or low at any given time. He is very expressive of his own feelings and also sensitive to the feelings of others. He is effective in ministry to people, and is very creative in his approach to accomplishing tasks. He may become easily depressed if things don't go the way he would like for them to. This personality combination is quite rare, as many of the characteristics of these two types are mutually exclusive.

Sanguine-Phlegmatic/Phlegmatic-Sanguine

This individual is a delight and pleasure to be around. He is comfortable around people and makes them feel comfortable. He is outgoing and easy going at the same time. He has a high level of tolerance for others, and his good sense of humor helps keep things in perspective. His greatest weakness is a lack of follow-through. While he may volunteer easily for projects, he may have difficulty getting the job done.

Choleric-Melancholy/Melancholy-Choleric

This individual is highly motivated and very productive. He not only sets goals but stays   on schedule and sees them through to their desired end. He is likely to be a talented individual, and is not inhibited to use his God-given talents in the service of the Lord. He may be self-centered and more concerned with his own agenda than the "big picture." He may be hesitant to make big commitments, but will sacrifice whatever is necessary to accomplish the things he has committed to.

STEP 1 *The Captain's Compass*
- Your Personal Vision
- Your Ministry Vision

STEP 2 *Look at the Map*
- **Your Plan for Planning**
- **Ministry Review**
- **Planning Team Evaluation**

STEP 3 *Watch for Obstacles and Opportunities*
- Task Summaries
- Job Descriptions
- Historical Growth Statistics—Bible Study
- Historical Growth Statistics—General Church Criteria
- Community Demographics
- Obstacles and Opportunities
- Space Utilization

STEP 4 *Get Your Equipment Ready*
- Ministry Flow Chart
- Organizational Chart
- Communication System

STEP 5 *Plot Your Course*
- Ministry Leader Planning Worksheet
- The Ministry Plan
- The Master Calendar
- The Financial Plan
- Communication Plan

STEP 6 *Look Over the Next Hill*
- Long-Range Ministry Plan
- Growth and Capacity Analysis
- Growth Projections
- General Church Criteria
- Building Plan Schedule and Expenditures
- Long-Range Financial Plan

STEP 7 *Get on the Trail*
- Monthly Planning Worksheet

LOOK AT THE MAP

The next step in the planning process is to take a good, hard look at the current conditions of your church: the strengths and weaknesses of each area of your ministry and the culture of the planning process itself. Some of us err by failing to plan, and others make the mistake of making rigid, inflexible plans as though we are omniscient and know the future. The Bible encourages us to enjoy the blessings of the day without worrying about tomorrow, but not worrying does not mean we shouldn't plan. In fact, planning allows us to enjoy the present by reducing anxiety about the future. As pastors and church leaders, we must be able to identify and anticipate the needs of our people tomorrow while we rejoice in the goodness of God today. Good planning involves good listening—to the Lord and to those we serve. Step 2 focuses on this listening process to determine the condition of our flocks so our plans will reflect the Lord's direction and so we can effectively serve Him, our flock, and our community.

The Bible encourages us to enjoy the blessings of the day without worrying about tomorrow, but not worrying does not mean we shouldn't plan. In fact, planning allows us to enjoy the present by reducing anxiety about the future.

PLANNING TO PLAN

Before you jump into the planning process, it is wise to think about the process itself. In fact, one of the most important steps is "planning to plan." A clear focus and direction can prevent you from getting bogged down in details or getting off track. Some important factors to consider are selecting your planning team, getting good data, and assessing resources.

Selecting a Planning Team

Even the most astute plan written on your own will be inferior to a plan carefully crafted by a good team. Involving others gives you more objective data, and also gives participants a sense of goal ownership. When other people contribute to the plan, they are far more likely to defend it and to marshal resources to accomplish it.

The members of this team should have two main characteristics: loyalty to the pastor and loyalty to the purposes of the church. Under those two main criteria, the team should consist of people with diverse backgrounds and diverse opinions in order to find creative solutions.

Your planning team has very important duties. First, they will be entrusted with the responsibility of translating godly direction into strategic steps of action.

In the vast majority of churches, the pastor will be the leader of the planning team. The members of this team should have two main characteristics: loyalty to the pastor and loyalty to the purposes of the church. Under those two main criteria, the team should consist of people with diverse backgrounds and diverse opinions in order to find creative solutions.

Form a planning team with a good cross-section of gifted and mature people, those with wisdom and discernment, men and women, young and old, and be sure they are not all just like you. Some need to be people who "color outside the box," and some need to be those who specialize in creating artistry inside the box. Depending on the size of the church, your team may be as few as three people for a bi-vocational church, and as many as seven for larger churches. In very large churches, each of the major ministry segments will have their own planning teams, and these will then report to a central team, which may be led by the senior associate on the staff.

Be wise about the people you include. Invite mature people of varied orientations to join the process so you will avoid "group think." Some people, such as the pastoral staff and lay leadership, need to be an integral part of the entire process. Your church leadership needs to be adequately informed, but all of them do not need to be on the planning team itself. You may want to select individuals who are not a part of the recognized church leadership in order to get a broader perspective of the needs and possibilities. Keep the size of your team workable so that you don't get bogged down in endless discussions.

Your planning team has very important duties. First, they will be entrusted with the responsibility of translating godly direction into strategic steps of action. Second, they must be individuals who are loyal to the pastor's leadership and committed to the spirit of unity even when they have differing opinions. Third, they must be spiritually sensitive to discern the difference between man's ideas and God-given inspiration for direction. Fourth, your team must be comprised of people who will become deeply involved in the planning process and are willing to devote time and energy to it. Ownership and successful implementation of the finalized plan begins with your planning team. Keep in mind that *how* your team plans determines *what* they plan.

With planning teams, beware of personal agendas which can lead to frustration and fractured leadership. Each member must be willing to set aside his or her personal agenda in lieu of what is in the best interest of the body (Mark 8:27-38; Luke 24:44-49).

Encourage the team to be open and transparent with their opinions. The prerequisites of loyalty to the pastor and their commitment to be led by God's Spirit should form a bond among them. As the team works together, the synergy of their different strengths produces a wholesome result, and any disagreements build trust instead of threatening it. Involving others can be a time-consuming process, but it is very productive. Not involving others in planning gives people the message that you don't value their input and leadership.

Have the team first establish a skeleton of your plan, and then put meat on its bones. Have a key leader or two, probably the pastor and an articulate lay leader, draft the plan on paper. Bring the first draft to the team for review and comments, then send it back to the writers for a second draft. This process continues until the plan is clear and compelling. The plan is then shared with the church body in a worship service or a business meeting. It should be presented in an attractive way—both a written version and a verbal explanation using powerful visual images.

Your congregation needs to become committed to the plan because they are the ones who will implement and finance it. If the planning team includes a broad representation of the congregation, the people in the pews will feel more confident that the plan will meet their needs. Also, if every segment has been given the opportunity to express their opinions in some way, they are more likely to accept the final plan. This process of involving many carefully selected people in information-gathering and planning requires skill, patience, and hard work, but it reaps rich rewards.

As you present your plan for approval, don't come to the business meeting (or any other decision-making body) with an attitude that suggests, "This plan has been hard work. You had better approve it tonight!" Instead, have a servant's heart and patiently explain the Kingdom benefits of your plan if you want people to be receptive.

Getting Good Data

Solomon wrote:

> "By pride (or presumption) comes nothing but strife,
> but with the well-advised is wisdom" (Proverbs 13:10).

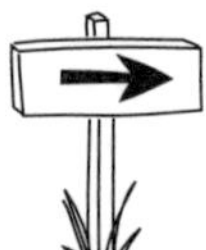

Take time to get the accurate data about the present situation, as well as historical data so you can see the trends.

We often presume we know what people think and feel about certain programs or people (and we usually believe that they see things exactly as we do!), but if we are wrong, our plans will be off base. Take time to get the accurate data about the present situation, as well as historical data so you can see the trends. For instance, your youth Sunday school program may have grown when you began a day-care program, but it may have plateaued when each class reached a certain size due to facility limitations.

Attendance at worship, Sunday school, small groups, or seminars can be traced fairly easily. Monthly offerings usually follow seasonal cycles, but giving may also reflect the congregation's attitude about very positive or negative events in the church's life. It is important to determine if a trend is seasonal or situational.

Other examples of data which may be helpful are:

— Hard data: income, expenses, attendance, trends, number of people at new events, etc.
— Subjective data: How people feel about the style of worship, type of music, sermon content and application, teaching, stewardship, quality of fellowship and supportive relationships, etc.

We will look at how to gather this data later, but for now, simply realize that this is a vital part of the planning process. There are several avenues for collecting reasonable, accurate data for your planning process. Surveys of the congregation can give you broad perspective, but be careful not to create expectations that every person's individual desires will be met. Reports from specific committees will give you facts and trends. Focus groups often provide very meaningful feedback when the participants are selected wisely. Of course, always consider the quality and quantity of information. A pet peeve of a few outspoken church members can seem like an overwhelming and conclusive statement of fact. Be sure to get information from some of the "quiet" people, too. Getting good data takes time and effort, but it will shape the entire direction of your planning process and ultimately, the direction of your church.

Getting good data takes time and effort, but it will shape the entire direction of your planning process and ultimately, the direction of your church.

Assessing Resources

Time, facilities, money, and leadership are resources which must be considered for any direction or activity — new or existing. Though all activities have their congregational champions, they are not equally important. Prioritize the emphases and events which are most important to the direction of the church at this point in its life.

Assess the existing resources to determine how time, money, facilities, and key leadership can be used most effectively. Of course, leadership is your most important resource. The lack of time, money and facilities usually can be overcome by creative approaches, but the lack of strong godly leadership is a serious deterrent to the future of your church. Leadership development must be one of your highest priorities.

Many of us try to do too many things without having the resources to accomplish them. Remember: Quantity follows quality. Focus on a few things and do them well. As additional leadership is developed, more breadth and depth can be added to your ministry.

The Schedule for Planning

Don't rush the planning process, but on the other hand, don't let it drag on endlessly. When a pastor is new to a church, I encourage him to make no significant changes for several months. During this time, he can get to know his staff and lay leaders better, gauge the attitudes of his leaders and his congregation more accurately, and uncover any land mines that threaten to blow up if he takes a wrong step.

I don't want to give anyone a specific timetable for planning because there are so many variables for any particular church situation. Choose your planning team wisely, and move forward at a pace that accomplishes your purposes. When the plan takes shape, move on to implementation so the fruit of your planning can be realized. And watch what God does in the lives of people in your church and your community!

One of the first steps in planning, and indeed, one that determines the very direction of your church, is to develop a ministry philosophy. We have already outlined a leadership philosophy for the role of the pastor, including the three functions of pastoral leadership. Here we want to determine the specific values and style of ministry the church will employ. Over the years, many different philosophies have been articulated. The vast majority of them focus on several key elements of the life and growth of a church. At the end of Step 2, you will find a worksheet to help you think through your church's ministry philosophy.

Most churches with whom I've been associated use the Bible study hour on Sunday morning as the most significant

Of course, leadership is your most important resource. The lack of time, money and facilities usually can be overcome by creative approaches, but the lack of strong godly leadership is a serious deterrent to the future of your church.

DETERMINE YOUR MINISTRY PHILOSOPHY

place to incorporate new people into the life of the church. Leadership teams were established in each class, and job descriptions were drafted to clearly outline specific responsibilities, such as outreach and inreach leaders, greeters, refreshments, communication (letters to newcomers and a monthly letter to all class members), teaching, parties, and care-giving. These classes are promoted during the announcements in worship, and the pastor uses illustrations about God's work in these classes in his sermons. The message is clear: You need to be a part of these classes! This is where God is at work in our church!

Still others have a very significant small group ministry. Many models for small groups exist today. Some focus on topics of interest, some include people from geographic areas of the city, and some are designed for particular demographic groups in the congregation, like young couples. Information about these groups is included every week in the bulletin, and sermon illustrations often describe how God is working in these environments. Group leaders are carefully picked and trained, and newcomers are encouraged to join a group so they will make strong friendships.

Consider your ministry philosophy very carefully, and articulate it clearly so your leaders and your congregation understand your church's commitment to express the heart of God to those inside and outside the church. As you write it, focus on reaching the lost as well as teaching and strengthening the body of believers. All other programs will complement this central priority of proclaiming the Word of God. As you consider your ministry philosophy, you may want to visit one or two in your area to broaden your vision of what God might want to do in your church. Tradition is valuable, but sometimes tradition is a straightjacket. Many pastors do the same things in the same way year after year without asking, "God, what do You want to do here? Stretch my mind and my heart to grasp all that You want to do, and equip me to do it."

Consider your ministry philosophy very carefully, and articulate it clearly so your leaders and your congregation understand your church's commitment to express the heart of God to those inside and outside the church.

THE NECESSITY OF LEADERSHIP DEVELOPMENT

Hundreds of books have been written on leadership. Many of them are very informative and insightful. The growth of any organization, both quantitatively and qualitatively, is based on the growth of competent leaders. The number of followers may expand faster than the number of leaders required to serve them. This creates a leadership vacuum. The leadership base must continually be expanded for healthy and dynamic growth. Far too often, pastors are focused on doing the ministry themselves, and they neglect the essential element of developing other leaders. Perhaps they have never seen good models of leadership development, and perhaps their academic training didn't devote enough emphasis to this subject. The ministry grows, they believe, when they work harder and do more. So that's what they do. They want to see God touch as many lives as possible, so they become consumed by every ministry of the church, giving hands-on direction to evangelism, visitation, administration, children's ministry, and trying to meet every need. By the time they get home, they are exhausted. As we have noted, the average tenure of service for pastors in a church in America is only two-and-a-half years. I believe that a good-hearted but wrong-headed emphasis on the pastor's own personal ministry, instead of developing others, is one of the main reasons for this alarming statistic. Many work as hard as they can as long as they can, but they may never reach their potential because of misspent time and energy.

Developing leaders certainly takes some time and energy, but the benefits are exponential as these men and women get involved in advancing God's Kingdom. And the results are even greater when many of these learn the skills of leadership development themselves. The elements of leadership development aren't obscure. They are readily obvious, but they require a genuine commitment for the long-term process to be a success. These elements include:

Developing leaders certainly takes some time and energy, but the benefits are exponential as these men and women get involved in advancing God's Kingdom.

— *Recruiting:* The call to follow Christ boldly is for every believer, and all of us can lead others in one way or another. This is primarily a call to service.
— *Selecting:* The team leader assesses the strengths and weaknesses of each person to see who is qualified for each role and responsibility.
— *Mentoring:* Before placing someone in a key position of responsibility, young recruits should work under a proven leader to learn the skills and absorb the perceptions necessary for effective service.
— *Placing:* The leadership team can assess the needs of the church and the qualifications and gifts of the person to find the best fit for effective service.
— *Coaching:* The Bible is quite explicit about putting untried people into responsible positions in the church. This is a recipe for serious problems! Good coaching is essential, and it includes regular input and feedback, as well as lots of encouragement and celebration of successes.

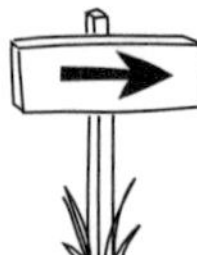

Don't just keep doing the same old things and expect dramatic change. You may need to break the mold and find a new way of thinking and doing ministry if your you want your church—and the individuals in it—to grow.

— *Maximizing:* Ministry leaders need to see themselves as resource providers for every person serving with them. They can suggest articles to read, seminars to attend, and countless other resources to equip their people to do the work of the ministry for which they are responsible.

— *Multiplying:* Eventually, many of those who are doing the ministry well can become multipliers. They will learn to select, mentor, coach, and maximize the effectiveness of those under them, and the leadership base continues to grow.

Read books, talk to friends who are successful at developing leaders, and find churches where you can go to see what they are doing in this area of ministry. Don't just keep doing the same old things and expect dramatic change. You may need to break the mold and find a new way of thinking and doing ministry if your you want your church—and the individuals in it—to grow.

AN ATMOSPHERE OF FAITH

Nothing is too great for the God of the Universe. He can work miracles. We have the unspeakable privilege of being His emissaries in this adventure.

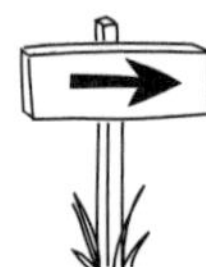

As your planning team meets over the course of the planning process, take time for devotions in God's Word, to encourage one another often with promises and examples of faith, and to stimulate one another to trust God for great things.

In this phase of preparation and assessment, take a look at your expectations and the attitudes of other leaders in your community of faith. If God has called you to lead the lost to the Savior, help the weak to walk and the strong to run, you can be excited that God will accomplish what He has called you to do! Many passages of Scripture tell of God's great desire to honor our faith if we will trust Him. Nothing is too great for the God of the Universe. He can work miracles. We have the unspeakable privilege of being His emissaries in this adventure. Perhaps you need for the Lord to refresh your sense of expectancy. Step 1 was focused on that very topic: refreshing your personal vision for your own life and your vision for how God wants to use you. Now, it may be time for you to encourage other leaders in your church to pray, to study the Scriptures, and to trust God to fulfill His promises in His way and in His timing. You might look at passages such as Jeremiah 29:11-14, Isaiah 40:27-31, Isaiah 64:1-4, II Timothy 1:7, and other faith-building, encouraging texts.

Remember that faith is centered, not in ourselves, but in Christ. Steps of faith take us outside our comfort zone, where we must depend on God's goodness and power to accomplish His will. But we are never alone, either in the planning phase as we chart out those steps, or in the implementation phase where we may be tested at particular times. As your planning team meets over the course of the planning process, take time for devotions in God's Word, to encourage one another often with promises and examples of faith, and to stimulate one another to trust God for great things.

DISCERNMENT AND PRAYER

Most evangelical leaders are primarily men and women of action. We get our marching orders from the Word of God and the Spirit of God, and we move out confidently to do His will. It is wise for us, however, to take a bit more time to listen carefully and reflect on God's leading so that we make sure we have heard all He wants to say to us before we set out. Spiritual disciplines are required to gain and maintain a closer walk with the Lord. Instead of just reading the Word, we need to genuinely meditate on Scripture and let the Holy Spirit direct our thoughts so we can apply the truth more specifically. Instead of just listing our needs to God in prayer, we need to sit quietly before Him and let His Spirit guide us, comfort us, and challenge us to believe Him even more. Fasting for a day or more is a wonderful practice to focus attention on the Lord and His desires. The goal is not to show how spiritual we are, but to tap into the thoughts of God and let Him guide us.

In my own life, I have learned that even though I was sure I understood God's teaching on a subject, I sometimes acted without the Spirit's confirmation. With maturity, I've learned to wait with more consistency for that "still, small voice" that whispers, "This is the way. Walk in it." No, the reliability of the Word hasn't changed, but I am now more consistent in applying His truths in relationships, in the selection of leadership, in structuring a ministry, and in the direction and timing of a project. I am often reminded that Jesus spent the whole night in prayer before He chose the Twelve. If the Son of God felt the need to pray that long and that intently before selecting His men, how much more do I need to pray so I discern God's leading?

Instead of just reading the Word, we need to genuinely meditate on Scripture and let the Holy Spirit direct our thoughts so we can apply the truth more specifically. Instead of just listing our needs to God in prayer, we need to sit quietly before Him and let His Spirit guide us, comfort us, and challenge us to believe Him even more.

THE SCRIPTURES AND PLANNING

Throughout the testimony of Scripture, we find God's chosen ones receiving and implementing His plans to advance His Kingdom. Abraham was led by God and made plans to leave his homeland and enter Canaan. He planned carefully how to find a wife for his son, Isaac. Jacob was more than a planner; he was a schemer who plotted how he could take away his brother's blessing. His example is a warning signal to each of us who might be tempted to substitute carnal desires for God-centered motivation. David planned his campaigns and the unification of Judah and Israel. Paul planned his missionary journeys to take the gospel to the ends of the earth. In all of these, we find examples of listening to God, and being flexible to change plans when God led in a different direction. The Proverbs say a lot about the planning process. They offer us a template of principles to guide our thoughts:

Proverbs 16:1
"The preparations of the heart belong to man,
But the answer of the tongue is from the Lord."

Proverbs 16:9
"A man's heart plans his way,
But the Lord directs his steps."

Proverbs 18:13
"He who answers a matter before he hears it,
It is folly and shame to him."

Proverbs 13:16
"Every prudent man acts with knowledge,
But a faithful ambassador brings health."

Proverbs 13:19
"A desire accomplished is sweet to the soul,
But it is an abomination to fools to depart from evil."

Proverbs 14:8
"The wisdom of the prudent is to understand his way,
But the folly of fools is deceit."

Proverbs 15:22
"Without counsel, plans go awry,
But in the multitude of counselors they are established."

Proverbs 18:15
"The heart of the prudent acquires knowledge,
And the ear of the wise seeks knowledge."

Of course, there are many other passages throughout the Scriptures that give us insight, encouragement, and direction. As you pray and plan, saturate your mind with God's Word so your purposes are in line with His purposes, and so your plans reflect the values and direction He wants you to take.

Your church's vision statement tells people, "This is who we are." This vision provides the benchmark for your values ("Which principles and practices are important to us?") and planning ("Where does God want us to go?"). Many churches, however, don't have a clearly defined vision statement. They simply do what has been done in the past, or they adopt the latest trend and try to implement it without tailoring it to fit their particular situation. The results of the first is to remain stagnant, and the results of the second is to confuse your people and compromise your leadership by changing direction too often. The "wind of the Spirit" is as necessary to determine the direction of the church as the wind of nature is for a sailboat to stay on course and reach its destination.

A vision statement consists of the principles, fundamental beliefs, and attitudes that guide church leadership, and the church body, to live out those concepts in real life. Pastoral leadership must have a well-defined purpose. The absence of a clear philosophy usually leads to "Christian fatalism," a belief that, "Whatever happens must be the will of God." I'm sorry to say that our Lord is blamed for many failures of poor leadership and poor planning. If you don't have a clear vision, you may arrive somewhere and not know why. The absence of a clear vision often leads to:

Ministry that is driven from crisis to crisis, which is characterized by:
— wasted energy,
— missed opportunities,
— missed deadlines,
— unproductive work by the always-busy pastor, staff, and lay leaders,
— leaders reacting to pressures of the moment instead of progressing toward the future, and
— the pastor serving as a spiritual ambulance, on call to take care of every need in the church.

Ministry guided by church fads, which is characterized by:
— trying the latest thing in organizational structure, curriculum, and philosophy,
— changing direction with each new trend that comes along, and
— confusing people because they can't remember which fad you're following now.

YOUR CHURCH'S VISION STATEMENT

The absence of a clear philosophy usually leads to "Christian fatalism," a belief that, "Whatever happens must be the will of God."

Ministry shackled by tradition, which is characterized by:
— being unaware of the many good alternatives,
— sacrificing cultural relevancy, and
— being stuck in the same old system doing the same old things over and over; wishing things were different but not bold enough to challenge the status quo.

At the end of this chapter, take time to pray, reflect, and write your church's vision statement. It will guide your thinking and prayers as you continue to plan.

A CLOSER LOOK

Imagine that you are looking at them through the eyes of a wise, perceptive advisor who has no axes to grind and nothing to hide. You are simply being objective about the strengths and weaknesses of each ministry of your church

It is now time to take a good look at every program in your ministry. As you enter a shopping mall, you usually see a graphic layout of the stores and an arrow that indicates: "You are here." Until we know where we are, it is impossible to go where we would like to be. And in this metaphor, if the arrow indicates that you are in more than one place, it will take real wisdom to determine the next step you need to take. As you review and evaluate your church programs, strive to be totally unbiased and objective. Imagine that you are looking at them through the eyes of a wise, perceptive advisor who has no axes to grind and nothing to hide. You are simply being objective about the strengths and weaknesses of each ministry of your church. The categories of your assessment include:

The Ministry's Strengths

List every area of ministry in your church, and ask these questions about each one:

— In what ways are people being reached and edified through this ministry?
— Is there a spirit of joy in their fellowship and service?
— Does the ministry reach and satisfy all the needs in this area? If not, identify those not currently being met.
— What adjustments are required to permit this ministry to flourish?
— Does this ministry enhance the overall program of the church, or does it seek its own independence?

Each ministry should be examined in detail, down to the point of its impact on individual church members. For example, the pastoral ministries can be assessed by looking at the effectiveness of the ministry to the sick, the grieving, the needy, families in crisis, and biblical counseling. Examine each element of each area of your ministry, from worship to janitorial services, from education to administration.

Focus your attention on the evidences of growth, health, and those things worthy of praise. Chart out the growth you have seen in each area on the worksheet at the end of this chapter . . . and thank God for His faithfulness!

The quality of leadership makes or breaks any organization. In the church, we need leaders with integrity as well as skill in their arena of ministry. A godly character is not optional, and a willing, servant spirit is not negotiable. We need leaders who exemplify the character of our Lord, and who use their God-given abilities to build up the body of Christ.

THE LEADERSHIP AND ITS STRUCTURE

I know a pastor who is very disciplined in his personal and spiritual life. He is up early each morning, and he spends quality time in prayer each day. His teaching and preaching reflect the meticulous research in his preparation. Each day is carefully planned to be sure he accomplishes as much for the Lord as possible. But this dear pastor has one chief flaw: He assumes that each person on his staff is just like him, but they aren't. He is intrinsically motivated, and never needs a boot to get him going. In fact, he would feel terribly guilty if anyone ever had to tell him to work harder. A couple of his staff members, however, are not nearly so disciplined. One of them takes advantage of his senior pastor's assumptions and only works about half the time. Another is at the office a lot, but he doesn't organize his time well. Most of his time is spent on administrative details that could be handled by someone else.

The senior pastor doesn't delegate well. He assumes that if he is a good enough example, the others will follow his cue and work diligently and effectively. He avoids conflict at all costs, so he only corrects those on his staff when they have really blown it badly. And when that happens, his outburst at the problem makes him feel guilty, and his staff gets angry at him. He tends to spiritualize their problems, and he believes that if he prays more for them, they'll become more committed and disciplined. Certainly, prayer is appropriate and essential, but change is unlikely unless work habits and the will to serve are addressed directly.

This pastor is a wonderful, good-hearted man of God. He is an outstanding teacher and counselor, but he has overlooked some key factors in his role as the senior pastor. His assumptions may be well-intentioned, but they lead to

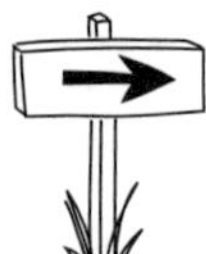

Good intentions are not enough to build effective teams of staff and lay leaders.

misunderstanding, poor delegation and control, and resentment instead of harmony on the staff. Usually, resentment doesn't surface, but it smoulders just below the surface.

Good intentions are not enough to build effective teams of staff and lay leaders. We need clear principles and workable practices of selection, delegation, training, and oversight.

Selection and Delegation

Leadership expert Robert Rosen wrote about the need to move the hearts of those we select for our leadership teams. He observed,

> "Leaders see the whole organization, thanks to their singular vantage point. Successful leaders make the whole greater than the sum of its parts. They take charge of the organization and feel a sense of obligation and responsibility for making things happen. This can only occur if the leader has a mental image of the ideal organization he wants to create. To come close to the ideal, he must share his vision with others, enlist their ideas and support, and help people see where they fit in. Leaders must celebrate—and balance—the diverse voices within their organization. The voices must blend; otherwise there is just noise. Creating this harmony is the challenge of any leader."[5]

I am convinced that God raises up leaders, but we are responsible to develop them for the Kingdom's sake and so they reach their potential.

I am convinced that God raises up leaders, but we are responsible to develop them for the Kingdom's sake and so they reach their potential. Second and third generations of leadership should exceed the capability of their mentors, but this rarely happens because to mentor promising, rising leaders is not perceived as an important role of leadership.

The constant need to balance resources

We have looked at the three functions of the office of the pastor. We have extended those three functions into a suggested formula of three tracks around which the church leadership and ministry can be programmed. With the function and form in mind, it is appropriate to focus now on the needs of the people. This is the defining point for church programming. When old traditions outlive contemporary needs, or when programs are adopted only because the church

5 Robert. H. Rosen, *Leading People*, (New York: Viking Press, 1996), p. 32.

down the street is doing them, programs become the tail that wags the dog. The only reason to organize a program is to satisfy the needs of the people. After a church membership grows beyond several families, the pastor's limited capacity can't meet all of their needs. Notice, I said *capacity* not *capability.* Acts 6 gives a solution for this overload through the selection and ordination of deacon servants to assist in the administrative and support functions of the church. Selecting these servants, though, is not a guaranteed solution, even when the deacon body is exceptionally loyal and dutiful. We also need to build and cultivate more young leaders to be ready to assume these important roles. God usually raises up leaders in specific areas of ministry (e.g., youth, children, teaching roles, evangelism, etc.). It is our responsibility to identify the strengths of new leaders and put them in roles that broaden their horizons beyond the narrow focus of a specific ministry so they grasp the overall church organization and perspective. The increasing needs of a growing church require a constant balancing of resources at the pastor's disposal, and finding competent leadership should be a continual priority for the pastor.

Delegate or die

With the prospect of adding lay leaders and staff, the pastor finds himself in a dilemma. He is well aware that he, as the shepherd, will be accountable to God for his ministry and care of the flock. He is caught between his own inability to meet all their needs and his reluctance to assign some responsibilities to someone else. How can this be done without placing some of the precious flock in the hands of a "hireling"? This is often a difficult time of transition. It requires the pastor to spend considerable time in prayer and meditation to find the best solution.

Ultimately, we can measure the quality of our leadership by the passion and energy of those we have selected to minister with us. Dr. Jack Weber, Professor of Management at the University of Virginia observed, "The bottom line is that leadership shows up in the inspired action of others. We traditionally have assessed leaders themselves. But maybe we should assess leadership by the degree to which people around leaders are inspired."

Find someone who balances your strengths

The first step in finding that person to whom you can delegate with trust is to know and understand yourself and

The increasing needs of a growing church require a constant balancing of resources at the pastor's disposal, and finding competent leadership should be a continual priority for the pastor.

Ultimately, we can measure the quality of our leadership by the passion and energy of those we have selected to minister with us.

Another pastor is on the other end of the spectrum. He is a very compassionate man who loves to affirm people, but he despises conflict. This man also hired people who were like him. Their staff meetings are full of encouragement, but hard decisions are often put off.

We need to choose staff and lay leaders who will bring balance to our leadership team, and then we need to value their individual contributions so they excel in their gifts instead of simply melting into the pastor's mold.

your own needs. The pastor must honestly evaluate his strengths, weaknesses, and spiritual gifts, and he needs to ask himself, "What am I really accomplishing?" He can list the various elements of ministry that are required of him, and assess his performance in each one. A good way to start is for a pastor to ask himself, "What is it that I don't like to do?" The answer to this question may indicate a lack of spiritual gifting. The importance of this ministry self-analysis cannot be overestimated. I call it a time of "ego-alteration." To the degree that a man will spend time with the Lord in prayer and fasting, his needs will be made known by the Lord. If a person is genuinely humble, God will begin to reveal certain characteristics He wants to cultivate in his personal life, while correspondingly, the Lord also develops aspects of his ministry plan.

Pastors often look for staff and lay leaders who are much like themselves. A pastor may feel more comfortable with those of similar strengths and perspectives, but the ministry is weakened by such lack of balance. I know a pastor who is a strong leader and a quick decision-maker. He hired staff who are just like himself, individuals who are opinionated and shoot-from-the-hip. They enjoyed robust conversations, but some of the pastoral ministries of the church, as well as the planning process itself, suffered because these men collectively didn't see the need to do patient and thorough research.

Another pastor is on the other end of the spectrum. He is a very compassionate man who loves to affirm people, but he despises conflict. This man also hired people who were like him. Their staff meetings are full of encouragement, but hard decisions are often put off. That church environment is certainly pleasant, but momentum is often reduced due to a malaise of empathetic group therapy. They could be finding adventure by sailing in new waters, but they seem to be much happier not making waves.

It takes a wise leader to see the need for staff and lay leaders who are very different from himself, but this wisdom pays tremendous dividends in blending and balancing strengths so the ministry benefits from a multitude of gifts. Hiring people who are gifted in different ways, however, doesn't guarantee the benefits of diversity. If a person does not have the freedom or personal motivation to major on his strengths, his contribution is neutralized. We need to choose staff and lay leaders who will bring balance to our leadership team, and then we need to value their individual contributions so they excel in their gifts instead of simply melting into the pastor's mold.

A significant contribution that Southern Baptists have made to the organized church over the years has been the specialized training of ministry staff, such as, educational directors, ministers of music, youth ministers, and others. The specialized church staff, though, has prompted "the categorical calling" of staff, that is, obtaining and assigning staff for predetermined, traditional roles without consideration of other important factors.

It is appropriate for staff to be assigned special areas of ministry according to their gifting and abilities. Their highest priority, however, must be complementing the gifts and abilities of the pastor. Only then will the office of the pastor realize its greatest leadership potential in meeting the needs of the entire congregation. If this occurs, each staff member will find fulfillment in his role in the ministry, and the pastor will enjoy his most productive and fulfilling leadership role as his weaknesses and time deficiencies are balanced by the strengths of the staff members.

Find staff and lay leaders who are committed to building God's Kingdom, not their own

When staff or lay leaders are called to create or build certain ministries, that is usually what they do . . . sometimes independent of other ministries of the church and independent of pastoral and spiritual authority. Unless the pastor is very deliberate in outlining the responsibilities and expectations, "kingdom building" results because people do what is right in their own eyes. Many pastors would say that they and the church were better off before a hastily acquired staff member came on board. Haste led to poor judgment in his selection. The greater emphasis was placed on *where* he would serve rather than *how* he would function.

Many pastors would say that they and the church were better off before a hastily acquired staff member came on board.

Building a Leadership Team

There are no vending machines where we can insert our requests and receive the perfect staff members or lay leaders. Selection is the first criterion for building a ministry team. There is no formula for selecting the right person, but the determining signature of God is a unity of spirit among all who participate in the selection process. Some of us are wowed by people with great skills, but I much prefer someone with a great heart. It is easier to teach skills than to teach heart.

Some of us are wowed by people with great skills, but I much prefer someone with a great heart. It is easier to teach skills than to teach heart.

Many pastors use manuals, resumés, hearsay, and guess-work instead of spiritual discernment in selecting staff. Take time to pray, and take even more time to listen. One pastor gave this advice: "Make people decisions very slowly." Don't rush to pick someone. Take time to reflect, to interview several people, and try to see that person in several contexts. Look for character and heart as well as skills. And remember, working with people is never an exact science. Even the Lord Jesus Himself had one who betrayed Him, and all but John deserted Him at His greatest moment of need. Use good sense, take your time, and pray for God's clear discernment.

There are many staff-related problems, but I want to focus on these three: failing to make the adjustment to the next level of leadership, being threatened by others' successes, and competing loyalties. As a church grows, it will get to the point where the pastor simply cannot shoulder all the leadership burden as the only staff member, and he needs full-time assistance. Too often, the decision to hire additional staff comes when the pastor's schedule and the demands of ministry are incredibly burdensome, and he doesn't take the time to equip and train the new staff member. The pastor assumes the new person will take a lot of his burden, and he is disappointed when the new staff member fails in performance and in choosing priorities. The new associate, too, feels confused and angry because he came to serve on a team but is left alone and without direction. One of the tasks of training this new staff member is to broaden his grasp of the entire scope of the ministry so he comprehends "how all the pieces fit." This understanding helps him coordinate his efforts with other ministries, and it prepares him to assume greater responsibility in the future.

Whenever you hire a staff member, whether it is the first or the twenty-first associate, anticipate the time it will take to welcome, initiate, and train that person to be a fully invested, deeply committed member of the pastoral team. The effectiveness of synergy and the joy of ministry can be gained by planning wisely to equip this new person for his role on your staff.

A second staff problem I've noticed is that some pastors are threatened by a staff member's recognition or successes. I've even known some pastors who hired weaker people so they would look better in the eyes of people in their churches. A secure man will try to hire a competent, secure person, but an insecure, easily threatened man will tend to hire someone not as qualified as himself, and perhaps, someone

Whenever you hire a staff member, whether it is the first or the twenty-first associate, anticipate the time it will take to welcome, initiate, and train that person to be a fully invested, deeply committed member of the pastoral team.

who is very insecure. In both cases, the leader reproduces himself.

When those on our staff succeed, we need to celebrate! In fact, a good leader is the staff's biggest cheerleader and the first to celebrate any accomplishment. Jealousy over the appreciation shown to another on the staff is a sure way to wreck the team and kill the vision of building God's Kingdom.

A third common problem that can occur on staff teams is when the staff have competing loyalties. When a new senior pastor comes, many on the leadership team were probably chosen by the previous pastor. Depending on the circumstances of the previous pastor's departure, the staff may still be loyal to him and refuse to support the new pastor. I've seen new pastors close their eyes and assume this problem would go away, only for it to explode later. At the other extreme, a new pastor may also walk in and fire most of the staff for disloyalty if they express kind thoughts about the previous pastor. Those who come into an established church need a large measure of discernment and diplomacy. Your goal, of course, is to win the loyalty of the staff with your integrity, your vision, and your good humor. As you exhibit those qualities with consistency, most people will be won over. After a few months, those who are still reluctant to follow may exhibit their continued displeasure and choose to leave. If not, a pastor cannot allow an unhappy staff member to spread dissatisfaction to the church family.

The leadership assessments in this Step (and the writing of job descriptions later) will clarify expectations and create open lines of communication. All of us need to know what is expected of us so we will be encouraged when we perform well. Clear expectations and affirmation give us a sense of well-being and fulfillment. If we, as leaders, fail to communicate our expectations clearly, we leave people wandering aimlessly about and wondering what to do. Some will simply give up because they don't want to risk trying something on their own without support, and others will charge ahead and try to achieve what they think is right. Too often, however, leaders with insufficient direction build independent ministries and followings, which can cause great trouble down the road. Clear communication between a pastor and his staff is a protection against these kinds of problems.

In your communication, make the accountability structure very clear. The question, "Who is responsible?" needs an instant answer. Three words define accountability: awareness, acceptance, and attitude.

When those on our staff succeed, we need to celebrate!

Your goal, of course, is to win the loyalty of the staff with your integrity, your vision, and your good humor.

Most of us can readily overlook mistakes that are made by someone who loves God and genuinely wants to do his best, but even a skilled person has a negative impact if he has a rotten attitude.

Awareness of a person's responsibility for a task comes when he genuinely understands not only the task itself, but the task's relationship to the vision of the church. This grasp comes through dialog with those who are delegating the responsibility, a communication which focuses on all aspects of the duties: the goal, the process, and the relationships.

Acceptance of the task occurs when the person "owns" the vision that is imparted to him. The task is no longer an arbitrary time-filler. Instead, it becomes an extension of that person's own identity and ministry vision.

Attitude is the characteristic that so often defines a good or a not-so-good team player. Most of us can readily overlook mistakes that are made by someone who loves God and genuinely wants to do his best, but even a skilled person has a negative impact if he has a rotten attitude. A person with a good attitude lives by the admonition: "And whatever you do, do it heartily, as to the Lord and not to men" (Colossians 3:23). Look for people with gracious spirits and teachable hearts. I'm not equating *teachable* with *passive*. Even lions have to learn to hunt!

Far too often, I've seen pastors shake their heads at staff or lay leaders who have "a bad attitude." Asking a few questions, however, sometimes reveals that the pastor has never defined his expectations for that person. At least some of the time, therefore, the person's grumbling and delays in completing tasks are the result of muddy expectations and little, if any, communication from the pastor. Take the time to communicate clearly and forthrightly. I believe it will make a tremendous difference in your leadership team.

Use the interview questions in the exercise at the end of this chapter to guide your conversation with your staff and ministry leaders. As you talk with them, look at them as a team as well as individuals. Conduct team-building exercises to increase trust and effective working processes.*

Your Analysis

I encourage you to interview each person on your leadership team, staff and lay leaders, and ask questions such as:

— What do you really enjoy about your role here?
— What would you say is your greatest contribution to our ministry?

*Consider using the *DISC Behavioral Profile* or *Building Powerful Ministry Teams* from Next Level Leadership Network. Contact them at: www.NextLevelLeadership.com.

— Which spiritual gifts has God given you?
— How can I help you employ those gifts more effectively?
— What ministry opportunities would you like to have that you don't have already?
— Describe your ministry responsibilities.
— What is your vision for growth in these areas? What is your plan for developing leadership?
— What can we do to help our team work together more effectively?
— What would you like to be doing in five years? in ten years?
— Is there anything in your life or your past that would be objectionable to us and our church?

Also, conduct an assessment of your support staff to determine their strengths and experience. You can use a variation of the interview questions used with the pastoral staff and lay leaders, but the listing of responsibilities will need to be more detailed and comprehensive.

Not every problem is a spiritual one. Years ago, Dallas Seminary professor Dr. Howard Hendricks said, "Don't attempt to manage spiritual problems or spiritualize management problems." This is a cardinal principle in working with people. Some of the problems on staff teams are because of poor time management. As people learn to prioritize their work, list their goals for each day and schedule their time, many problems of bad attitudes vanish and more work gets done for the Kingdom.**

THE BUDGET AND ITS STRUGGLE

In many churches, the programs (and consequently, the church's potential for growth) are controlled by the dollars available. The shortage of funds eliminates vision and elevates bookkeeping above blessings. God-given vision balances finances with faith-planning. If inspirational leaders are controlled by narrow, inflexible budget processes, accomplishments will plateau instead of pointing to the promise of the future. It is imperative that the finances of the church be in the hands of godly, visionary, responsible people who understand the heart of the pastor and his vision. Good and godly financial planning is not a hindrance. It can provide a springboard for accelerating God's vision for your church.

Good and godly financial planning is not a hindrance. It can provide a springboard for accelerating God's vision for your church.

**Note: You may want to look at the *On Mission Life Planner* as a resource to help your staff and support staff with time management. For more information, go to: wwwonmissionlifeplanner.com

Many pastors and committees confuse their budgets with their financial plans. The plans are the strategies to provide resources for the ministry; the budget is the yearly projection and tracking system to keep up with income and expenses. Pastors and their leadership will serve the church well by developing a comprehensive, long-range financial plan, including their philosophy of:

— how stewardship is to be taught in the church, from the pulpit, in classes, in newsletters, etc.;
— how needs are communicated;
— the perspective on tithing and other forms of giving;
— debt, when and if it is acceptable to borrow;
— the normal cycles of giving in the church and the expectations of the cash flow in each up and down time of the year;
— how to conduct capital campaigns;
— the system of oversight by each ministry;
— when and how designated funds are established;
— the percent of the annual budget that needs to be kept in reserve for emergencies;
— the strategy and responsibility for long-range planning; and
— how financial decisions are made.

The budget, then, is the compilation of each ministry's anticipated funding needs based on the vision of the pastor and the ministry team. Quite often, the monetary estimates will be negotiated up or down based on past performance and new program requirements. Certainly, we need to be realistic, but our ministries need to be vision-driven, with faith that God will provide what He calls us to do. A necessary step in this process, and one that is too often overlooked, is the communication of the vision with passion and clarity. I've found that if the vision is compelling, people respond with open hearts and open wallets. They are thrilled to be a part of God's great work. It is our responsibility to receive that vision from God, and then to communicate it practically and powerfully to our people. In most cases, they will respond and give very generously.

At the end of this chapter you will find a financial assessment worksheet, including the topics outlined in this section. Go over these issues with your planning team, and be sure to include at least the chairman of the stewardship committee in this discussion. With this input, a wise chairman can lead his committee with a clear focus on the church's goals.

THE DEACONS AND THEIR SERVICE

The pastor-deacon relationship is strong because of two factors: the high spiritual requirements in selecting deacons and the commitment to real spiritual ministry on the part of each deacon.

The deacon body (or a similar lay leadership board) embodies the greatest asset or liability in the church. Sanctioned by God to be a relief to the pastor and a remedy for many of the needs in the church family, this servant body can extend, multiply, and maximize the effectiveness of the church if it serves with vision and vigor, but it can be one of the biggest hindrances to the church's purpose if there is lethargy or strife.

Some churches organize so that a staff member, elder, or deacon is in charge of each major ministry. Under their leadership, other deacons and lay leaders serve in capacities that fit their gifts, experience, and desires. In many churches, however, the deacon body is simply an advisory board that has little hands-on responsibility for the operation of the church. One of the best examples of an effective deacon body is the one at my own church. The pastor-deacon relationship is strong because of two factors: the high spiritual requirements in selecting deacons and the commitment to real spiritual ministry on the part of each deacon. The pastor is secure enough in his own leadership position to allow the deacons to function according to their spiritual gifts, while they understand the role and responsibility of the pastor and allow him to be the God-ordained spiritual leader of the church.

One of the biggest complaints I have heard from pastors is that a particular deacon or a small group of them has become, in effect, the pastor's adversary. Real power, it seems, rests in the hands of a disgruntled person or two who command the respect (or fear) of others. Perhaps they feel threatened by the new vision of the pastor, or perhaps the pastor has failed to win their hearts because he demanded their allegiance instead of patiently and personally communicating his passion and purposes. One of the main goals of any pastor is to structure his lay leadership and communicate with them so that the Kingdom is advanced instead of hindered. Some pastors need to do some remedial work to rebuild trust, and some need to be bolder in sharing their vision with the deacons. Ultimately, you will want to find men who are genuine servants of God, who speak truth with conviction, and who are committed to reaching the lost, comforting the hurting, and building up the body of Christ.

If these qualifications result in your deacon body remaining small, so be it. You and the church will benefit from having a smaller group of men who love God, are loyal to their pastor, and have servants' hearts.

The selection and ordination of a deacon has life-long consequences. He may rotate in and out of active service, but even when he is not a part of the functioning deacon body, others probably still think of him as a deacon. Selection, then, is of paramount importance, and the Bible gives specific guidance and prerequisites to prevent frivolous and hasty choices. Look for spiritual maturity, wisdom, and proven leadership. If these qualifications result in your deacon body remaining small, so be it. You and the church will benefit from having a smaller group of men who love God, are loyal to their pastor, and have servants' hearts.

I encourage you to review your strategy and philosophy of the role of deacons, and move toward the biblical model of responsibility and accountability. Having been both a deacon and a minister, I have discovered that most conflicts among pastors and deacons arise due to a lack of knowledge of what the Bible teaches about their respective roles and responsibilities. If a deacon understands that he is disobedient to God's Word when he doesn't allow the pastor to be the spiritual leader of the church, he is more apt to follow than to fight. Deacons must also realize that all the matters of the church, from preaching to office administration and the budget, are within the scope of spiritual leadership. And the pastor must realize that, while he has the authority of leadership, he is not a dictator but the "chief of servants." Mutual respect between the pastor and the deacons must be preserved and strengthened at every point and at all times to assure unity of spirit. This will defeat Satan at his favorite point of attack on the church. Ask the Lord for wisdom about how to instill in your deacons a solid grasp of biblical roles so this group of men can serve most effectively in the future.

THE ADMINISTRATION AND ITS STABILITY

Administration must also include the orderly networking of programs. This need is at the heart of every aspect of the church, and it is just as much a part of the spiritual ministry of the church as preaching and teaching.

Administration is the planning, organizational strategy, and oversight of ministries and support services of the church, and it is especially linked to the budget and financial strategies to provide resources to support the network of ministries in the church. Administration is often perceived as only the narrow scope of daily operations (answering the phone, cleaning the building, fixing the air conditioning, and paying the bills), but this perspective compromises the potential for strong ministry management. Administration must also include the orderly networking of programs. This need is at the heart of every aspect of the church, and it is just as much a part of the spiritual ministry of the church as preaching and teaching.

If pastors focus only on the public aspects of ministry and neglect administration, ministry effectiveness is inevitably compromised. After all, preaching and counseling give immediate feedback, while administration is often behind the scenes. But good administration is the foundation that allows all the other ministries, those visible and those invisible, to flourish. Some critical tools of good administration are an organizational chart, job descriptions, a good planning process, the calendar, and the financial plan.

A necessary ingredient for good decision-making is dependable information. Many of us make decisions based on the complaints or suggestions of one or two people, or we choose a direction after we hear someone else succeeded by doing it. There's nothing wrong with getting input from a few people or learning from others' successes and failures, but we need to develop a strategy and system that provides excellent information so our decisions will be well-informed. Most churches have some kind of regularly scheduled leadership meeting at which the pastor can hear reports from each ministry leader. These ministry leaders, in turn, need to provide opportunities for those in their charge to give them input and feedback.

Information comes in two forms: objective and subjective. We need objective statistics about how many people attended meetings, costs and income, and other quantitative assessments. But we also need to hear how people felt and were affected by those programs. Make sure you get input on both. It's not a success, even if a lot of people come to an event, if they felt deflated there. They probably won't come back. Some people are very intuitive and can give you excellent feedback in their subjective analysis. Value their input as much as the objective numbers others give you. The quality of decisions is a direct reflection of the quality of the information, so design a system that allows you to get good, accurate information.

Of course, the size of the church introduces variables in how goals will be set, pursued, and accomplished. The basic principles of leadership and organization, however, are the same for the very small church with a bi-vocational pastor to the very large with its multiple staff. The challenge for any size is to keep it simple, keep it relational, and keep it biblical.

At the end of this chapter, each ministry leader will be asked to conduct a review of the strengths and needs in his or her particular ministry. At this time, the planning team can

THE CHURCH AND ITS SIZE

The challenge for any size is to keep it simple, keep it relational, and keep it biblical.

review the strengths and needs of the church at large. You will, of course, be more familiar with the church's history while you've been there, but take time to find out what happened during the years before you arrived. You may find that the patterns of obstacles and opportunities have been around for a lot longer than your tenure.

Changes in the direction and leadership structure of the church, changes in the style of worship from traditional to contemporary, and similar shifts in direction are catalysts in changing growth patterns. You may also find that some of those who have been a part of the church for years don't feel comfortable with these changes. In your analysis, note how any changes like these have affected the church's growth. Also, note how these changes were communicated to the church family. Communication, not the change itself, often determines the effect on the fellowship.

Look for patterns and trends, and examine carefully the points of change in leadership and in any demographic shifts. In some churches, the neighborhoods have changed in the past few years from stable, rural or small town environments to an incorporated suburban sprawl of a major city. This change brings great opportunities to reach highly mobile young people, but it often threatens the stability of the "old guard." Tension and conflict between the old and the new can be seen as insurmountable obstacles that will wreck the church, or they can be seen as opportunities for growth. We need God's wisdom to know His heart and His ways in these situations.

TAKE A STEP

The worksheets at the end of this Step are designed to help you, your planning team, and your ministry leaders take stock of your current ministry situation. I encourage you to find some of the most creative people in your church to join the planning team to brainstorm to find fresh ways to expand the ministry where it is doing well and to resolve any problems where they exist. The needs of the church, defined by opportunities and obstacles, will help determine your program for the coming year, and the program will then determine your delegation of responsibilities to your leaders. The program will also shape the decisions surrounding the finances of the church, and some adjustments may need to be made in allocation of funds to be sure the priority programs are adequately funded. Far too often, I've seen the cart of finances placed before the horse of programs which are developed to meet the needs of the people. Money, or the lack of it, becomes the primary determining factor in decisions. Don't let finances rule the programs in your planning process! The first step is to clearly identify the needs. That is what your analysis in Step 2 is all about.

Taking a look at your current situation requires time and energy, but it is absolutely essential for good planning. Take time to be thorough. You won't need to do this every year. Once is enough if you do a good job and gather the information you need to get an accurate appraisal of your church. Each subsequent year's analysis will simply add to your understanding and perspective of how God has worked in your church.

If you involve ministry leaders in the assessments, be sure to give them clear instructions and a deadline for when you need the information. Patiently answer any questions. You want them to understand your purpose for asking them to get involved. This isn't just busy work; it is a part of the strategic planning process to fulfill your vision for your church. At every opportunity, share your hopes, dreams, and vision for what you believe God wants to accomplish.

The core exercises for Step 2 are:

— Your Plan for Planning,
— Ministry Review,
— Planning Team Evaluation,

and additional exercises which may help you are:

— Your Church's Ministry Philosophy,
— Your Church's Vision Statement,
— Ministry Leader/Staff Interview,
— Analysis of Administrative Processes, and
— Financial Assessment.

I encourage you to find some of the most creative people in your church to join the planning team to brainstorm to find fresh ways to expand the ministry where it is doing well and to resolve any problems where they exist

YOUR PLAN FOR PLANNING

— *Who?:* The pastor.

— *Why?:* To select the best team and chart the best course for the planning process.

— *How?:* You may have already selected your planning team, and indeed, that team may be your core leadership for your ministry. You may, however, want to add someone who "thinks outside the box" to stimulate the team's thinking and expand your vision. Choose this team carefully, then use this planning exercise to get your bearings and outline your overall strategy for the planning process.

— *Then what?:* After this crucial step, you will be ready to implement the planning process.

YOUR PLAN FOR PLANNING

Reflect on the following and record your thoughts:

1. Who needs to be included on the planning team? What specific roles (if any) will each of these people play? (gathering data through surveys or focus groups, specific ministry team planning, etc.)

    Name ________________________________ Role ________________________________

    Name ________________________________ Role ________________________________

    Name ________________________________ Role ________________________________

    Name ________________________________ Role ________________________________

    Name ________________________________ Role ________________________________

2. How can you get clear, objective records of the past few years? Is that information readily available?

3. How will you communicate your vision and expectations of the planning process to your ministry leaders? your congregation?

4. Outline your general planning schedule here. Include information gathering and assessments, the actual planning procedure, scheduling, reporting to the congregation, and final approval of the plan. Be sure to include tentative due dates for each stage of the process.

MINISTRY REVIEW

— *Who?:* The pastor and the planning team will evaluate the church as a whole, ministry leaders will evaluate their programs and events (such as education, music, youth, missions, etc.).

— *Why?:* This assessment will show you where your leaders perceive God at work, and where they believe more needs to be done to meet the needs of people.

— *How?:* Ask ministry leaders to conduct an evaluation of the strengths and areas which need improvement in the ministries they lead. They may want to do this evaluation themselves, or better, they may choose to conduct it with their ministry team. Give them a deadline of when you need their assessments handed back to you.

— *Then what?:* When the evaluations are completed and turned in, you will be ready to do your own assessment of each ministry based on their input.

Ministry Responsibilities and Tasks

Note: You may want to give each ministry leader a list of the topics you want assessed, as well as the specific questions you want answered. Here are some topics and categories of service for each major ministry area. Change these to fit your organizational structure:

MUSIC
- Style of music
- Choir
- Selection of songs
- Special presentations
- Instrumentation
- Worship style

WORSHIP SERVICE
- Flow
- Visitor perceptions
- Preparation
- Announcements
- Bulletin
- Greeters/signage
- Multiple services
- Worship style

SERMON
- Content/topics
- Helpfulness
- Clarity
- Length

CHILD CARE
- Facility
- Cleanliness
- Staff/Child ratio
- Program
- Volunteers

CHILDREN & YOUTH MINISTRY
- Facility
- Staff/Student ratio
- Program
- Quality of leadership
- Volunteers

DISCIPLESHIP & EDUCATION
- Sunday school
- Small groups/Bible studies
- Teacher training
- Leadership development

EVANGELISM & MISSIONS
- Training
- Implementation
- Education

STEWARDSHIP
- Monthly giving
- Special needs
- Budgeting
- Accounting
- Capital funds

COMMUNITY COHESIVENESS
- Fellowship groups
- Athletic programs
- Special events

CARE-GIVING
- Pastoral counseling
- Lay care-giving
- Tele-care
- Support groups
- Recovery groups
- Referral to competent professionals

PRAYER MINISTRIES
- Corporate & community prayer gatherings
- Prayer chain

SPECIAL MINISTRIES
- Singles' program
- Seniors' program
- Family ministries
- Niche ministries
- Cooperative efforts with other churches
- Seminars & conferences

FACILITIES
- Exterior and grounds
- Interior
- Heating, A/C, aesthetics
- Accessibility and parking
- Sound and lighting
- Location
- Janitorial services

Ministry Review

Your Name _______________________________ Responsibility _______________________________

List every ministry area below and reflect on the following questions. Summarize conclusions that suggest specific changes in program or leadership assignments. Use additional paper if necessary.

1. In what ways are people being reached and edified through this ministry?
2. Is there a spirit of joy in their fellowship and service?
3. Does the ministry reach and satisfy all the needs in this area? If not, identify those not currently being met.
4. What adjustments are required to permit this ministry to flourish?
5. Does this ministry enhance the overall program of the church, or does it tend toward its own independence?

Ministry Area: _______________________________ Person Responsible: _______________________________

Your responses to the questions above: _______________________________

____

____

____

____

____

____

____

____

____

____

____

____

____

____

Suggested changes or improvements: _______________________________

____

____

Ministry Area: _________________________ Person Responsible: _________________

Your responses to the questions above: ____

____

____

____

____

____

____

____

____

____

____

____

Suggested changes or improvements: ____

____

____

Ministry Area: _________________________ Person Responsible: _________________

Your responses to the questions above: ____

____

____

____

____

____

____

____

____

____

____

____

Suggested changes or improvements: ____

____

____

PLANNING TEAM EVALUATION

— *Who?:* The planning team.

— *Why?:* To conduct a thorough assessment of each ministry area in the church based on the input from the ministry leaders.

— *How?:* When the ministry teams' reviews are handed to you, you will conduct your analysis of each ministry area. The leaders' reports will give you valuable grass-roots input, and now you will add your own analysis. You will probably find that some ministries of the church are flourishing because they are well-led, but others—vital ministries—lack bold and loving leadership.

I encourage you to add a creative person or two for this evaluation to help you think of new ideas and new approaches to meet people's needs. Use this time as a brainstorming session, and encourage these new ideas, even if they are "out in left field." You may find that some of these seemingly off-the-wall ideas evolve into a genuinely great concept that will help to meet your people at their point of need.

— *Then what?:* This assessment will be the foundation for much of the decision-making during the planning process.

PLANNING TEAM EVALUATION

Use the Ministry Review sheets turned in by each leader. Take time to assess each one using the following questions (you will need extra paper for these questions):

For each ministry:

1. What would you say are the strengths of this ministry? How do we see God at work here?

2. How is leadership being developed in this ministry? Is there a clear, comprehensive plan to expand the leadership base? If so, how is it working? If not, what steps need to be implemented to develop leaders?

3. What facets of this ministry are particularly strong?

4. What are the strengths and needs of the leader?

5. How can we help this person be even more effective?

6. Who are the rising leaders in this ministry?

7.　Our recommendation for this ministry:

— regarding the ministry leader:

— regarding recruiting, selecting, training, and placing rising leaders:

— regarding existing programs:

— regarding new programs:

8.　Review each segment of the organizational chart and answer these questions:

— What (or who) is killing your vision and sapping your strength?

— What essential ministry goals aren't being achieved?

— Look at each segment on the organizational chart. What is your vision for this area? In what ways is the church falling short?

— Who is out of place on the organizational chart?

— What are common complaints by the congregation?

— What skills do staff need training in? . . . lay leaders?

YOUR CHURCH'S MINISTRY PHILOSOPHY

— *Who?:* The pastor and the planning team, with ministry leaders.

— *Why?:* To identify and clarify the church's values and systems.

— *How?:* Use this time to listen carefully to what each person perceives is the church's direction and culture. You may be surprised!

— *Then what?:* This discussion may allow different opinions to be aired and resolved, and perhaps, it will clarify direction for the group. Both are good outcomes. You can then move on to the church vision statement.

YOUR CHURCH'S MINISTRY PHILOSOPHY

Take some time to reflect on how your church accomplishes its purpose. Answer these questions:

1. As you look around your church family, what are some obvious evidences of changed lives?

    — What events, programs, or people did God use to move in these people's hearts to change their lives?

2. How is leadership developed? (What is your strategy to select, equip, and provide resources for your leaders?)

3. How do people experience genuine Christian fellowship?

4. How and where are they encouraged to ask for help to meet their needs?

5. What is the decision-making process on the staff level and/or the top levels of leadership in the church?

6. How is responsibility delegated? How is oversight provided?

7. How are financial needs communicated to the congregation?

— Is there a good spirit of giving for regular financial needs and for special opportunities?

8.   How is the church presented to the community? How do people hear about the church?

9.   What would make people want to come the first time?

10. What would make them want to come back?

11. How are people encouraged to serve?

12. What systems are in place or need to be developed to recruit, select, train, model, and oversee those who serve?

13. What aspects of the church genuinely excite the pastor? the staff? the lay leaders? the people in the pew?

14. When, where, and how is this excitement communicated?

15. What churches are good models for you? What are they doing that is attractive and fits your situation?

16. In summary, what would you say are the essential elements of your church's ministry philosophy?

YOUR CHURCH'S VISION STATEMENT

— *Who?:* The pastor and the planning team with the ministry leaders, or perhaps, a subgroup of the ministry leaders who give their recommendation to the planning team.

— *Why?:* As a product of the discussion on your ministry philosophy, your leadership team can formulate a succinct, clear vision statement to serve as a benchmark to keep your church on track with God's will.

— *How?:* This exercise is often more difficult than you may think! But a gripping, heart-felt, easily stated vision statement is worth the effort. Take time to brainstorm and find the right phrases that capture the heart of what God has called your church to be and do.

— *Then what?:* Many churches put this statement on their letterhead, bulletins, and other church correspondence because it captures the heart of God's calling.

YOUR CHURCH'S VISION STATEMENT

You have taken time to identify your ministry philosophy. Now articulate your vision statement. You may want to have a statement that is fairly long and involved, one which describes what you believe God wants to do in and through your church. Others will want their vision statement to be a slogan that can be put on a banner or a business card, one that is easily remembered by everyone who hears it.

Brainstorm with those on your staff and leadership team to find the right words and phrases that express your vision. Don't be surprised if this takes some time. Few churches finalize their vision statement on the first try.

— What do you want your vision statement to accomplish?

— Who will use it? Where? How?

Complete each statement:

1. Our proven areas of strength are (We have succeeded at):

2.   Our proven areas of weakness are (We have not succeeded at):

3.   The three words that best describe our church are:

   ____

   ____

   ____

4.   Our church is unique because:

5.   The most attractive things about our church are:

6. If we could write the perfect scenario of what we believe God has prepared us to do in the ministry of our church, it would be:

7. As we read Scripture, we see that God is telling His church to:

8. If we knew we couldn't fail, we would do the following within our ministry:

9. For our church, success in ministry looks like:

10. The kind of people who make up our church are:

11. The kind of people our church wants to attract are:

12. For us to achieve the goals we feel God wants us to focus on we will have to:

13. Write several words and phrases that reflect your vision for your church:

14.   Now write your final vision statement for your church. (Use action words to accentuate your purpose and strong commitment to move forward.)

MINISTRY LEADER/ STAFF INTERVIEW

— *Who?:* The pastor, with each ministry leader and staff member.

— *Why?:* To open lines of communication and find out what really motivates each person in leadership so you can tailor each person to the right responsibility and accountability style.

— *How?:* Use the questions in this exercise to stimulate conversation. Find a time when you will not be hurried or distracted, possibly away from the church offices. Explain that you are asking strategic leaders for their input. As you ask these questions, follow up with others to find out more about what the person really feels and desires.

— *Then what?:* These interviews will help you shape your organizational chart and job descriptions.

MINISTRY LEADER/STAFF INTERVIEW

Use these questions as a launching pad for discussion:

1. What do you really enjoy about your role here?

2. What would you say is your greatest contribution to our ministry?

3. Which spiritual gifts has God given you?

4. How can I help you employ those gifts more effectively?

5.   What ministry opportunities would you like to have that you don't have already?

6.   Describe your biggest frustrations.

7.   Describe your ministry responsibilities.

8.   What is your vision for growth in these areas? What is your plan for developing leadership?

9. What can we do to help our team work together more effectively?

10. What would you like to be doing in five years? in ten years?

11. How can I help you reach your personal goals? What can I do to encourage you more in your walk with the Lord?

ANALYSIS OF ADMINISTRATIVE PROCESSES

— *Who?:* The planning team.

— *Why?:* To examine how administrative processes are conducted in the church to determine the strengths and needs in organization, planning, and communication.

— *How?:* Answer the questions in this exercise.

— *Then what?:* You will identify strengths in communication and reporting, and you will find weaknesses that need to be corrected.

ANALYSIS OF ADMINISTRATIVE PROCESSES

1. Draw an organizational chart of your ministry as it exists today.

2. Review the following questions to help you analyze the existing administrative processes at your church for each of the major responsibilities on the organizational chart:

    — Who is in charge?

    — How are other leaders in that area recruited and selected?

— How are responsibilities delegated?

— How is information gathered?

—How are decisions made?

—How is vision communicated?

—How are programs, the calendar, and budgets drawn up?

—How are results measured?

FINANCIAL ASSESSMENT

— *Who?:* The planning team and the chairman of the stewardship committee.
— *Why?:* To analyze the church's policies for establishing and implementing the financial plan, budget, and communication about giving.
— *How?:* Answer the questions in this exercise.
— *Then what?:* This assessment identifies the strengths and weaknesses of your financial strategy and policies. You will address these in the process of financial planning in later Steps.

FINANCIAL ASSESSMENT

A church's financial plan is the practical and expectant vision for providing resources for its ministry plan for the coming year. A budget, on the other hand, is the projected line-item allocation for expenditures for specific expenses. It is very important to separate visionary financial planning from a detailed budget mindset. When budgetary limitations are allowed to determine the program of the church, the God-given vision is compromised. This essentially replaces the power to lead with simple arithmetic. Your planning team, with input from your financial leadership, can discuss these elements of your strategy for your financial plan:

1. How is stewardship taught in the church (from the pulpit, in classes, in newsletters, etc.)?

2. How are needs communicated to the body?

3. What is the church's perspective on tithing and other forms of giving?

4. What is your philosophy and policy about debt (when and if it is acceptable to borrow)?

5. Describe the normal cycles of giving in the church and the expectations of the cash flow in each up and down time of the year.

6. What is your strategy in capital fund-raising?

7. How are the expenses for each ministry supervised and evaluated?

8. When and how are designated funds established?

9. What is the percent of the annual budget that needs to be kept in reserve for emergencies?

10. What is the strategy and responsibility for long-range planning?

11. How are financial decisions made?

STEP 1 *The Captain's Compass*

- Your Personal Vision
- Your Ministry Vision

STEP 2 *Look at the Map*

- Your Plan for Planning
- Ministry Review
- Planning Team Evaluation

STEP 3 *Watch for Obstacles and Opportunities*

- **Task Summaries**
- **Job Descriptions**
- **Historical Growth Statistics—Bible Study**
- **Historical Growth Statistics—General Church Criteria**
- **Community Demographics**
- **Obstacles and Opportunities**
- **Space Utilization**

STEP 4 *Get Your Equipment Ready*

- Ministry Flow Chart
- Organizational Chart
- Communication System

STEP 5 *Plot Your Course*

- Ministry Leader Planning Worksheet
- The Ministry Plan
- The Master Calendar
- The Financial Plan
- Communication Plan

STEP 6 *Look Over the Next Hill*

- Long-Range Ministry Plan
- Growth and Capacity Analysis
- Growth Projections
- General Church Criteria
- Building Plan Schedule and Expenditures
- Long-Range Financial Plan

STEP 7 *Get on the Trail*

- Monthly Planning Worksheet

STEP 3

WATCH FOR OBSTACLES AND OPPORTUNITIES

Some situations, like the influx of many young couples into your church, are clear opportunities, and some, such as the constant criticism of a respected and powerful layman, seem like insurmountable obstacles. In the most difficult circumstances, we need to remember that God is good and sovereign. He will accomplish His purposes if we trust Him, even if those purposes are to purify our hearts and show us how dependent we are on Him. Every obstacle, if seen from His perspective, is an opportunity for growth—maybe not the kind of growth we envisioned, but instead, growth of our character. And sometimes, opportunities bring their own obstacles. Movement creates friction, but the oil of the Holy Spirit lubricates and liberates us for more growth.

A church of 600 in Texas welcomed two young couples to their fellowship. These couples are sharp, attractive, and love God with all their hearts. Not long after they came, their friends—and they have a lot of friends—began attending the church. After a few months, the chairman of the deacons remarked, "There hasn't been a Sunday in the past several months that I haven't seen several couples in worship that I've never seen before. They just keep coming!" These two couples formed a classic network of influence, and soon, a new Bible study was formed, full of excitement and growth. The entire church was energized by the scores of young couples who became active, enthusiastic members of the church.

The law of unintended consequences, however, reared its ugly head. The childcare system of the church, which had been near capacity before the addition of all these new young couples and their children, became seriously overburdened. Volunteers simply couldn't keep up with the demands, so the leadership decided to hire ladies to work during the Sunday morning Bible study and worship hours. The initial complaints

In the most difficult circumstances, we need to remember that God is good and sovereign. He will accomplish His purposes if we trust Him, even if those purposes are to purify our hearts and show us how dependent we are on Him.

that their children weren't being cared for soon turned to thanksgiving.

These young couples wanted to go to discipleship classes on Wednesday nights, but the hired childcare workers weren't available for that time. The classes, which had been planned with such vision, died because there wasn't enough childcare for those who wanted to attend.

One deacon commented, "I'm glad to have all these young people, but they ought to volunteer to help with childcare."

"No," one of the pastors told him, "we want them to feel like this is a place where they are fed spiritually before they are asked to serve."

"Fine," the deacon retorted, "we've fed 'em. Now let 'em serve." Then he added, "If they gave more, we'd have enough money to hire workers for Wednesday night, too." (Some churches don't believe it is appropriate to hire childcare workers at all. They believe it is the duty and privilege of the church body to care for their own children, so they only accept volunteers from among their own membership for this role.)

As this book is being written, church leaders are analyzing this situation and determining a plan. We'll see how the Lord leads this church or how the leadership responds to take advantage of so many young couples joining the church.

The childcare dilemma is common to many churches. We've all seen those in charge of childcare recruiting, plead, twist arms, and threaten to get enough volunteers. We can imagine that those who receive the benefits of this ministry should be the first to help provide services, but many churches don't want to ask young mothers and fathers to miss worship and Bible study. The solution for one church may be different from another. Wise leaders are devoted to prayer about the specifics of each situation.

Many churches experience conflict over the style of worship. Older members value the traditional hymns, but the younger generations enjoy contemporary styles. And the volume. . . . Church leaders are caught between reaching out to the young families and youth who will be the leaders of the future, and the older generation who currently funds the church's ministry.

Amid these opportunities and obstacles, disagreements too often become personal attacks. Instead of seeking understanding, people complain that their needs aren't being met, and they accuse others of not caring. They threaten to leave the church, and in some cases, they follow through with their threats. Lay leaders, and sometimes staff, take sides and polarize the situation instead of maintaining cool heads and resolving it. It is essential that a good leadership team be in place, with properly defined roles and a proper perspective, to handle obstacles and opportunities.

In this Step, we will look carefully at those circumstances which are roads forward or roadblocks for you and the vision God has given you.

In the last chapter, you reviewed the strengths of your staff and key lay leaders as you interviewed them. Now we want to look more objectively at the total performance of each leader (particularly the staff and support personnel), his or her responsibilities, job description, work habits, time allotment to each task, effectiveness, and fulfillment. This process can be threatening to people, so assure them that your goal is to shape each person's role so he will be most fulfilled. You want to maximize each person's gifting and design roles that provide the most opportunities for growth, both for the person and for the Kingdom. Of course, no one will have a job that fits him 100 percent, but that should be our objective. In this chapter, you will take the next step of writing (or rewriting) clear job descriptions for each leader and support person in your ministry.

Use the exercises at the end of this chapter as communication tools to open or continue dialog with your leaders. Share your heart and listen to each person's desires and goals. Then trust the Lord to give you wisdom to design a role that encourages, challenges, and maximizes that person's contribution to the ministry of the church.

Your staff, support personnel, and possibly, selected lay leaders, will fill out Task Summaries to note how they actually spend their time on the job, then they will put these activities into groups of duties in the Job Descriptions. Lay leaders probably won't fill out the Task Summaries in great detail, but it will be helpful for them to complete the Job Descriptions worksheet. As they share their assessments with you, affirm them in the things they are doing well. If adjustments need to be made, assume that the problem is your lack of clear communication, not their unwillingness to do the job. However, after you have communicated clearly and often, if the job is still not being done, you can address leaders with confidence and clarity because you have made your expectations known and supervised the work over a period of time.

REVIEW LEADERSHIP ASSIGNMENTS, JOB DESCRIPTIONS, AND WORK PRACTICES

Then trust the Lord to give you wisdom to design a role that encourages, challenges, and maximizes that person's contribution to the ministry of the church.

Let's face it: We all have weaknesses, both personally and in our ministries. During this assessment, we will uncover a number of obstacles that prevent our churches from functioning as it should. In some cases, this analysis will bring inappropriate attitudes to the surface, and in other cases we will find that we haven't been bold or clear enough in our leadership. Don't point too many fingers. Be honest, be objective, and be willing to hear from others who may have a different perspective than you do.

I find that most organizations, including churches, have a problem with communication. The leader thinks he has communicated his heart and direction clearly, but those under him haven't understood for some reason. Many of the problems we encounter would be solved if we would learn to speak without making assumptions and to listen without "interpreting" too much. The exercises at the end of this Step give you opportunities to reflect with your staff, lay leaders, and planning team on these questions:

— What (or who) is killing your vision and sapping your strength?
— What essential ministry goals aren't being achieved?
— Look at each segment on the organizational chart. What is your vision for this area? In what ways is the church falling short?
— Who is out of place on the organizational chart?
— What are common complaints by the congregation?
— In what skills do staff and lay leaders need training?

REVIEW THE GROWTH HISTORY OF YOUR CHURCH

At the end of this chapter, you will evaluate the overall growth history of your church for the last several years, targeting your analysis on each specific ministry, especially the demographic groups in Bible study: children, youth, singles, young marrieds, middle aged, and seniors, as well as the church at large. You may find that one or two groups have grown significantly, but in others growth has stagnated. Analyze the reasons for the growth curve for each group, including leadership, programming, facility limitations, and demographic shifts.

I suspect you might discover that significant growth is the result of quality leadership, men and women who have a vision for reaching and involving people, and who are skilled at building relationships. Ultimately, the most growth comes when leaders recruit and equip other leaders so the impact is multiplied.

As our nation's population grows, once rural lands and small towns are swallowed up by urban sprawl. The idyllic settings, traditional expectations, and the slow pace of many generations of those who attended a church are caught off-guard by the changes that occur when rapid demographic change takes place. Recently I drove through a bustling section of North Atlanta which only a few years before was farmland and a few hamlets. The churches in that area, like bedroom communities near cities across the country, have had to either change or turn down tremendous opportunities.

If your church is considering a building program, find out what road systems are planned for the surrounding area. In many cases, these plans are established by the county, city, and state several years in advance of actual construction and are available as public information in regional planning offices. You will be wise to find out what those plans entail before you start shoveling dirt.

The Census Bureau or the North American Mission Board can provide resources to inform you about the demographics of your community. You may think you already have a good understanding of these statistics, and your vision and programming may reflect your insights, but don't assume your perceptions are accurate. Do the research. Get the statistics, and you may be surprised by what you learn. For example, many of the communities in our country have seen an enormous increase in the number of Hispanics. Does your church reach out to them? Recently statistics show that the number of unmarried couples forming households has risen dramatically in the past decade. Are you teaching about the sanctity of marriage? On the other hand, do people from those homes who are seeking God feel welcomed at your church? In every community, there is a tremendous need for specialized ministry to single-parent families.

When you get the statistics, analyze them carefully. You may want to ask some engineers and social workers to form a sub-committee to review the statistics and give a report to your planning team.

You can begin your search for demographic data by going to www.census.gov or calling the North American Mission Board. Your local library also may provide resources for you. Then complete the Community Demographics worksheet at the end of this chapter. A good analysis of your community's demographics will surface some obstacles and opportunities your planning team needs to address.

RESEARCH YOUR COMMUNITY'S DEMOGRAPHICS

Don't assume your perceptions are accurate. Do the research. Get the statistics, and you may be surprised by what you learn.

EXAMINE SPACE UTILIZATION

Some churches don't think through how to maximize their facilities. The same classes meet in the same rooms year after year, and indeed, generation after generation, without thought of what would be most effective.

Most churches are notorious for not using their facilities very effectively. In some ways, that's the nature of an organization that uses its main meeting room only one or two days a week, and most other rooms are used just as rarely. Even then, some churches don't think through how to maximize their facilities. The same classes meet in the same rooms year after year, and indeed, generation after generation, without thought of what would be most effective.

As a church grows, some of the facility questions and concerns are:

— space for nursery and children's ministries;
— sound system requirements for worship;
— women's groups and classes during the week;
— a place where the noise of youth ministries doesn't bother others;
— the distance between children's rooms and adults;
— ample hallways;
— restroom that accommodate seniors as well as young parents with infants;
— wheelchair accessibility;
— adequate parking facilities; and
— when, how, and where to build new facilities.

Ask ministry leaders to do a brief space utilization analysis so you will know each of their needs. Using the Space Utilization worksheet at the end of this chapter, consider your existing space and how it is used in light of your growth history and your programming needs. If one group is growing and another declining, why should the size of their rooms remain constant? Look for trends and changes. You will use this information later in the planning process to determine your space needs for next year, and you will use it in your long-range planning to determine your facility needs for the next five to ten years.

The following pages are worksheets to help your planning team analyze the opportunities and obstacles that your church faces. As you work through them, ask the Lord for wisdom and insight, as well as the courage to be objective. All of the assessments in this Step are core exercises, including:

— Task Summaries,
— Job Descriptions,
— Historical Growth Statistics—Bible Study,
— Historical Growth Statistics—General Church Criteria,
— Community Demographics,
— Obstacles and Opportunities, and
— Space Utilization.

TASK SUMMARIES

— *Who?:* Your staff, support personnel, and other ministry leaders.
— *Why?:* To obtain a detailed record of work actually performed. This provides a human resource file for future hiring. It also provides the basis for a detailed and accurate job description.
— *How?:* Ask them to keep a log of everything they do for a month (preferably an "average" month).
— ***Then what?:*** Use this information in filling out the Job Descriptions worksheet.

Task Summary

Ministry _______________________ Position Title _______________________ Name _______________________

Please list the various tasks in "bullet" form that are required to carry out your ministry. Check (✔) daily, weekly, or monthly as it applies. Order or sequence is not important. Use additional paper if necessary.

Task

Task	daily	weekly	monthly
______________________________________	❏ daily	❏ weekly	❏ monthly
______________________________________	❏ daily	❏ weekly	❏ monthly
______________________________________	❏ daily	❏ weekly	❏ monthly
______________________________________	❏ daily	❏ weekly	❏ monthly
______________________________________	❏ daily	❏ weekly	❏ monthly
______________________________________	❏ daily	❏ weekly	❏ monthly
______________________________________	❏ daily	❏ weekly	❏ monthly
______________________________________	❏ daily	❏ weekly	❏ monthly
______________________________________	❏ daily	❏ weekly	❏ monthly
______________________________________	❏ daily	❏ weekly	❏ monthly
______________________________________	❏ daily	❏ weekly	❏ monthly
______________________________________	❏ daily	❏ weekly	❏ monthly
______________________________________	❏ daily	❏ weekly	❏ monthly
______________________________________	❏ daily	❏ weekly	❏ monthly
______________________________________	❏ daily	❏ weekly	❏ monthly
______________________________________	❏ daily	❏ weekly	❏ monthly
______________________________________	❏ daily	❏ weekly	❏ monthly
______________________________________	❏ daily	❏ weekly	❏ monthly
______________________________________	❏ daily	❏ weekly	❏ monthly
______________________________________	❏ daily	❏ weekly	❏ monthly
______________________________________	❏ daily	❏ weekly	❏ monthly
______________________________________	❏ daily	❏ weekly	❏ monthly
______________________________________	❏ daily	❏ weekly	❏ monthly
______________________________________	❏ daily	❏ weekly	❏ monthly
______________________________________	❏ daily	❏ weekly	❏ monthly
______________________________________	❏ daily	❏ weekly	❏ monthly
______________________________________	❏ daily	❏ weekly	❏ monthly
______________________________________	❏ daily	❏ weekly	❏ monthly
______________________________________	❏ daily	❏ weekly	❏ monthly

Ministry **Education**   Position Title **Minister of Education**   Name _______________

Please list the various tasks in "bullet" form that are required to carry out your ministry. Check (✔) daily, weekly, or monthly as it applies. Order or sequence is not important. Use additional paper if necessary.

Task

Task		daily	weekly	monthly
Personal Quiet Time		☑ daily	☐ weekly	☐ monthly
Meet with Pastor		☐ daily	☑ weekly	☐ monthly
Review and Develop Training Materials		☐ daily	☐ weekly	☑ monthly
Teachers Meeting		☐ daily	☐ weekly	☑ monthly
Go over Calendar Events		☐ daily	☑ weekly	☐ monthly
Meet with Individual Leadership		☑ daily	☑ weekly	☑ monthly
Counseling Appointments		☐ daily	☑ weekly	☐ monthly
Review Church Statistics		☐ daily	☑ weekly	☐ monthly
Read/Respond to Mail		☑ daily	☐ weekly	☐ monthly
Study for Teaching/Preaching		☐ daily	☑ weekly	☐ monthly
Preach/Teach		☐ daily	☑ weekly	☐ monthly
Meet with Finance Committee as required		☐ daily	☐ weekly	☑ monthly
Discipleship of Teachers		☐ daily	☐ weekly	☑ monthly
Deacon's Meeting		☐ daily	☐ weekly	☑ monthly
Order/Approve Purchases		☑ daily	☐ weekly	☐ monthly
Meet with Education Committee		☐ daily	☐ weekly	☑ monthly
Meet with Building Committee		☐ daily	☑ weekly	☐ monthly
Correspondence		☑ daily	☐ weekly	☐ monthly
Pre-marital Counseling	**as required**	☐ daily	☐ weekly	☐ monthly
Conduct Weddings	**as required**	☐ daily	☐ weekly	☐ monthly
Conduct Funerals	**as required**	☐ daily	☐ weekly	☐ monthly
Baptisms		☐ daily	☑ weekly	☐ monthly
Plan and Carry Out Teacher Fellowships	**quarterly**	☐ daily	☐ weekly	☐ monthly
Monitor Teacher Performance		☐ daily	☑ weekly	☐ monthly
Approve Sunday School Materials Being Taught	**quarterly**	☐ daily	☐ weekly	☐ monthly
Manage Space Use		☐ daily	☐ weekly	☑ monthly
Meeting with Committee on Committees		☐ daily	☐ weekly	☑ monthly
Task Force/Special Projects		☐ daily	☐ weekly	☑ monthly
Review Department Budgets		☐ daily	☐ weekly	☑ monthly
Review Staff Prospect		☐ daily	☑ weekly	☐ monthly
Develop and Coordinate Educational Plan		☐ daily	☐ weekly	☑ monthly

JOB DESCRIPTIONS

— *Who?:* Your staff, lay leaders, and support personnel.

— *Why?:* To analyze and appreciate how each person is using his time to carry out responsibilities, to determine how much time is consumed for each major function, then to give feedback so each person's role is fine-tuned.

— *How?:* After all staff members, lay leaders, and support people fill out the Task Summary, instruct them to categorize their work into no more than five major duties. They will then estimate, based on the Task Summary, the percent of time spent for each of the major categories. Lay leaders may use an abbreviated form of the Task Summaries to move ahead to the Job Description exercise. Having each leader write his or her own job description has tremendous benefits. It tells you not only how people are spending their time, but also how they have prioritized their work. As the pastor, your priorities for them may be significantly different. For example, you may find that a pastor is spending a third of his time on administrative details that a secretary should be doing. It's quite possible that a pastor or staff person may be spending an exaggerated amount of time counseling instead of meeting other needs in the church family. Or you may find that someone is actually more efficient than you thought. Use this time to clarify your expectations and make your desires known. Be sure to encourage each person in every way you can.

— *Then what?:* When you determine how your leaders and support people actually spend their time, you will have a basis to affirm them and make any adjustments in their roles so they will be more effective individually. As you review each leader's contribution, you will have the capability to focus or re-focus the church ministry. Write your comments on the "Supervisor's Remarks" section of the form to maintain focus, clarify expectations, and select and place new leaders in the future.

Job Description

Position Title: _______________________   **Name:** _______________________

Reports to: _______________________   **Date:** _______________________

List major responsibilities along with their respective duties. Indicate the percentage of your time required to carry out each of these major responsibilities. Space for "Supervisor's remarks" is provided for input and discussion.

Major Responsibilities (no more than five):	% of time required:	Supervisor's Remarks:
I. _______________________ • • • • •		
II. _______________________ • • • • •		

Major Responsibilities (no more than five):	% of time required:	Supervisor's Remarks:
III. ___________ • • • • •		
IV. ___________ • • • • •		
V. ___________ • • • • •		

Job Description

Position Title: Minister of Pastoral Care   **Name:** _______________

Reports to: Pastor   **Date:** _______________

List major responsibilities along with their respective duties. Indicate the percentage of your time required to carry out each of these major responsibilities. Space for "Supervisor's remarks" is provided for input and discussion.

Major Responsibilities (no more than five):	% of time required:	Supervisor's Remarks:
I. **Pastoral Counseling** • Biblical counseling (by appt./walk-in emergency/phone) • Provide relevant educational resources • Provide referrals in long-term situations • Enlist/train lay counselors • Oversee support groups (if needed) • Prepare & maintain counseling records • Review any resources to be used in counseling	**40%**	
II. **Pastoral Care** • Hospital visitation • Minister on-call • Hospital to home follow-up calls • Home visitation • Bereavement	**25%**	

Major Responsibilities (no more than five):	% of time required:	Supervisor's Remarks:
III. **Ministerial Functions** • Weddings/Counseling • Funerals • Baptisms	**7.5%**	

IV. **Prayer Ministry**
 • Track classes on prayer
 • Watch Man on the Wall
     Monthly newsletter
 • Inner Room prayer ministry
     Prepare weekly devotional
     Prepare weekly entries (World, National, State)
 • Update emergency needs
 • Power House Prayer Teams
 • Special prayer events
	20%	

V. **Administrative/Support** • Assist Senior Pastor as needed • Staff meetings • Worship Service counselor • Teach Sunday School • Encourage membership • Teach Discipleship classes	**7.5%**	

Job Description

Position Title: **Education Secretary**   **Name:** _______________

Reports to: **Minister of Education**   **Date:** _______________

List major responsibilities along with their respective duties. Indicate the percentage of your time required to carry out each of these major responsibilities. Space for "Supervisor's remarks" is provided for input and discussion.

Major Responsibilities (no more than five):	% of time required:	Supervisor's Remarks:
I. **Secretary to Minister of Education** • Handle incoming & outgoing calls & e-mails. Type correspondence and perform all clerical duties. • Scheduling in church calendar and special mailings • Synchronize calendar • Special Projects	**35%**	
II. **Sunday School Coordination** • Statistics, attendance sheets, Pastor's class lessons, announcements, promotion, class maintenance, church letter, special lessons, special topic books, quarterly literature, maintain S.S. boxes, interact with S.S. teachers, dept. directors and other leadership, post attendance, maintain current lists of S.S. teachers and classes, coordinate with outreach secretary, classroom signs, disaster relief.	**25%**	
II. **Secretary to Singles Minister** • Provide clerical assistance, handle correspondence and special mailings.	**5%**	

Major Responsibilities (no more than five):	% of time required:	Supervisor's Remarks:
IV. **Secretarial Support** Men's Ministry • Business Luncheon • Men's retreat • Men's Ministry Council Women's Ministry • Clerical assistance, name tags and prayer list for weekly Morning and Evening Bible Study • Maintain current mailing list and prepare special mailings • Women's Ministry Council • Ladies Night Out; brunches; seminars, conferences and retreats Discipleship Ministry • Brochures, posters, Sign-up sheets, literature Cancer Conquerors • Maintain current mail list. Prepare and mail bi-weekly card. Prepare scripture cards	**25%**	
V. **Miscellaneous** • Obtain quotes and order office and S.S. supplies, books, cassettes, videos and other items as required. Tract ministry • Attend monthly "all-staff" and Bi-weekly meetings.	**10%**	

HISTORICAL GROWTH STATISTICS— BIBLE STUDY

— *Who?:* The planning team.

— *Why?:* This exercise may tell you that you are doing exceptionally well with some groups in your church, but that others are being inadvertently overlooked. The number of people attending Bible study is a good indication of the strength, health, and growth of the church.

— *How?:* Chart the Bible study growth of each target audience in your church for the last five to ten years. On the Program Analysis, consider leadership changes, significant programs, and any other factors that influenced the effectiveness of your ministry to this group.

— *Then what?:* This data will show you how much you are growing, and then you can determine which areas need more vision to stimulate growth, better leadership, or more resources to capture the growth the Lord is producing. This information will be used in planning programs to meet the needs that are revealed in this exercise.

Historical Growth Statistics
Bible Study

	Yr. -10	Yr. -9	Yr. -8	Yr. -7	Yr. -6	Yr. -5	Yr. -4	Yr. -3	Yr. -2	Yr. -1	Present Yr.
Preschool (Average Attendance)											
Percentage increase/decrease*											
Children (Average Attendance)											
Percentage increase/decrease											
Youth (Average Attendance)											
Percentage increase/decrease											
Adults (Average Attendance)											
Percentage increase/decrease											
Total Bible Study											
Percentage increase/decrease											

Note: Each age division assumes Sunday a.m. on campus.
* To calculate percentage of increase/decrease, subtract previous year (ex. Yr -10) from current year (ex. Yr. -9) and divide by previous year (ex. Yr. -10).

Historical Growth Statistics
Bible Study

	Yr. -10	Yr. -9	Yr. -8	Yr. -7	Yr. -6	Yr. -5	Yr. -4	Yr. -3	Yr. -2	Yr. -1	Present Yr.
	1991	1992	1993	1994	1995	1996	1997	1998	1999	2000	2001
Preschool (Average Attendance)	37	38	39	42	45	46	45	46	48	52	54
Percentage increase/decrease*		2.7%	4.1%	6.4%	7.0%	1.9%	-1.8%	2.5%	5.8%	6.4%	5.7%
Children (Average Attendance)	37	38	39	42	45	46	45	46	48	52	54
Percentage increase/decrease		2.7%	4.1%	6.4%	7.0%	1.9%	-1.8%	2.5%	5.8%	6.4%	5.7%
Youth (Average Attendance)	29	30	31	33	35	36	35	36	38	40	43
Percentage increase/decrease		2.7%	4.1%	6.4%	7.0%	1.9%	-1.8%	2.5%	5.8%	6.4%	5.7%
Adults (Average Attendance)	160	164	171	182	195	198	195	199	211	224	237
Percentage increase/decrease		2.7%	4.1%	6.4%	7.0%	1.9%	-1.8%	2.5%	5.8%	6.4%	5.7%
Total Bible Study	262	269	280	298	319	325	319	327	346	368	389
Percentage increase/decrease		2.7%	4.1%	6.4%	7.0%	1.9%	-1.8%	2.5%	5.8%	6.4%	5.7%

Note: Each age division assumes Sunday a.m. on campus.
* To calculate percentage of increase/decrease, subtract previous year (ex. Yr -10) from current year (ex. Yr. -9) and divide by previous year (ex. Yr. -10).
 Example: Year -9 inc/dec percentages: Bible Study Ave. Attd.: (269 - 262 = 7) / 262 = 2.7%

Program Analysis
Historical Growth Statistics—Bible Study

Review the data collected from the Historical Growth Statistics, and analyze the causes of growth (or the lack of growth) in each target group in your church. On this form, chart each year's size, the leadership, shifts in demographics, significant programming, or other factors that have had an impact on the growth pattern.

	Yr. -10	Yr. -9	Yr. -8	Yr. -7	Yr. -6	Yr. -5	Yr. -4	Yr. -3	Yr. -2	Yr. -1	Present Yr.
Nursery											
Preschool											
Children											
Youth											
Adults											

For your purposes, adults can be
broken down in categories such as:

	Yr. -10	Yr. -9	Yr. -8	Yr. -7	Yr. -6	Yr. -5	Yr. -4	Yr. -3	Yr. -2	Yr. -1	Present Yr.
Singles											
Young marrieds											
Medians											
Seniors											
Total											

Note: Each age division assumes Sunday a.m. on campus.

HISTORICAL GROWTH STATISTICS— GENERAL CHURCH CRITERIA

— *Who?:* The planning team.

— *Why?:* This analysis measures the quantitative pulse of the church in all areas, including Bible study attendance.

— *How?:* This form combines the statistics you reviewed about Bible study attendance in the last form with church membership, baptisms, and finances.

For a period of five to ten years (the longer the better), chart the growth of the church in the categories provided. The categories on this form are the ones you will use to project growth in your future plans. Don't be overwhelmed or discouraged by the amount of detail required for this chart. Find the best available source of data for this history, and realize that your accuracy at this point will greatly enhance the accuracy of your projections for the future.

— *Then what?:* This information will be part of the foundation for projecting growth for your annual and long-range plans.

Historical Growth Statistics
General Church Criteria

	Yr. –10	Yr. –9	Yr. –8	Yr. –7	Yr. –6	Yr. –5	Yr. –4	Yr. –3	Yr. –2	Yr. –1	Present Yr.
Church Membership											
Percentage increase/decrease*											
Bible Study (Average Attendance)											
Percentage increase/decrease											
Worship (Average Attendance)											
Percentage increase/decrease											
Baptisms											
Finances											
Budget Receipts											
Percentage increase/decrease											
Designated Gifts											
Building Fund											
Total Gifts											
Percentage increase/decrease											
Operational Budget											
Percentage increase/decrease											

* To calculate percentage of increase/decrease, subtract previous year (ex. Yr. –10) from current year (ex. Yr. –9) and divide by previous year (ex. Yr. –10).

Historical Growth Statistics
General Church Criteria

	Yr. -10	Yr. -9	Yr. -8	Yr. -7	Yr. -6	Yr. -5	Yr. -4	Yr. -3	Yr. -2	Yr. -1	Present Yr.
	1991	1992	1993	1994	1995	1996	1997	1998	1999	2000	2001
Church Membership	1050	1072	1108	1177	1268	1289	1294	1332	1402	1484	1548
percentage increase/decrease*		2.1%	3.4%	6.2%	7.7%	1.7%	0.4%	2.9%	5.3%	5.8%	4.3%
Bible Study (Average Attendance)	262	269	280	298	319	325	319	327	346	368	389
percentage increase/decrease		2.7%	4.1%	6.4%	7.0%	1.9%	-1.8%	2.5%	5.8%	6.4%	5.7%
Worship (Average Attendance)	287	304	321	348	384	395	391	412	438	469	511
percentage increase/decrease		5.9%	5.6%	8.4%	10.3%	2.9%	-1.0%	5.4%	6.3%	7.1%	9.0%
Baptisms	11	13	17	21	26	16	19	23	18	27	28
Finances											
Budget Receipts	$432,962	$458,608	$487,254	$528,986	$597,246	$619,033	$611,127	$638,535	$687,285	$729,415	$802,183
percentage increase/decrease		5.9%	6.2%	8.6%	12.9%	3.6%	-1.3%	4.5%	7.6%	6.1%	10.0%
Designated Gifts	$15,000	$15,000	$15,000	$20,000	$20,000	$20,000	$25,000	$25,000	$30,000	$30,000	$30,000
Building Fund			$3,000	$3,000	$5,000	$5,000		$7,500	$7,500	$7,500	$7,500
Total Gifts	$447,962	$473,608	$505,254	$551,986	$622,246	$644,033	$636,127	$671,035	$724,785	$766,915	$839,683
percentage increase/decrease		5.7%	6.7%	9.2%	12.7%	3.5%	-1.2%	5.5%	8.0%	5.8%	9.5%
Operational Budget	$395,248	$418,963	$444,101	$472,967	$503,710	$528,896	$539,474	$561,053	$589,105	$621,506	$658,796
percentage increase/decrease		6.0%	6.0%	6.5%	6.5%	5.0%	2.0%	4.0%	5.0%	5.5%	6.0%

* To calculate percentage of increase/decrease, subtract previous year (ex. Yr -10) from current year (ex. Yr. -9) and divide by previous year (ex. Yr. -10).
Example: Year -9 inc/dec percentages: Bible Study Avg. Attendance: (269 - 262 = 7) / 262 = 2.7%

COMMUNITY DEMOGRAPHICS

— *Who?:* The planning team.

— *Why?:* To see how the community is changing, so that you can meet people's needs by planning programs for targeted groups.

— *How?:* Meet with the civil planning agencies of the city or county to determine what changes are planned for housing, road systems, sewers, etc. Review the Census Bureau statistics and answer the questions in this exercise. This worksheet is designed to help you understand the shifts that are taking place in your community so you can be more effective in planning the right programs to meet real needs.

— *Then what?:* This information will be used as you analyze the obstacles and opportunities your church faces.

COMMUNITY DEMOGRAPHICS

List the insights you learned from the city or county planning agencies. Itemize those factors that are, or will be, affecting your growth potential:

After reviewing the Census Bureau statistics for your community, and perhaps researching other pertinent sources, summarize your findings.

1. How has your community changed in the past decade (numerically, racially, by household income, etc.)?

2. What audiences (by age group, income level, and race) are you reaching now?

3. What audiences are you not reaching very effectively?

4. What kinds of programs might reach more people in your community with the gospel?

What kinds of programs might work effectively to teach, disciple, and shepherd the various people in your community?

How are these programs different from what you are doing now?

5. How can your church present itself to the community most effectively so people will take advantage of your ministry?

6. What are your greatest areas of opportunity to reach your community for Christ?

OBSTACLES AND OPPORTUNITIES

— *Who?:* The planning team.

— *Why?:* To identify the open doors the Lord has provided in your community, as well as the obstacles that hinder your ministry in these areas.

— *How?:* As a summary of the analysis of the Historical Growth Statistics and your Community Demographics, examine the opportunities for growth and the obstacles that may prevent that growth.

— *Then what?:* You will use these insights as you plan programs, assign responsibilities, and finalize your plans.

OBSTACLES AND OPPORTUNITIES

Now that you have assessed the current strengths and needs of each ministry and identified any shifts in the community demographics over the past few years, it is time to look at the areas that offer the greatest hope for growth and the biggest obstacles to that growth.

Obstacles

1. In which ministry areas do the leaders need additional training in order for them to be more effective?

2. In what ways is mediocrity, dead tradition, and lack of vision stealing enthusiasm and progress?

3. Is conflict taking the focus off Christ and taking energy away from His purposes?

4. Can you detect evidences of spiritual conflict and the opposition of the enemy?

5. What would you say is the biggest obstacle to your church's growth?

Opportunities

1. What ministries of the church are seeing the greatest growth?

2. Which of your leaders have unusual vision and energy to serve God?

3. What target groups (by age, economics, or ethnicity) are expanding in your community?

4.   What doors has God opened that you haven't yet walked through?

5.   If God worked—really worked—in your church and in your community, what would it look like?

SPACE UTILIZATION

— *Who?:* The planning team.

— *Why?:* To help you assess the current effectiveness of your facilities, especially the space required during the time of maximum facility use, on Sunday morning.

Good planning requires a knowledge of the exact square footage of each room in your church so you can determine how much of it is being used effectively and efficiently. Many times, relatively simple changes can make a big difference in the usefulness of a room. If additional space is required, an accurate assessment of present usage is your first step in planning.

For this exercise, you will need at least one, and perhaps several, schematics of your church's floor plan, as well as a weekly schedule of events and a calendar of special events. Gather the information provided by the ministry leaders, and make sure you ask them to outline their needs for space and their suggestions for meeting those needs.

With this information, plot where every class, meeting, and event takes place on the campus, including special events like conferences and weddings. For each one, note how many people attend, using a range of attendance if it fluctuates to any degree. Also, be sure to assess the quality of the meeting facilities regarding sound, lighting, access, etc.

Examine these issues:

1. What are the most common complaints about your facilities?

2. Which meetings, classes, and events have ample room? Which are currently cramped? Which have too much space for the group to feel comfortable?

3. What are the needs expressed by the ministry leaders?

4. How are you currently addressing the needs of:
   —entrances to the building on crowded days,
   —exits on those days,
   —space for nursery and children's ministries,
   —sound system requirements for contemporary worship,
   —women's groups and classes during the week,
   —a place where the noise of youth ministries doesn't bother others,

—the distance between children's rooms and adults,
—ample hallways, and
—adequate parking facilities.

5. How can you plan your facility use to conserve energy and save energy costs?

6. Assess your facility insurance, costs and coverage.

7. Outline your suggestions for improving the use of your facilities.

8. What are your suggestions for additional space? When, how, and where will you build them?

— *How?:* Answer the questions on the worksheet, then use the form to chart the actual use of rooms at your church according to four groupings: worship, music, age groupings for Bible studies, and support services (such as offices, maintenance, and storage). You may need to get this information from each of your ministry leaders, or your church office may have that data. Ask a secretary or someone on the planning team to help you gather the accurate square footage for each room.

— *Then what?:* This information will be used in your analysis of space requirements as you formulate annual and long-range plans.

Space Utilization

Function	Sq. Ft. Per Person	Current Sq. Footage	Average Attendance		
			Current Year	Capacity 100%*	Capacity 85%**
Worship	11				
Auxilliary Space (i.e. Foyer, Restroom)					
Education					
Preschool	35				
Children	25				
Youth	15				
Adults	10				
Total Classroom Square Footage					
Auxilliary Space (i.e. Hallways, Storage)					
Music Rehearsal					
Kitchen/Fellowship					
Activities/Family Life					
Administration					
Other					

*To calculate capacity 100%, divide the square footage of the area by the square foot per person.
**To calculate capacity 85%, divide the square footage of the area by the square foot per person and multiply by .85.

Space Utilization

Function	Sq. Ft. Per Person	Current Sq. Footage	Average Attendance		
			Current Year	Capacity 100%*	Capacity 85%**
Worship	11	10,000	511	909	773
Auxilliary Space (i.e. Foyer, Restroom)		2,000			
Education					
Preschool	35	2,100	54	60	51
Children	25	1,600	54	64	54
Youth	15	800	43	53	45
Adults	10	2,600	237	260	221
Total Classroom Square Footage		7,100	389	437	372
Auxilliary Space (i.e. Hallways, Storage)		2,000			
Music Rehearsal		1,250			
Kitchen/Fellowship		3,300			
Activities/Family Life		6,200			
Administration		2,200			
Other					

*To calculate capacity 100%, divide the square footage of the area by the square foot per person.
**To calculate capacity 85%, divide the square footage of the area by the square foot per person and multiply by .85.

STEP 1 *The Captain's Compass*
- Your Personal Vision
- Your Ministry Vision

STEP 2 *Look at the Map*
- Your Plan for Planning
- Ministry Review
- Planning Team Evaluation

STEP 3 *Watch for Obstacles and Opportunities*
- Task Summaries
- Job Descriptions
- Historical Growth Statistics—Bible Study
- Historical Growth Statistics—General Church Criteria
- Community Demographics
- Obstacles and Opportunities
- Space Utilization

STEP 4 *Get Your Equipment Ready*
- **Ministry Flow Chart**
- **Organizational Chart**
- **Communication System**

STEP 5 *Plot Your Course*
- Ministry Leader Planning Worksheet
- The Ministry Plan
- The Master Calendar
- The Financial Plan
- Communication Plan

STEP 6 *Look Over the Next Hill*
- Long-Range Ministry Plan
- Growth and Capacity Analysis
- Growth Projections
- General Church Criteria
- Building Plan Schedule and Expenditures
- Long-Range Financial Plan

STEP 7 *Get on the Trail*
- Monthly Planning Worksheet

GET YOUR EQUIPMENT READY

Those intrepid hikers who tackle significant stretches of the Appalachian Trail, Big Bend in Texas, or climb Mt. Whitney in California all spend plenty of time looking at the map and getting ready for the trip. They may spend weeks or even months gathering information and learning the nuances of the trail because they don't want to be caught off guard once they begin. In the final days before they hit the trail, they make their final preparations and check all their equipment to be sure it is ready for the journey. In the same way, all the preparation so far in the planning process has given us information. Now it is time to organize our resources so we will be ready to discern our church's course for the future.

Now it is time to organize our resources so we will be ready to discern our church's course for the future.

STRATEGY AND STRUCTURE

By this time, some of those reading this book have already accomplished many of the things we have discussed. They have spent time with the Lord to shape their personal vision and they have looked at their gifting and experience to identify their personal ministry vision. They have formed a planning team and have conducted extensive research, and they are ready for the next step. Others, however, are reading this book through cover to cover before taking the first step.

If you haven't yet begun to plan, you may want to finish reading the book and getting your arms around the entire process before starting. Whenever you are ready, begin your preparations with protracted, open-hearted time with God to hear from Him. Don't take another step until you have been refreshed in His grace and directed by His wisdom. When you have a sense of His presence and leading, select your planning team and develop your strategy and timetable for planning. Conduct your research and gather information using reports from ministry leaders, demographic analysis, and insights from your planning team. You will gain insight from objective facts as well as by listening to subjective perceptions from those you serve. In this process, you will find out that some people are a wealth of knowledge. They are your scouts, and they will contribute greatly to your planning process.

Be sure to involve ministry leaders in the process. Open communication during this stage often yields a deep well of insight, for you and for them. You may find that some of them aren't doing as much as they can because they need more direction from you, and you may find that some are simply out of place. They may not be skilled or gifted in the areas where they serve. Many have wonderful hearts but need additional training or resources to do a great job. And some (bless their hearts!) are skilled, gifted, self-motivated, and effective. They need little guidance. These, however, should be considered exceptions to the rule. The vast majority of those who serve need regular encouragement, training, and shepherding.

As church leaders go through these steps, many of them become aware for the first time that the decision-making process in their churches is cumbersome. There may be a tendency at this point to find short-cuts, but don't let this happen. If information-gathering and communication are neglected, decisions may be made in a vacuum or based on the opinions of a few. Remember, "By pride (or presumption) comes nothing but strife, but with the well-advised is wisdom" (Proverbs 13:10).

The gathering of information also reveals strengths and uncovers flaws in the system of delegation and control. Some of those in responsible positions simply have been left on their own. They don't share the pastor's vision because they don't know how it applies to their specific ministries. They may continue to flounder month after month because no one is giving them encouragement and feedback. They feel confused and lost. They want to serve effectively, but they lack direction or training, or both. Even if the pastor is clear in his communication, sometimes people simply don't understand his heart and direction. He needs to encourage them to ask questions, clarify his direction, and be patient.

Your desires for the church will be communicated through the specifics of your church's annual Ministry Plan, the Financial Plan, and the Master Calendar (these will be completed in Step 5). In preparation for writing these, Step 4 helps you analyze the basics of how your ministry network

There may be a tendency at this point to find short-cuts, but don't let this happen.

is designed and how the responsibilities are delegated to accomplish the church's programs.

Don't be discouraged if and when you find deficiencies in your current system. If you find them, you can correct them, but if they remain hidden, they will continue to hinder your church's effectiveness for years to come. Learn to welcome the truth. Instead of being threatened by these deficiencies and assuming they make you look like a failure, thank people for their honesty. See every need as an opportunity for growth. That positive, faith-oriented attitude will do wonders to build your leadership team!

You have received valuable information from your ministry leaders about the current condition of their areas of service, and your team has come further than you might think in determining the course for the next year. At this point, take some time to construct a Ministry Flow Chart, which is a graphic representation of the network of ministries within your church structure, and an Organizational Chart, which identifies the people who are responsible and accountable for each program. This exercise goes back to the basic principle of first identifying the needs of the people, which determines the type of ministry, which then determines the qualities of the leader who can take responsibility for each ministry.

As you look at the Ministry Flow Chart, the size of the church and the complexity of the program will determine how you subdivide its ministry groupings. Consider putting the networks of your ministries into three to five major groups according to three criteria: their functions, their relationship to one another, and their need to be centralized for the best support of the entire church program. It is easy to see that worship and music fall into a single category. Similarly, the many classes in the church are grouped under education. The area of administration should be as broad as the size and complexity of the programs require it to be, extending from just a bookkeeper and janitor (roles assumed by many pastors of small churches), to a full finance office, human resources, food services, computer systems, and staff coordinator in a large church. Pastoral care or missions may be another major segment which needs to be separated into a category for effectiveness and efficiency.

Of course, churches may have particular philosophies of ministry that dictate a specific grouping of programs. The key in designing your Ministry Flow Chart is to discern a communication path from the office of the pastor through the

See every need as an opportunity for growth. That positive, faith-oriented attitude will do wonders to build your leadership team!

Consider putting the networks of your ministries into three to five major groups according to three criteria: their functions, their relationship to one another, and their need to be centralized for the best support of the entire church program.

various programs to meet the needs of the person in the pew. The priority of meeting personal needs is then balanced with the priority of equipping people to serve others. For various reasons, not every program will fall neatly into a category. For example, in many churches, outreach is the responsibility of the Bible study classes, but it may be wise to create a separate division of evangelism to focus more attention on this crucial area.

After you complete the Ministry Flow Chart, match your leadership to these roles on the Organizational Chart, which shows the relationship of each person to the office of the pastor and to one another. The design of the chart used in this book indicates a team approach instead of the traditional, top down, "Christmas tree" design. Finalizing your Organizational Chart requires godly discernment for selection and placement. A small church may need only a few lay leaders, but in large churches, most of the key leadership may be full-time staff.

To take full advantage of a particular leader's time and talents, the final Organizational Chart may have some crossed lines. That is not only acceptable; it is desirable. A flexible and creative Organizational Chart doesn't violate the purposes of responsibility and accountability for leaders who head more than one area of ministry as long as communication is clear and strong. For example, your administrator or minister of education may have gifts and a passion for missions. If time permits him to do a good job in both of these ministry responsibilities, allow him to oversee both areas.

DEVELOP A LEADERSHIP POSITION MANUAL

A clearly outlined leadership position manual enhances effective teamwork. This manual should include job descriptions, spiritual gift assessments, and personality profiles for each leader and support personnel. In small churches, this manual will include lay leaders who are responsible for key ministries in your church. In medium-sized churches, there is usually a mix of staff and lay leaders in charge of ministries. The value of this manual is to better understand your key personnel, the ones who serve in strategic assignments and those who speak for you to the congregation and the community. Understanding their gifts, strengths, and weaknesses enables you to more accurately perceive their hearts and their actions as they serve. An accurate assessment of your leaders and support people will enable you to assign teams of people with different and complementary gifts and personalities. As they balance one another, these teams can be more effective, and serious mistakes can be avoided.

A most important facet of the culture of business and ministry relationships is the reporting structure: who reports to this person, and to whom does that person report. An organizational chart does not create a culture of leading and following. It is designed to show the paths of communication to achieve the objectives of the ministry. A healthy church culture is developed when the body of leaders accepts and follows the goals and processes of the church. Complete acceptance of authority and accountability, however, is often difficult to achieve. Some of us give every indication that we are totally supportive of the system, but we find ways to excuse ourselves from the "letter of the law" if that law proves to be inconvenient. "After all," we may say, "administrative processes aren't the Ten Commandments." That's true, but when a pastor and church leaders have agreed on an operating system but one chooses to go his own way, he is practicing deceit. And that deceit undermines trust. I have noticed that some of us are more adept at teaching and preaching on authority than we are at submitting to authority ourselves. We find it much easier to be authoritative than submissive, but this spells doom to unanimity. Spiritual leaders must set the standard for organizational integrity. Integrity is more than the absence of moral failure; it is the presence of humility and the willingness to obey, even when it is inconvenient. Remember, accountability is inextricably interwoven with authority, regardless of where we find ourselves on the organizational chart.

All of us are accountable to the highest authority of all, our great and loving God. Authority in the church is certainly God-ordained. Even Jesus was under the authority of the Father, and He did all things that the Father commanded Him to do. The pastor is not only under the authority of God; he is also under the authority of the congregation. The one who is unwilling to be submissive to authority disqualifies himself from leadership, but the willingness to submit reveals the qualities of humility and servanthood. Those in authority should focus on the positives, and address the negatives in ways that build up instead of tearing down. Offer help, not criticism. One of the best things you can say when someone is struggling with his responsibilities is: "How can I help you?"

I have noticed that some of us are more adept at teaching and preaching on authority than we are at submitting to authority ourselves.

One of the best things you can say when someone is struggling with his responsibilities is: "How can I help you?"

As a team leader, plan and conduct meetings that are fun and encouraging. Plan to focus on success stories, and celebrate each one. Appreciate people for their willingness to be involved in God's work, even if they aren't the most gifted and successful. Offer ideas and suggestions, but remember that each person has a unique blend of motivations, experiences, gifting, and personality. In too many cases, only our favorites receive our praise, while others long to hear a kind word of affirmation from us. Know your people, acknowledge their achievements, encourage them according to their gifts and personalities, and tailor your admonition and instruction to help them serve the Lord most effectively.

WHEN TO HIRE STAFF

Planning is a continual balancing of the needs of the people, the programming to meet those needs, and the finances to support those programs with appropriate resources and staffing.

Certainly, each staff member will have targeted responsibilities, but their first calling is to the Lord, to the pastor's vision, and to the team, not to that specific ministry in the church.

One of the most common questions I am asked is, "When should we hire another staff member?" This one is closely followed by its corollary, "What role should that person fill?" The overarching principle is that the needs of the people determine the program, and the program determines the personnel needed. Planning is a continual balancing of the needs of the people, the programming to meet those needs, and the finances to support those programs with appropriate resources and staffing.

The factors which determine when, how, and who to hire for a staff position varies widely from church to church. Of course, the needs of the church and the desire to find people with complementary gifts should be high on the list. Finances always play an important part, however, choosing and placing the right person should result in significant advancement in the church's edification of its people. In addition, adding staff should accelerate growth, which in turn enhances the stewardship program of the church. Of course, calling people to staff positions should never be for economic reasons, but for the spread of the gospel and the building up of the saints. Wise leaders recognize the need to be prudent and purposeful in the use of tithes and offerings so the ministry of the gospel is advanced as much as possible.

As you add staff, be sure to avoid "categorical calling," that is, as you recall, the concept that a staff member is totally focused, and consequently isolated, on one category of the ministry, such as educational directors, ministers of music, and youth ministers. Certainly, each staff member will have targeted responsibilities, but their first calling is to the Lord, to the pastor's vision, and to the team, not to that specific ministry in the church. He may be asked (and indeed, will almost certainly be asked from time to time) to take on responsibilities outside his initial job description to fulfill the needs of the church. If a person holds tightly to his perceived categorical calling, he will be hesitant to help whenever and wherever he is needed, but if he understands that his role is larger than his specific job description, he will gladly serve where he is needed. As the church grows, his role and responsibility will grow, too. And more importantly, he should be growing in his spiritual life as well as his professional capability. If he sequesters himself in a rigidly protected category of ministry, he may miss the most promising and fulfilling ministry of his life. Complementary gifting, a servant's heart, and a calling to extend the pastor's vision are essential ingredients in each staff member and lay leader's calling.

Adding staff is not always the answer. Many churches would benefit more by selecting and equipping lay volunteers. Strong leadership development is the first priority of a healthy, growing church. Sometimes pastors are not considered to be good managers, but that is true of many people in virtually all professions. I prefer to think that a pastor's priority requires him to first to manage and organize himself and his preaching ministry. After that, he may have little time to coordinate all the demands of the ministry. In those cases, God will provide laity to take up the slack, or perhaps an additional staff member will be needed to extend the leadership of the pastor and to equip the laity to serve strategically.

In many churches, God has already begun to call out lay leaders who have a commitment to Christ, loyalty to the pastor, and a vision for an area of ministry. A lay leader who is integrally involved in serving God, his pastor, and his church may be a strong candidate for a staff position. The testimony of many people is echoed in my own experience: As God prepares this person for the ministry, He is also preparing the ministry for the person. Then, when the timing is right, the person and the ministry are brought together. In almost every church, lay leaders are being groomed by the Lord and by their involvement in ministry for greater involvement. Perhaps as they continue to excel in lay ministry, God may speak to their hearts about the ministry as a vocation. I believe pastors would be wise to look at their lay leaders as a primary source of staffing to meet the needs of their people. If he senses God's leading and timing, the pastor should approach the lay people with the idea that God may be calling them to greater service. A man who is known by his pastor and peers and who has proven himself in their service

A lay leader who is integrally involved in serving God, his pastor, and his church may be a strong candidate for a staff position.

All too often, poor performance is overlooked, or in an attempt to avoid confrontation, someone else is asked to take up the slack created by an underachieving person.

is a much greater "known quantity" than one who is interviewed several times.

On the opposite end of the continuum, what do you do about an employee who is not performing well? In business, options are clear cut, and action can be swift. In the church, however, the options are not so clear, and the time of decision and implementation is often quite prolonged . . . and rightfully so. The ideal solution is a win/win situation in which the harmony of the church fellowship is preserved and the individual is encouraged to find purpose and fulfillment in ministry.

All too often, poor performance is overlooked, or in an attempt to avoid confrontation, someone else is asked to take up the slack created by an underachieving person. Avoiding these issues, however, greatly hinders effective leadership and team building. Many leaders avoid effective confrontation at the cost of their own integrity and the respect of their staff teams. Confrontation certainly is not to be pursued aggressively nor publicly, but resolution seldom results from avoiding the issues. Don't wait until the situation is a crisis. Even a low grade temperature is a sign of poor health and needs to be addressed before greater problems arise.

The goal of confronting poor performance is always to help the person who is struggling. When this proves to be impossible, however, a different course must be taken. In all cases, documentation of each step is essential. The first step is to attempt to determine if the problem is a spiritual one or if it stems from incompetence or poor relational skills. If it is a spiritual problem, the focus is restoration of the person's relationship with Christ, and the course of action is shaped by the principles of Scripture. If the person's response is improper or inadequate, move through the successive levels of leadership (according to Matthew 18:15-20) to indicate to the person the unanimity of spirit on the part of the leaders of the church. Further resistance by the person requires a swift removal before the cancer of bitterness and rebellion can spread. However, this decision should be communicated to him in a loving and appropriate manner.

If a spiritual problem is uncovered and the person is appropriately repentant, steps should be taken to affirm his ministry potential, or perhaps to find a more appropriate ministry area where he can serve. Sometimes you will be able to find a more suitable ministry within the framework of your church, but on occasion, another church might provide a better place for this person to serve effectively. If another pastor or church is brought into the picture, both the individual and his former pastor should be very transparent with those who interview him. Leadership styles and team dynamics are very different in churches, and it is entirely possible that an individual may fit better on one team than another. Strive to find the proper role and the proper environment for each person. Conflict resolution is the responsibility of leadership, not a problem to be avoided.

Conflict on a staff or leadership team occurs when a person's safety or significance is threatened. When someone gets attention in a high profile ministry, jealousy can surface among the other leaders. I've seen conflict occur most often when staff felt overlooked, when they were asked to report to someone lower on the perceived pecking order, and when expectations of them were perceived as unrealistic. Honest and open communication is the best solution to these problems. If we fail to talk openly about them, they can fester for months or years and taint the entire ministry of the church. If they are identified and addressed appropriately, however, understanding and healing can occur. If the two people can't work things out on their own, I suggest they find a third party, respected by both and as objective as possible, to serve as mediator. If the two are willing to speak truth and genuinely try to understand each other, most conflicts can be resolved. Many times, however, "triangulation" occurs when one person talks to a third party about the other. This may be defended as "sharing a concern," but in reality, it is manipulation and gossip. This is not a proper way to resolve a relational problem.

There are few occasions when termination is appropriate, but in those rare cases, the process needs to be undertaken with caution and patience. After every effort has been made to avoid termination, each affected segment of the church body needs to be informed with as much—or as little—detail as is deemed suitable. Those who love and respect this person need to understand the reasons behind the proposed action, so take time to explain why and how the decision was made. The process you take is every bit as important as the final decision.

Conflict resolution is the responsibility of leadership, not a problem to be avoided.

As I have worked with scores of churches across the country, one of the factors that I've seen which contributes greatly to a strong team ministry is its system of communication up and down the authority structure. We will look briefly at elements of healthy communication on the leadership team, within the church family, and in the community.

DEVELOP A COMMUNICATION SYSTEM

Good communication is both an art, requiring sensitivity and perception, and a science, requiring workable structures so the network of interaction can flow smoothly and regularly.

Even though we live in a high-tech world, nothing can take the place of old-fashioned, personal interaction.

On the Leadership Team

A leader is only as effective as the quality of the people he chooses and the information he gets. Ministry leaders and staff need to be careful to give the pastor accurate and objective information. In larger churches, a senior associate may serve to coordinate the flow of communication to and from the pastor. This service frees the pastor from many time-consuming conversations and allows him to focus on his true calling. My pastor has said, "The pastor needs to be free to do what only he can do—not free *of* work, but free *to* work." A pastor, however, must not become isolated from the heartbeat of every facet of his church. Good communication is both an art, requiring sensitivity and perception, and a science, requiring workable structures so the network of interaction can flow smoothly and regularly.

In the Church Family

We live in the information age, and churches are learning how to use every means available to communicate with their people. Bulletins and newsletters still work well, but many churches also use websites to provide daily updates to their people. A growing number of churches have home pages for major ministries so those involved can ask for help or get the information they need on a daily basis.

Even though we live in a high-tech world, nothing can take the place of old-fashioned, personal interaction. At this point, I want to insert a caution about the use of automated, preprogrammed telephone systems in churches. When people call the church, they usually want personal contact. The last place for impersonal (though often expedient and less expensive) service is the church. Make sure your communication is genuine and personal.

Face-to-face conversation is the core of good communication in a church family. Good communication, as we all know, doesn't taken place until a spoken or written word is understood by the hearer or reader. We can't assume that simply speaking or writing accomplishes this genuine understanding without appropriate feedback.

When the size of the church grows beyond the point when the pastor can address each issue for each person, he needs to carefully choose people to interpret messages for him. When we try to communicate with someone who speaks a language we don't understand, we need an interpreter who understands both languages. In the same way, pastors need to choose "interpreters" who understand the "language" of the pastor as well as the "language" of the people in the pews. These interpreters, from senior staff to church receptionists, communicate the pastor's vision to the people. Even the minister of music is an interpreter of the pastor's heart and style in his selection of worship hymns and choruses. I cannot overemphasize the need for a pastor to carefully consider the selection and training of those who may be speaking for him so that they understand his heart and his vision for their areas of ministry. Communication in the church family is tremendously important, so the pastor needs to choose wisely those who hold those strategic and privileged positions of speaking for him.

In the Community

Depending on the scope of a church's ministry, its "community" may be a small town, a part of a city, or a national audience. To be a good citizen of the community, the pastor and his leaders need to be good listeners to prove they want to build relationships as well as have an impact for Christ.

Preaching and teaching the Word of God may take a variety of forms. Some are effective as the Holy Spirit produces fruit, but some have proven to be quite ineffective if we are simply trying to build our own reputations and our own kingdoms. The style of communication to your community can be tailored to fit your situation, including service projects, outreaches, newspaper articles and other media, classes, and a host of other possibilities. Whatever form and style you choose, make sure the materials, events, and communication are known for their excellence. After all, quality produces quantity.

The exercises at the end of this chapter are designed to help you finalize your organizational structure, develop an effective reporting system, and evaluate and plan your communication system.

The core exercises include:

— Ministry Flow Chart,
— Organizational Chart, and
— Communication System.

Communication in the church family is tremendously important, so the pastor needs to choose wisely those who hold those strategic and privileged positions of speaking for him.

Whatever form and style you choose, make sure the materials, events, and communication are known for their excellence. After all, quality produces quantity.

TAKE A STEP

MINISTRY FLOW CHART

— *Who?:* The planning team.

— *Why?:* To show how the major divisions of the ministry extend from the office of the pastor and reach out to touch the lives of each church member. The number of major ministry divisions will vary from church to church depending on factors such as the size of the church, the philosophy of ministry, and the number of pastoral staff. Each division, such as education, represents ever-widening circles of leadership and participation until every person and every activity is included in a ministry responsibility.

— *How?* Divide your ministry, regardless of its size, into no more than five major groupings. For the church plant or bi-vocational pastor, these major headings may represent the families of the church. As churches grow in size and complexity, these groupings will take shape based on the vision of the pastor and the availability and capability of leadership.

— *Then what?:* After you complete this network of ministries and programs, you will proceed to the Organizational Chart to match specific leaders with those ministry roles and responsibilities.

Ministry Flow Chart
(Basic Design)

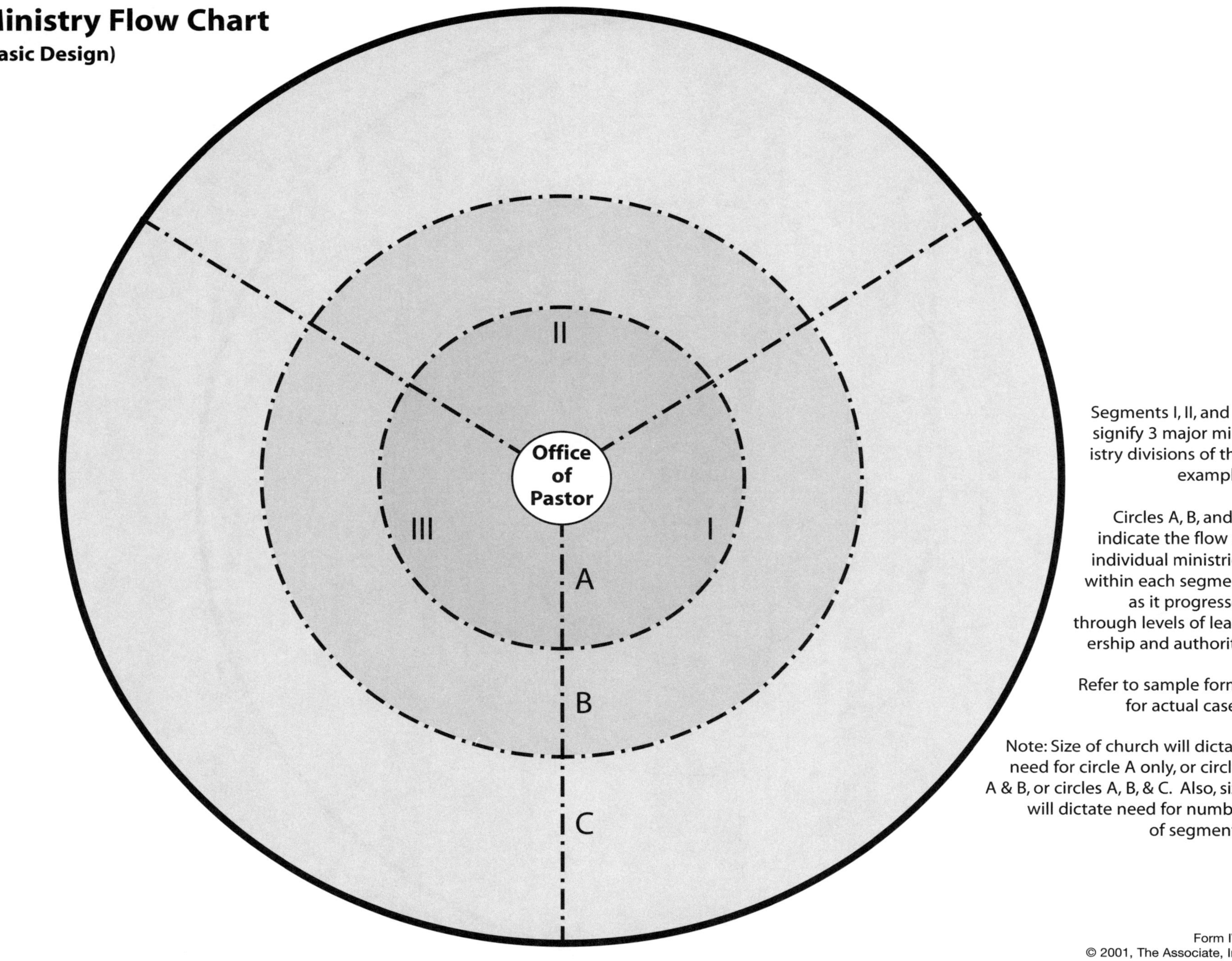

Segments I, II, and III signify 3 major ministry divisions of this example.

Circles A, B, and C indicate the flow of individual ministries within each segment as it progresses through levels of leadership and authority.

Refer to sample forms for actual cases.

Note: Size of church will dictate need for circle A only, or circles A & B, or circles A, B, & C. Also, size will dictate need for number of segments.

Form IV.1
© 2001, The Associate, Inc.

Ministry Flow Chart

Redesign this form to fit your church's organizational structure.

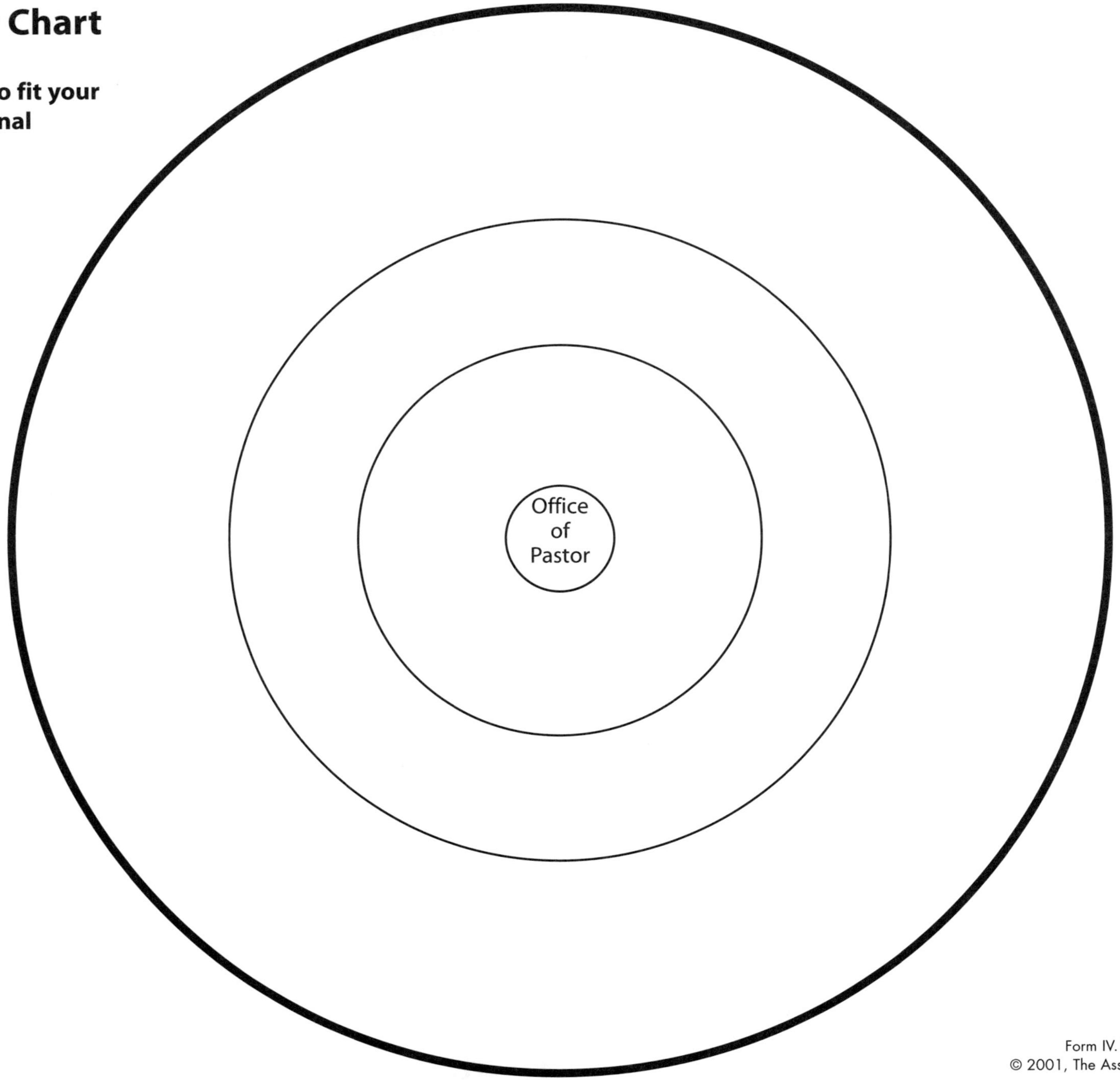

Form IV.1-worksheet

Ministry Flow Chart
(Sample A)

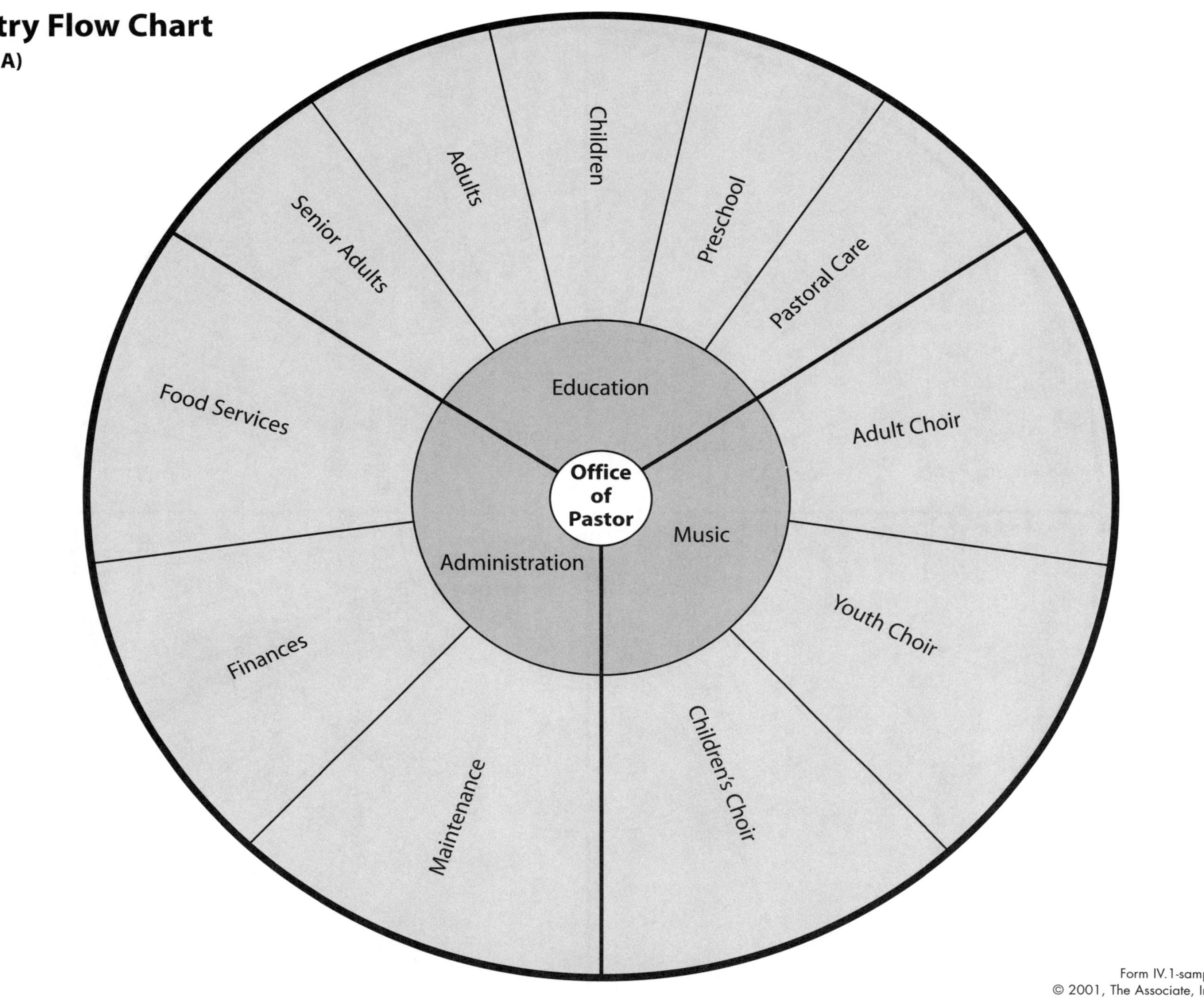

Ministry Flow Chart
(Sample B)

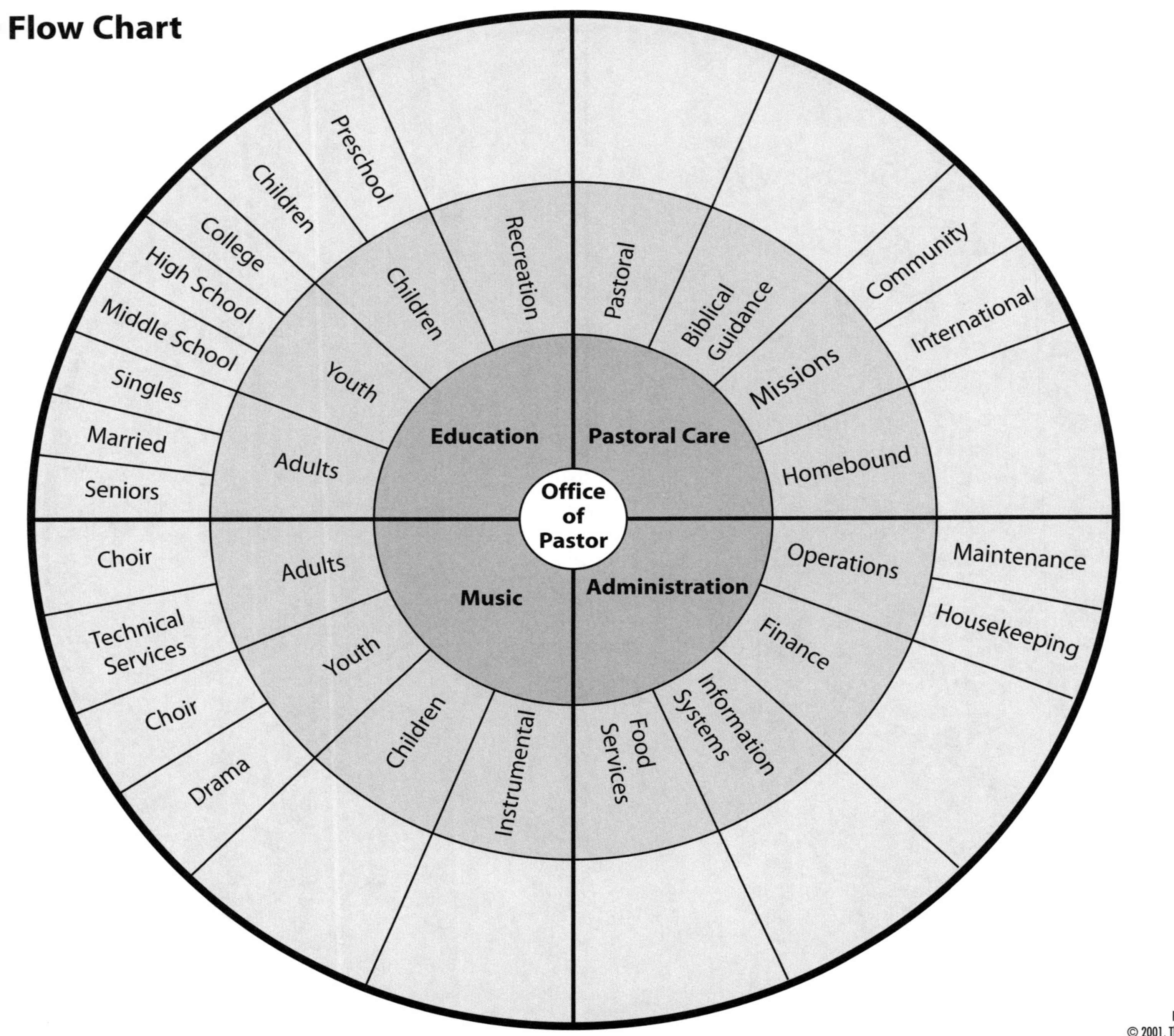

ORGANIZATIONAL CHART

— *Who?:* The planning team.

— *Why?:* To show the authority and accountability structure for each ministry in the church.

— *How?:* Assign leaders to each ministry identified in the Ministry Flow Chart. Most of those currently serving will continue in their present responsibilities, but some shifting may be required to match the needs, the vision, and the available personnel. Most churches will have at least three levels of responsibility outlined on their organizational charts, but larger churches will have several more levels as their growing pool of competent leaders is matched with the needs of the church.

Most organizations, including churches, use a traditional "Christmas tree" format for their organizational chart, but I recommend a relational format (see the example provided). The goal is to cluster teams around team leaders. On the traditional chart, individuals are more removed from the center of activity.

— *Then what?:* Your finalized Organizational Chart provides the team with a clear communication network so they can focus their combined resources on meeting the needs of the church.

Organizational Chart

(Basic Design)

Ministry leaders are identified by name in organizational boxes I, II, and III corresponding to the "A" division of responsibility on the Ministry Flow Chart (IV.1).

Supporting ministers, directors, etc. are identified by name in the next level of boxes and correspond to the "B" division of responsibilities on the Ministry Flow Chart.

Division "C" personnel can be shown by name adjacent to the division "B" person to whom they report.

Refer to sample forms for actual cases.

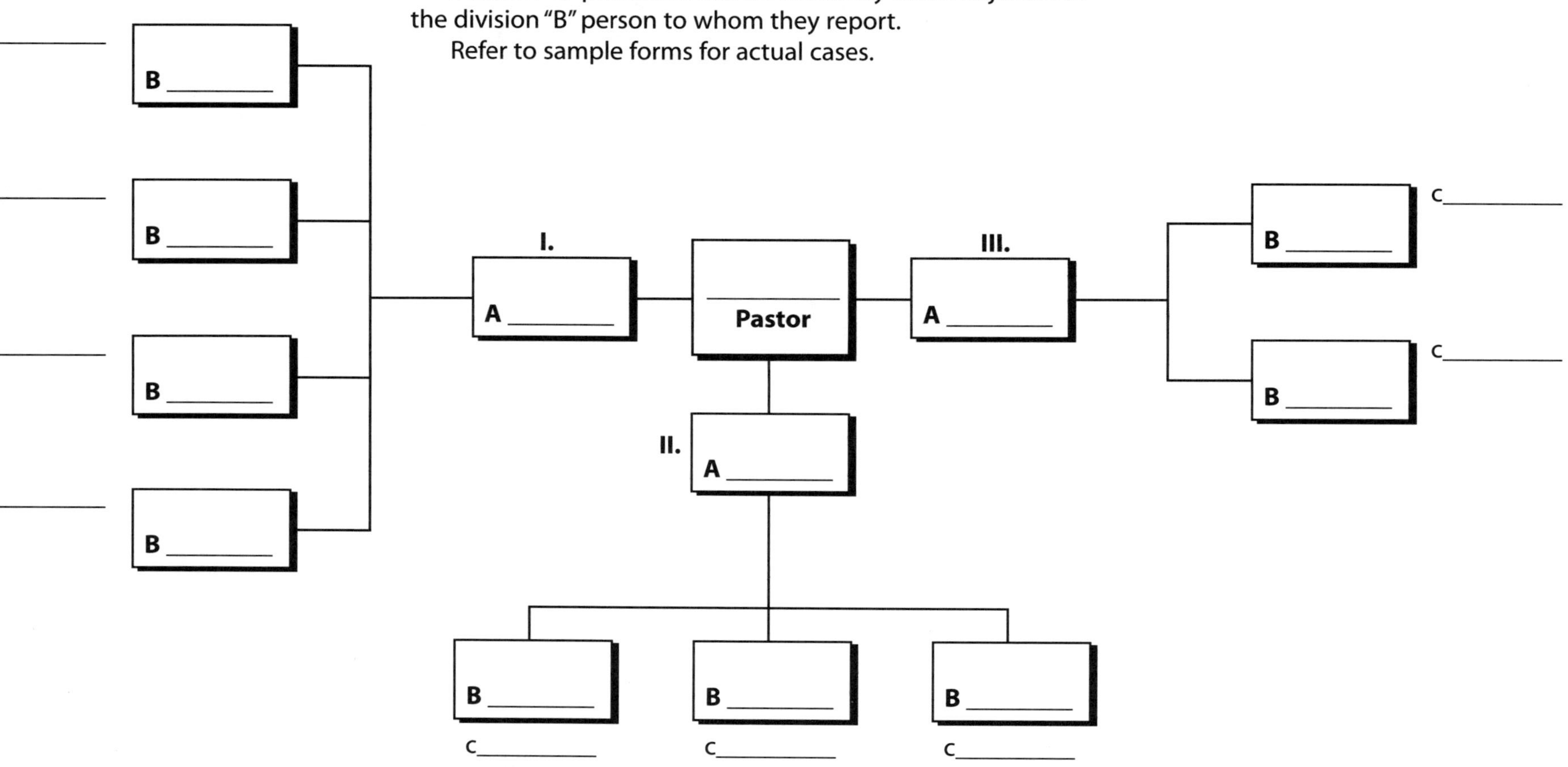

Form IV.2
© 2001, The Associate, Inc.

Organizational Chart

Design an organizational chart to fit your church's structure.

Organizational Chart
(Sample A)
Staff and/or Lay Leadership

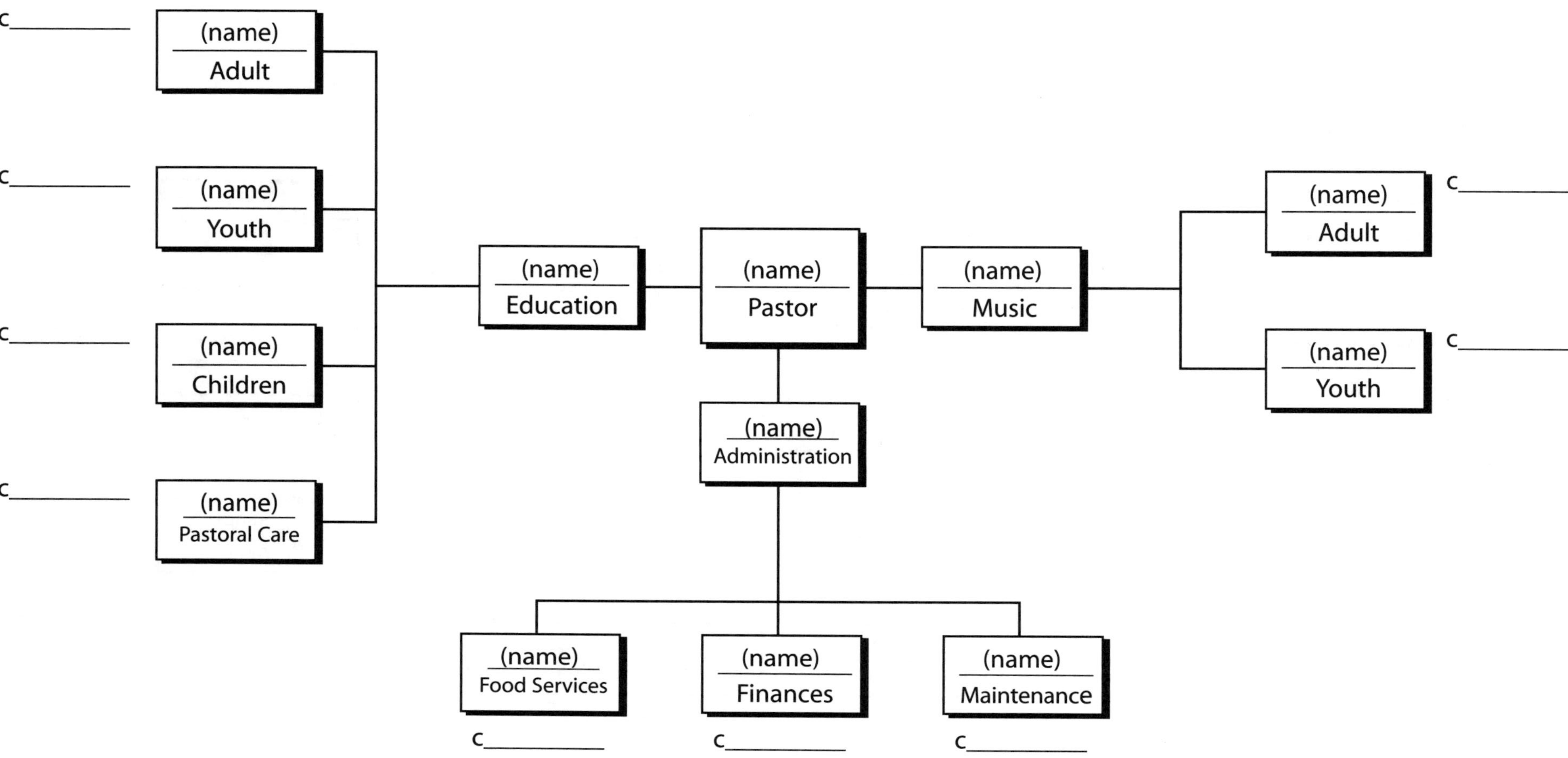

Organizational Chart
(Sample B)
Staff and/or Lay Leadership

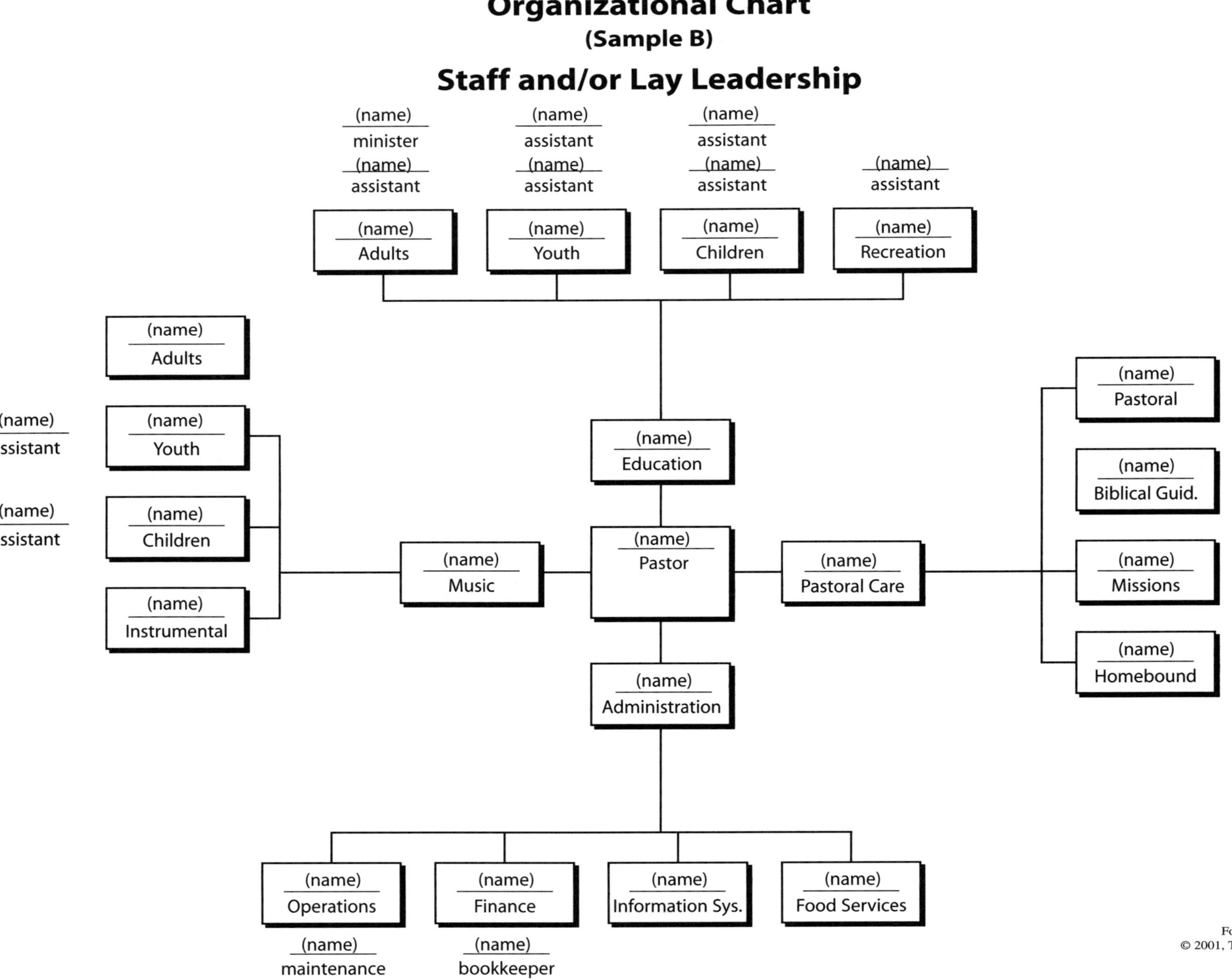

COMMUNICATION SYSTEM

— *Who?:* The planning team.
— *Why?:* To analyze how information is given and received on the staff, in the church family, and in the community.
— *How?:* For each segment of this exercise, you may want to get input from the staff and from selected ministry leaders who are responsible for communicating with the leadership team, the church family, and the community. Ask each ministry team to take time to answer the questions in this exercise, then have the ministry leader report to the planning team about their discussion. The planning team will assess the input from each ministry team and observe any trends or glaring needs.
— *Then what?:* Make any necessary adjustments to be sure communication in these three areas is clear and consistent.

COMMUNICATION SYSTEM

Ask each ministry team to take time to answer these questions, then have the ministry leader report to the planning team.

As you consider your church's communication style and effectiveness, consider these questions:

On the Leadership Team

— How is information gathered by each staff member and ministry leader? Is it primarily subjective or objective? How valuable is that information?

— Who are the most reliable interpreters among your leaders? How can you improve their liaison function to their areas of influence?

In the Church Family

— Evaluate each tool used to communicate to the congregation: bulletin, announcements, posters and banners, newsletter, classes, website, etc:

— Apart from the pulpit, how does the pastor communicate his vision with all the members and regular attenders?

— How can people express personal needs? To whom? When? Where?

— How can you use the web most effectively?

In the Community

— How are people in the community attracted to your church?

— How do visitors learn more about your church?

Summary

— What is your plan for upgrading your communication to:

. . . staff and ministry leaders?

. . . the church family?

. . . the community?

STEP 1 *The Captain's Compass*
- Your Personal Vision
- Your Ministry Vision

STEP 2 *Look at the Map*
- Your Plan for Planning
- Ministry Review
- Planning Team Evaluation

STEP 3 *Watch for Obstacles and Opportunities*
- Task Summaries
- Job Descriptions
- Historical Growth Statistics—Bible Study
- Historical Growth Statistics—General Church Criteria
- Community Demographics
- Obstacles and Opportunities
- Space Utilization

STEP 4 *Get Your Equipment Ready*
- Ministry Flow Chart
- Organizational Chart
- Communication System

STEP 5 *Plot Your Course*
- **Ministry Leader Planning Worksheet**
- **The Ministry Plan**
- **The Master Calendar**
- **The Financial Plan**
- **Communication Plan**

STEP 6 *Look Over the Next Hill*
- Long-Range Ministry Plan
- Growth and Capacity Analysis
- Growth Projections
- General Church Criteria
- Building Plan Schedule and Expenditures
- Long-Range Financial Plan

STEP 7 *Get on the Trail*
- Monthly Planning Worksheet

STEP 5

PLOT YOUR COURSE

You and your planning team have asked God for a vision of the future. You have done your homework by gathering pertinent information, talked to key ministry leaders to get their input, studied the demographics of your community, analyzed your organizational structure, and designed job descriptions. Now it is time to write your annual plan to distill your vision into a practical, workable format. By now, your vision probably has far exceeded one year. We will focus on long-range planning in Step 6, but if you don't have a practical and effective plan for the first year, it won't do much good to extend it into the future. This first year's plan, then, is crucial.

Now it is time to write your annual plan to distill your vision into a practical, workable format.

We briefly addressed the three elements of a church's plan in Step 1. We want to address these elements more fully at this point. The diagram which depicts church ministry and administration is a pyramid which points to the top, the pastor's personal and ministry vision. At the peak, the Chief Shepherd gives inspiration to the pastor. In turn, the pastor, with the anointing of the Holy Spirit, becomes the locomotive of leadership through whom three functional relationships are fostered: elder, shepherd, and bishop. These three functions form the primary tracks of ministry upon which the program of the church runs: the teaching, pastoring, and administrative ministries. These are also the functions that demand the ever-increasing involvement of leadership. Lastly, three components comprise the framework for operational planning and day-by-day operation. The final plan includes the Ministry Plan, the Master Calendar, and the annual Financial Plan. These form the base of the pyramid, giving practical support to the total program of the church. Each of these can, and should, be expanded into long-range plans.

THE THREE-FOLD FRAMEWORK FOR OPERATIONAL PLANNING

The final plan includes the Ministry Plan, the Master Calendar, and the annual Financial Plan.

Let's look at each of these components.

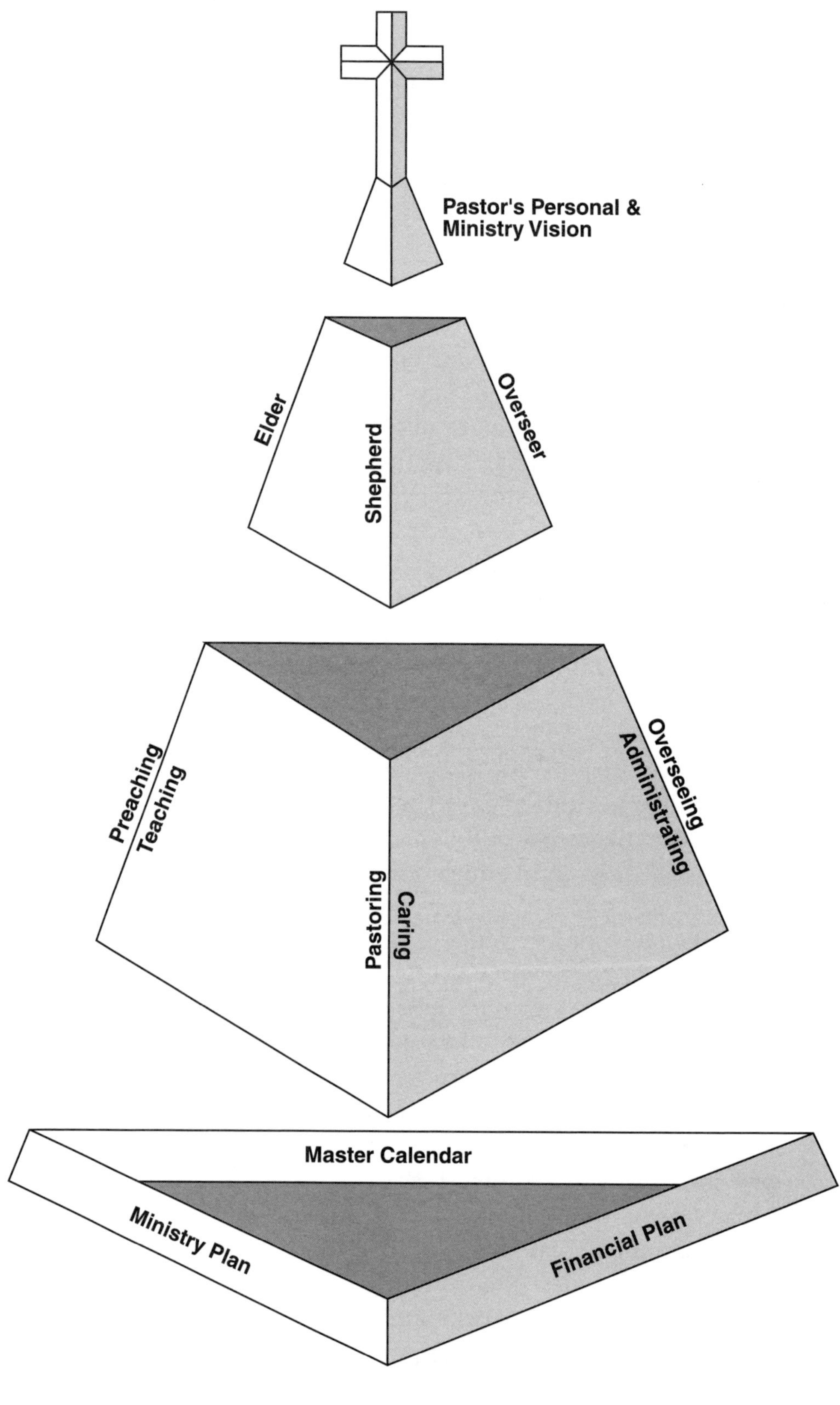

The Ministry Plan is the foundational tool for the day-to-day ministry of the church. Each program of the church is included in detail and is the result of planning based on the church's mission. Businesses have profit plans, marketing plans, and expansion plans. Surely, the church of our Lord Jesus Christ should look to the future with even greater anticipation than a secular organization. The motivation, though, is very different. In business, planning is designed to achieve profits. In the church, the motivation should be to help people experience the blessings of God and to expand our borders for the Kingdom's sake.

While the objectives may be different, the planning process remains quite similar. Some might insist, and correctly so, that you cannot "run" a church like a business. Over the last 20 years, I have become convinced that all good business principles are biblical principles. When we look carefully at business principles, they are primarily focused on relationships, and the authority for our relationships is the Bible. What good is it if we pray for the blessings of God if we have not made effective plans to optimize those blessings? Usually we don't know what to pray for or what to plan for because we haven't identified the hindrances to growth or the specific needs of the people. Our hearts must be prepared before we can ask, and our minds should be prepared to receive.

The Ministry Plan includes program input from every ministry leader of the church and is consistent with objectives established by the pastor. Early in the planning process, the pastor should meet with key ministry leaders to give them his broad objectives for the year. These objectives will come from his vision, inspired by the Holy Spirit, and his perspective of the church's need. The ministry leaders will be asked to incorporate these broad objectives into the development of their individual plans. If one of the pastor's objectives is evangelism, each leader (e.g., ministry leaders in education, music, pastoral care, etc.) will weave this emphasis into their activities so that the gospel is clearly and strongly communicated and so that new believers are incorporated into the life of the church.

As your overall vision is communicated to your leadership team, each ministry leader will set goals for the future. At this point, it is important for the shepherd to know his sheep. Some leaders are visionary and need only the broad strokes of the overall vision from you in order to chart the

THE MINISTRY PLAN

As your overall vision is communicated to your leadership team, each ministry leader will set goals for the future. At this point, it is important for the shepherd to know his sheep.

course for their segment of the ministry. If you give these people too many details, they become demotivated. On the other hand, some wonderful, faithful leaders will carry out your plans, but they simply cannot develop them on their own. Tailor this phase to fit the individual. For the visionaries, give them your vision and expectations, and ask them to come up with their own goals and plans. If they are close enough to your vision for the coming year, let them fly! If you feel their plans need some alteration, be sure to first affirm them and their creativity.

For those who need more direction (and that includes most of your ministry leaders), paint a more detailed picture of your vision and your expectations. Give them specific goals, and then ask them to draft their plans of how to reach those goals. In some cases, they need your help in writing these plans. Don't condemn them for a lack of vision and zeal. That's not the problem. Their gifts are simply different. If you give them tracks to run on, they will serve just as faithfully and capably as their visionary brothers. They require more of your time and energy on the front end of the planning process, but you can usually count on them to be diligent and thorough in accomplishing the tasks you outline for them.

Goal-setting is the part of the plan that determines specifically where your church is going. Goals are very specific, individualized, and measurable activities or events which are designed to accomplish parts of the vision. They are short-range statements about specific programs that explain how we are going to accomplish the long-range vision.

Steps toward goal-setting are:

1. Make sure goals are consistent with the vision. Never establish a major goal that runs counter to the stated purposes of the church. Always ask, "Does this get us closer to our overall purpose and vision?"

2. Get the facts. Goals should be established only after serious study. It is important to gather accurate information and facts before you establish goals. For example, if your goal is to upgrade the quality of music in your worship, it is essential that you know the desires of your congregation. Don't assume that the purchase of a new organ will bring excitement to worship if in fact the problem perceived by the majority of your congregation is that your

Goals are very specific, individualized, and measurable activities or events which are designed to accomplish parts of the vision.

sound system is inadequate or that many prefer something other than organ music.

3. Establish definitive targets. Where do you want to be? By when? What is your objective? What do you intend to accomplish? What is the anticipated result? Who will be in charge? Who will supervise? Remember: What gets measured gets done.

4. Determine a time-frame. How long will it take to reach your goal? Be specific. Be realistic. Write it down.

5. Get God's wisdom. God honors people of faith, people who aim high in setting goals. There is, however, an inherent problem when an organization sets goals that border on the impossible. If you set your goals too high, you and your people will experience frustration and confusion. Ask God for His wisdom, and help ministry leaders set goals that require the hand of God, but are not ridiculous. Some visionaries, of course, will set lofty goals. Usually, these people don't get discouraged if they don't meet these goals—they just set new ones. People working with them, however, may become disheartened by failure. Encourage these leaders to understand how their high goals can affect others.

6. Document progress toward your goals. Most ministries will have relatively few significant goals. Instruct leaders to select a few key goals and establish a system of follow-up and communication. Regular and enthusiastic progress reports stimulate motivation, action, and accountability.

When we trust God for great things, the ordinary becomes extraordinary

7. Get ready for change. A well-defined goal motivates people to take action and extend themselves to new levels. When we trust God for great things, the ordinary becomes extraordinary.

8. Pray for strength, flexibility, motivation and faith-filled optimism. Visionary and practical leadership is the key to achieving God-given goals. There are three kinds of people in life: those who make things happen, those who watch things happen, and those who don't know what's happening. Be a leader who, in God's strength, makes things happen. Stay positive, stay focused, stay joyful.

In setting goals for the church or for any segment of the ministry, anticipate change. Ask yourself and your leaders, "What will it look like when God takes us to the next level?" Expect more people to come to Christ and others to become more involved in the life of the church. Expect the need for additional space, the need for more leaders to shepherd those who have joined the church, and perhaps, criticism from those who don't like change. The purpose of setting goals is to foster change with powerful, positive results. Refusing to set goals invites stagnation, lethargy, and confusion.

Each individual ministry's plan should include new and creative programs as well as those that are routine and have been used effectively for many years. As you prepare each ministry leader for the planning process, be sure to explain these essentials: Every event which requires a calendar date and budget expenditures is to be listed. The programs are summarized under respective ministries, and each team presents its own plans for the upcoming year. Achievements can then be celebrated and monitored as the months progress.

After each ministry has listed its event schedule, the planning team needs to review and reconcile any conflicting dates. Similarly, the use of rooms, buses, or other church support items must also be reconciled among the scheduled events. From this process, the Master Calendar is created. Summarizing the cost of the program events, services, and materials will determine the annual church budget, which is a component of the Financial Plan. The Ministry Plan, which is compiled from the plans of ministry leaders and then refined by the planning team, is the basic document from which these two other major operational tools, the calendar and budget, are derived.

For each event on the calendar, be sure to include the entire spectrum of preparation, implementation, and follow through in the plan:

— *preparation:* including scheduling the speaker and the rooms, childcare, training of volunteers, etc. Be sure prayer is at the center of your preparations.
— *promotion:* including bulletin inserts, announcements in worship and in classes, targeted promotions through mailouts, newsletter articles, banners, radio and television ads, and any other option that is effective and reasonable. Tailor your promotions to fit your event.
— *set up:* including all the room needs, sound and light, the speaker's needs, the greeters, supplies, refreshments, etc.

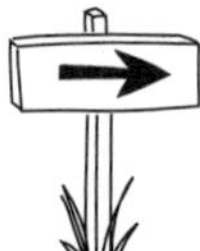

After each ministry has listed its event schedule, the planning team needs to review and reconcile any conflicting dates.

For each event on the calendar, be sure to include the entire spectrum of preparation, implementation, and follow through in the plan.

— *the event itself:* monitoring the comfort of the room, the power of the presentation, the effectiveness of the message, and communication of the next step for each person (the next event, how to get involved, etc.).

— *after the event:* thank you notes and appreciation for those who helped, clean-up, accounting, etc.

The church calendar is the tool of communication that not only assures ministry coordination but also communicates to the church family that everything is done decently and in order. The larger the church and the more diverse its programming, the more critical is the calendar. Having people show up at the same time and at the same place for different functions indicates a lack of organization. Programs must be scheduled to complement each other and to promote the God-given objectives for the year. Momentum in the church's spiritual growth is forfeited by ill-planned event scheduling. The broad, organized program, then, must complement the worship and proclamation of God's Word on Sunday morning. Justly or unjustly, the pastor is measured by the orderly and systematic way the total program of the church is conducted.

The distribution of the church calendar, in as much or as little detail as is appropriate, is of great value to the church members. Moreover, promotion of special events must not overlap other important functions. A chart displaying each week and month of the year, one that can be blocked out for individual events, is especially effective in large churches. The chart should not only display the times of those special, churchwide events, but also the promotional schedules and the follow-up periods. If the follow-up or afterglow of one event laps over into the promotion of the next, effectiveness is weakened. Also, endless and overlapping programs can produce a performance mentality rather than communicating a message. This gets into a "bigger and better syndrome" rather than addressing spiritual needs.

THE MASTER CALENDAR

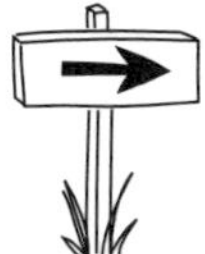

Programs must be scheduled to complement each other and to promote the God-given objectives for the year.

The Financial Plan is more than the budget of the church. It takes into consideration the financial integrity and viability of all financial factors, including indebtedness, current budget, and any future expenditures that can reasonably be projected. This is a most important operational tool, but it is not to be the instrument that drives the programs of the church. If program decisions are made by a finance committee which sees programs only through the lens of available dollars, the vision for growth can be stunted. Certainly, cost

THE FINANCIAL PLAN

The Financial Plan is more than the budget of the church. It takes into consideration the financial integrity and viability of all financial factors, including indebtedness, current budget, and any future expenditures that can reasonably be projected.

is an important factor, but this has to be weighed by the pastor, staff, and program leadership in keeping with the overall program focus for the year. Creative solutions, often in the form of adjustments in allocations, can solve most budgetary problems. Be careful, though, to make these adjustments thoughtfully. When you take money out of one bucket and put it in another, it is very important to communicate with those who are affected.

The value of an individual program should be determined prior to the beginning of a new year. Only at that time, in the context of the total church program, can most ministry emphases be properly evaluated. It is therefore important for the ministry teams to itemize each event within their ministries so they receive proper attention.

The Financial Plan is a derivative of the Ministry Plan, not vice versa. It is appropriate that anticipated program, support, and utility costs be projected monthly to establish an estimated cash demand. This estimated demand, projected against expected contributions, produces a cash flow schedule which is invaluable to financial leadership. Good planning will preclude many crisis decisions that may affect the overall program of the church.

WHERE THE RUBBER MEETS THE ROAD

The final stages of the planning process require a blend of visionary faith and ruthless realism.

The final stages of the planning process require a blend of visionary faith and ruthless realism. This part of the planning process is often the most difficult and frustrating, but it is absolutely essential if the plan is to be implemented. Each segment of the plan usually seems reasonable on its own, but when those segments are put together, you may realize that you have "overcommitted your resources." Perhaps there simply aren't enough people to provide leadership, not enough money, or not enough time to do all you want to accomplish. Priorities have to be set, and hard choices must be made.

Quite often, this stage of the planning process involves going back and revising the plan. Give yourself and the planning team plenty of time and encouragement. Trust God for wisdom about the hard choices. Consider the timing of events and programs. Some may have to be postponed until the next year, but this delay often gives time to plan and prepare to make them even more effective. "Wait" is much more palatable to people than "No."

Major events in your church's life need to be scheduled far enough ahead of time to provide plenty of time for preparation and promotion. Churches may plan major conferences two to three years ahead in order to secure the speakers they want. Of course, many events in the life of the church are fixed by the church calendar and occur every year, such as the Christmas and Easter musicals, vacation Bible school, and regularly scheduled meetings.

Be sure to plan your major events so two things happen: one, there are no competing events, and two, you have the time and energy to capitalize on the momentum generated by the event. I've seen churches schedule one large event one after the other. The promotion for one overlapped the next one. The people became confused, and the staff were exhausted. More often, I've seen churches put all their efforts into pulling off an excellent event, but they were so drained after it that they didn't have the time or energy to follow up and nurture the participants in their relationships with the Lord and the church.

I've seen churches put all their efforts into pulling off an excellent event, but they were so drained after it that they didn't have the time or energy to follow up and nurture the participants in their relationships with the Lord and the church.

FINALIZE YOUR PLAN

The form and style of a church's plan can be whatever the pastor and the planning team choose. A forms provided at the end of this chapter will help you draft and communicate your annual plan, but be sure to tailor it to fit your style. Some parts of the plan will have been developed by ministry leaders and submitted to the planning team for approval. These specific ministry plans, however, may include many details that aren't necessary to be included the overall annual plan, so the overall plan will probably contain only an abbreviated form of these more exhaustive ministry plans. The guidelines are that it be compelling and clear. To accomplish those objectives, I recommend:

1. Include a vision statement at the beginning. You may also want to add a brief statement of the long-term objectives of the church. Focus on how God wants to win the lost, build disciples, and form a loving community of believers.

2. The specific goals of each ministry in the church will form the Ministry Plan. Highlight any significant changes in direction, as well as your vision for how you anticipate these changes will make an impact on people for Christ.

3. Finally, the plan should include a synopsis of the Master Calendar and the Financial Plan for the coming year.

4. Proofread carefully to avoid misspelled words or other typographical errors.

These elements form the structure of the written plan. To add a creative touch, you may also want to include these suggestions:

5. To add warmth, include photographs of smiling people and those involved in ministering to others, as well as charts or graphs where they are needed to illustrate points.

6. Prepare a visual presentation such as slides or a PowerPoint presentation to present the plan to the leadership of the church and to the church.

Remember, this plan represents the vision God has given you and your church to accomplish His great purposes. Communicate this vision with joy and enthusiasm!

An annual plan may or may not require this level of detail in your presentation. Tailor the presentation of your annual plan to include as much information as necessary to communicate clearly. These guidelines, however, are essential for the presentation of a long-range plan.

PREPARE YOUR PRESENTATION

This important input from key leaders will help you polish your presentation before you present it to others, but more importantly, each of these people will now become a supporter and cheerleader.

After you write your annual plan, consider presenting it to your staff and some key lay leaders to get their feedback before you make your presentation to any other groups and the congregation. Ask the staff and lay leaders for constructive feedback. They may be able to save you from some awkward moments later by asking good questions now. They may make suggestions to strengthen your presentation. This will be a trial run of your final presentation. These leaders will help you anticipate many of the questions people will ask, and this process will enable you and your planning team to fine-tune your answers to these questions. This important input from key leaders will help you polish your presentation before you present it to others, but more importantly, each of these people will now become a supporter and cheerleader. They will be able to explain key elements of the plan and diffuse any misunderstanding or criticism. Their input and support will establish credibility and trust as the plan is implemented. Now you are ready to share the plan with key groups in the church.

Two factors that make a big difference in how a plan is received are the credibility of the people on the planning team and a careful communication process. If your congregation knows and trusts those on the planning team, they are likely to trust the plan. This the reason it is so important to select the team wisely, with a view toward the ultimate aim of having the members of the church gladly embrace, not just tolerate, your vision and plans. And secondly, before you share the plan with the congregation, communicate your plan to ever-widening circles of leadership in virtually every strata and segment of the congregation. I suggest you share your plan with two groups in particular: your deacon body (or a similar group in your church structure) and seniors. Both of these groups expect to be informed and to give feedback to the pastor. Typically, they represent the stalwarts of the church, and it is wise—especially for young pastors—to garner the support of these two important groups.

I suggest you share your plan with two groups in particular: your deacon body (or a similar group in your church structure) and seniors.

With the support and enthusiasm of these key groups, present your plan to the congregation. In my church, our pastor has presented our plans in a State of the Church message on a Sunday morning. You may think this is a strange thing to present during worship, but it is an exciting, uplifting, God-focused time for our body. As I have described this event to some pastors, they shook their heads and moaned, "We can't do that in our church." Every member of your congregation wants to be informed and involved in the vision of the church, so if you believe your plan is truly God's vision for your ministry, consider presenting it attractively and powerfully during a worship service. Think, pray, and prepare your presentation to speak to people's hearts and galvanize their commitment to Christ and to the church's mission. Be as creative in your strategy for presenting your plan as you have been in developing it.

When you present your plan, communicate with passion, enthusiasm, and clarity. Don't let yourself get bogged down mentally in all of the details and unanswered questions. Instead, as you prepare, think back on the vision God has given you. Focus on the benefits the plan will have to your church and your community. Our purpose is not simply to build buildings; facilities are tools to reach people for Christ and build people in their faith. Paint a strong verbal picture of how God will change lives as the plan is implemented, and if a new building is involved, include graphics to inspire people and pique their enthusiasm. Remember: Numbers often confuse, but pictures inspire.

When you present your plan, communicate with passion, enthusiasm, and clarity.

Consider asking a few members of the planning team or ministry leaders to share their enthusiasm for the plan, but be careful that the presentation doesn't become too long and detailed. If others share, make sure their messages are targeted and brief. As you think about presenting your plan to your congregation, consider painting a picture of God's vision for the future, not just one year, but for several years. Here are some guidelines for presenting your plan:

Introduce the presentation with appropriate Scripture that has challenged and encouraged you and your planning team.

1. Introduce the presentation with appropriate Scripture that has challenged and encouraged you and your planning team.

2. Connect the Scripture with the vision statement for your church, and specifically, for the next year and for the next several years.

3. Describe the spiritual dimensions and implications of your plan. How do you believe God is going to work?

4. Give a brief description of the plan for each ministry area, with bullet points for brevity and clarity.

5. Use pictures and other graphics instead of budgets and balance sheets.

6. Numbers, statistics, and dollars should only be presented in summary form.

7. Thank the planning team and ministry leaders who participated in developing the plan.

8. Use testimonials briefly but powerfully.

9. Ask each person to embrace the vision and the plan with whole-hearted support and believing prayer.

10. Share your vision with enthusiasm. You have every reason to be joyful if you believe your plan is really God's vision for your church and your leadership has had a part in formulating and fine-tuning it.

IN SUMMARY . . .

At this point, we have gone through the entire process, from analysis of the current effectiveness of each ministry to presenting the actual, final, one-year plan. Let me summarize this process:

1. The pastor spends time with the Lord to clarify his vision, on which the planning process depends.

2. The pastor selects the planning team (staff, lay, or a combination) with an eye toward the wisdom, creativity, and credibility of the group.

3. The planning team asks ministry leaders to complete an assessment of their ministries and propose plans for the coming year.

4. The ministry leaders submit these assessments and plans to the planning team, and the planning team then shapes these into the overall plan.

5. The pastor and the planning team work out any scheduling conflicts and budgetary concerns and give tentative approval when the calendar and finances seem satisfactory.

6. The plan is then finalized into the Ministry Plan, Master Calendar, and Financial Plan.

7. The plan is then presented to leadership groups (as it is appropriate) before presenting it in summary form to the congregation. This summary may include the budget and committee recommendations for the coming year.

8. A workable and effective annual ministry planning process will provide a template for this process for years to come. After this process has been completed successfully once, the pastor and the planning team will have confidence to revise it and fine-tune it each year to accomplish the vision God has given them.

After this process has been completed successfully once, the pastor and the planning team will have confidence to revise it and fine-tune it each year to accomplish the vision God has given them.

TAKE A STEP

In this step, you will finalize your plan for the coming year. The exercises in this step focus on the essential elements that comprise that plan:
— Ministry Leader Planning Worksheet,
— The Ministry Plan,
— The Master Calendar,
— The Financial Plan, and
— Communication Plan.

MINISTRY LEADER PLANNING WORKSHEET

— *Who?:* Ministry leaders.

— *Why?:* To help them clarify their visions, plan programs, and establish preliminary calendars and budgets.

— *How?:* The planning process for each ministry leader includes two parts: the Ministry Leader Planning Worksheet, which focuses on goals and responsibilities, and the annual Ministry Plan for that specific ministry.

Ministry leaders may choose to use the worksheet by themselves, or they may want to gather their ministry teams and go through this and planning process together. When they complete this worksheet, they need to fill out the annual Ministry Plan for their specific ministry area, including a detailed schedule of events for the coming year.

— *Then what?:* After completing the worksheet and the Ministry Plan for their area, ministry leaders will have identified several specific programs for the coming year. They will submit their ministry plans to the planning team for analysis, adjustments, and approval.

MINISTRY LEADER PLANNING WORKSHEET

Use this worksheet to help you plan effectively and specifically. If you have a team working with you, be sure to get their ideas and involve them in the planning process so they will have a sense of goal ownership.

1.   The pastor has specific expectations for your efforts. Describe these expectations; the vision for the ministry area, program, or event; and the specific goals to be reached:

2.   What people do you need to help accomplish these plans? How will you select them and delegate responsibility to them? How will you train them? How will you involve them in the planning process?

3.   For each specific goal, work out a detailed preliminary plan, budget, and schedule: (Use additional paper as needed.)

— Goal #1

— Goal #2

— Goal #3

4. What system do you have (or need) for follow-through, encouragement of your team, and control of time and money?

5. What system of evaluation is needed after the event or at regular intervals throughout the program?

6. Review your plans to be certain you've considered the following in your planning process:

— leadership (selection, training and supervision)

— budget

— facilities

— delegating and reporting system

— evaluation

— scheduling (especially in regard to other church events and programs)

THE MINISTRY PLAN

— *Who?:* The planning team.
— *Why?:* To focus all your resources on those activities that you believe will best fulfill the vision God has given you.
— *How?:* Collect the plans from each of the ministry leaders and analyze them to determine which ones take priority and which ones must be delayed for a while. Keep your vision in mind as you make these crucial decisions. If adjustments need to be made in a ministry leader's plans (and they often will), be sure to affirm his vision and passion, and explain your reasons thoroughly.
— *What then?:* The Ministry Plan will become an expression of your vision for the coming year, as well as the basis for developing the church calendar and budget.

Annual Ministry Plan

Ministry Area________________________________   Department________________________________

PROGRAM	CALENDAR		BUDGET - DOLLAR AMOUNT
Item or Event	Date(s)	Frequency/Time	Church Operation - $

Annual Ministry Plan

Ministry Area Music Ministry   **Department**

PROGRAM	CALENDAR		BUDGET - DOLLAR AMOUNT
Item or Event	Date(s)	Frequency/Time	Church Operation - $
Easter Services 2001	April 11, 13, 15, 2001	Annual, 6-9 pm	$1,200.00
Easter Services Visuals/Sets	April 11, 13, 15, 2001	Annual, 6-9 pm	$850.00
Senior Adult Choir Spiritual Enrichment Conference	April 23-28, 2001	Annual, all day	$1,000.00
Technical Training	May 19, 2001	Annual, 7-9 pm	$100.00
Children's Choir Fellowship	May 23, 2001	6-9 pm	$165.00
Adult Choir Fellowship	May 25, 2001	6-9 pm	$50.00
Music Camp	July 16-20, 22, 2001	Annual, all day	$350.00
Children's Choir Leader Conference	August 17-18, 2001	Annual, all day	$100.00
Children's Choir Leader Lunch	August 18, 2001	Annual, 12-1 pm	$100.00
Adult Choir Fellowship	August 24, 200	7-9 pm	$50.00
Leadership Training Materials	September 5, 2001	7-9 pm	$100.00
Adult Orchestra Fellowship	September 21, 2001	7-9 pm	$50.00
Adult Orchestra Fellowship	October 19, 2001	7-9 pm	$50.00
Ensemble Leaders' Appreciation Dinner	October 26, 2001	Annual, 7-9 pm	$75.00
Children's Choir Fellowship	November 14, 2001	6-7 pm	$165.00
Orchestra Christmas Concert Music	November 28, 30, 2001 December 2, 2001	Annual, 6-9 pm	$2,000.00
Orchestra Christmas Concert 2001	November 28, 30, 2001 December 2, 2001	Annual, 6-9 pm	$2,040.00
Adult Choir Fellowship	December 7, 200	7-9 pm	$50.00
Christmas Eve Services 2001	December 19, 24, 2001	Annual, 6-9 pm	$1,200.00
Christmas Eve Visuals/Sets	December 19, 24, 2001	Annual, 6-9 pm	$1,500.00
January Children's Choir Leader Appreciation Dinner	January 12, 2002	Annual, 11 am - 1 pm	$200.00
Adult Orchestra Fellowship	January 18, 2002	7-9 pm	$50.00
Technical Training	January 19, 2002	Annual, 7-9 pm	$100.00
Adult Choir Fellowship	January 25, 2002	7-9 pm	$50.00
Children's Choir Leaders Spring Workshop	March 9, 2002	Annual, 9 am - 2 pm	$700.00
Adult Choir Fellowship	March 15, 2002	7-9 pm	$50.00
Ensemble Leaders' Appreciation Dinner	March 22, 2002	Annual, 7-9 pm	$75.00
Leadership Training Materials	March 22, 2002	7-9 pm	$100.00
Technical Team Appreciation Banquet	March 29, 2002	Annual, 7-9 pm	$150.00

THE MASTER CALENDAR WORKSHEET

— *Who?:* The planning team.

— *Why?:* To make sure each event and program receives the time and attention it deserves, without competing unnecessarily with some other activity.

— *How?:* The worksheet provided gives you instructions about how to chart both ongoing and special events in your church.

— *What then?:* This calendar is designed specifically for your leaders to know when each event occurs, including the times for preparation and follow-up. The actual, comprehensive calendar doesn't need to be included in the final presentation to the congregation, but the dates of specific events will be a part of that presentation.

MASTER CALENDAR WORKSHEET

Find or design a two-year calendar (computer calendar software can be adjusted quickly, clearly, and easily), and plot your scheduled events on it. Make sure you plan all the preparatory activities (promotion and training) that need to occur, as well as the follow-up to capture the momentum generated by the event. Follow these guidelines for completing your Master Calendar:

1. First, plot all the normal events of each year, as well as the significant events in the life of church members, such as the beginning and end of school, Thanksgiving and Christmas holidays, Spring break, etc.

2. Plot all the events scheduled by each ministry leader.

3. Observe the conflicts and holes. Look for times when too many things are scheduled at the same time or too close together, and look for times when little is scheduled.

4. Inform the ministry leaders of the potential conflicts in scheduling, and get their input on resolving these.

5. Determine the best schedule to accomplish your church's vision. Trust God for wisdom as you assess the benefits and the costs (in time, personnel, and finances) of each event. Determine the priorities.

6. Present a draft of the calendar to your ministry leaders. Smooth out any remaining difficulties in the schedule, and enlist their cooperation.

7. Finalize the Master Calendar in a format that is clear and easily read, easily adjusted, and easily distributed throughout the year. This document may vary from the simplest of paper forms to a highly sophisticated, software system.

THE FINANCIAL PLAN

— *Who?:* The planning team.

— *Why?:* To chart the anticipated revenues and expenses of the coming year in order to be sure you have adequate resources to meet the needs. Your Financial Plan will include: current indebtedness, anticipated revenues, anticipated expenses, and fund-raising plans for the general operating budget and any capital expenditures.

— *How?:* Each ministry leader has provided a projected budget for the coming year. You have asked them to be creative and to have a great vision for God's work, and some of them may have given you a budget that is far in excess of what you believe God will provide. Therefore, you may need to make some adjustments in their funding requirements, just as you did for their programming plans.

— *What then?:* For most churches, the details of the budget probably don't need to be included in the presentation to the congregation, but you do need to include the projected budget that corresponds to the program plans for the coming year. People want to know if the totals in the financial plans are reasonable, but most of them aren't interested in the details of how office expenses are allocated.

Annual Financial Plan
Summary

	This Month			Year to Date	
	Budget	Actual	Annual Budget	Actual	Balance
Proposed Expenditures					
Operating Budget					
Debt Service					
Capital Improvements					
Total Budget Expenditures					
Anticipated Receipts					
Undesignated Receipts					
Designated Receipts					
Total Receipts					
Projected Cash Surplus/(Deficit)					

Monthly Budget Status

	This Month			Year to Date	
Account	Budget	Actual	Annual Budget	Actual	Balance
BUDGET INCOME					
Offering & Contributions					
(Non-Designated)					
TOTAL BUDGET INCOME					
DESIGNATED RECEIPTS					
BUDGET EXPENSES					
Missions					
Compensation					
Staff Salaries					
Payroll Tax (FICA)					
Retirement					
Medical Insurance					
Total Compensation					
Educational Ministry					
Preschool					
Preschool Supplies					
Total Preschool					
Children					
Children's Camps					
Children's Supplies					
Vacation Bible School					
Total Children					
Youth					
Youth Camps & Retreats					
Special Program					
Material & Supplies					
Total Youth					

Account	This Month		Annual Budget	Year to Date	
	Budget	Actual		Actual	Balance
Adult					
Retreats & Seminars					
Senior Adults					
Single Adult Ministry					
College Ministry					
Women's Ministry					
Total Adult					
Total Education					
Music Ministry					
Music Literature					
Leadership Trng & Fest. Reg.					
Children's Choirs					
Choir Activities & Supplies					
Robe Cleaning/Upkeep					
Total Music Ministry					
Pastoral Ministries					
Pastoral Care					
Biblical Guidance					
Total Pastoral Ministries					
Recreation Ministry					
Sports					
Rec. Equipment & Supplies					
Total Recreation Ministry					
Administration					
Office Support					
Hospitality					
Transportation					
Bookkeeping					
Food Services					
Total Administration					
Operations					
Utilities					
Maintenance & Repairs					
Janitorial Supplies					
Insurance					
Telephone					
Total Operations					
Other					
Special Projects					
Unscheduled Expenses					
Total Other Items					
TOTAL BUDGET EXPENSES					

Annual Financial Plan

Summary

	This Month		Year to Date		
	Budget	**Actual**	**Annual Budget**	**Actual**	**Balance**
Proposed Expenditures					
Operating Budget			$658,796		
Debt Service			$0		
Capital Improvements			$37,000		
Total Budget Expenditures			$695,796		
Anticipated Receipts					
Undesignated Receipts			$802,183		
Designated Receipts			$30,000		
Total Receipts			$832,183		
Projected Cash Surplus/(Deficit)			$136,387		

Monthly Budget Status

	This Month		Year to Date		
Account	**Budget**	**Actual**	**Annual Budget**	**Actual**	**Balance**
BUDGET INCOME			$658,796		
Offering & Contributions					
(Non-Designated)					
TOTAL BUDGET INCOME			$658,796		
DESIGNATED RECEIPTS					
BUDGET EXPENSES					
Missions					
Compensation					
Staff Salaries			$308,800		
Payroll Tax (FICA)			included		
Retirement			included		
Medical Insurance			included		
Total Compensation			$308,800		
Educational Ministry					
Preschool					
Preschool Supplies			$7,450		
Total Preschool			$7,750		
Children					
Children's Camps			$3,250		
Children's Supplies			$2,800		
Vacation Bible School			$3,600		
Total Children			$9,850		
Youth					
Youth Camps & Retreats			$8,450		
Special Program			$2,200		
Material & Supplies			$1,600		
Total Youth			$12,256		

| | This Month | | | Year to Date | |
Account	Budget	Actual	Annual Budget	Actual	Balance
Adult					
Retreats & Seminars			$1,080		
Senior Adults			$2,200		
Single Adult Ministry			$1,820		
College Ministry			$2,600		
Women's Ministry			$2,400		
Total Adult			$10,100		
Total Education			$39,956		
Music Ministry					
Music Literature			$14,050		
Leadership Trng & Fest. Reg.			$3,200		
Children's Choirs			$3,000		
Choir Activities & Supplies			$3,800		
Robe Cleaning/Upkeep			$1,100		
Total Music Ministry			$34,107		
Pastoral Ministries					
Pastoral Care			$3,250		
Biblical Guidance			$2,635		
Total Pastoral Ministries			$6,885		
Recreation Ministry					
Sports			$3,100		
Rec. Equipment & Supplies			$2,411		
Total Recreation Ministry			$7,711		
Administration					
Office Support			$3,800		
Hospitality			$1,600		
Transportation			$12,949		
Bookkeeping			$1,000		
Food Services			$22,500		
Total Administration			$41,849		
Operations					
Utilities			$46,500		
Maintenance & Repairs			$6,500		
Janitorial Supplies			$2,000		
Insurance			$21,000		
Telephone			$3,878		
Total Operations			$79,878		
Other					
Special Projects			$5,351		
Unscheduled Expenses			$2,500		
Total Other Items			$7,851		
TOTAL BUDGET EXPENSES			$658,796		

COMMUNICATION PLAN

— *Who?:* The planning team.
— *Why?:* To develop a strategy to help the church embrace the plan.
— *How?:* Determine the individuals and target groups who need to be informed personally about the plan, and work out a schedule to present it to them.
— ***Then what?:*** After you have talked to those who need to be informed, you may want some of them to share their enthusiasm for the plan, or a particular element of the plan, during your presentation to the congregation.

COMMUNICATION PLAN

Reflect on these exercises and questions before you communicate your plan:

1. Take some time to pray. Ask God for wisdom, patience, and enthusiasm as you anticipate questions about your vision and your plan. Determine to honor those who ask questions.

2. What questions do you anticipate in response to your plan?

    How will you answer each of them? (Be specific. It may be wise to role play your answers to see how they sound.)

3. Who are some individuals, and what are some small, targeted groups that need to hear the plan personally from the pastor or from someone on the planning team?

4. Write out a schedule for communicating your plan, including:
    — individuals and groups you want to talk to,
    — who will present the plan to them,
    — dates those presentations will be made, and
    — the date to present the plan to the congregation.

STEP 1 *The Captain's Compass*

- Your Personal Vision
- Your Ministry Vision

STEP 2 *Look at the Map*

- Your Plan for Planning
- Ministry Review
- Planning Team Evaluation

STEP 3 *Watch for Obstacles and Opportunities*

- Task Summaries
- Job Descriptions
- Historical Growth Statistics—Bible Study
- Historical Growth Statistics—General Church Criteria
- Community Demographics
- Obstacles and Opportunities
- Space Utilization

STEP 4 *Get Your Equipment Ready*

- Ministry Flow Chart
- Organizational Chart
- Communication System

STEP 5 *Plot Your Course*

- Ministry Leader Planning Worksheet
- The Ministry Plan
- The Master Calendar
- The Financial Plan
- Communication Plan

STEP 6 *Look Over the Next Hill*

- **Long-Range Ministry Plan**
- **Growth and Capacity Analysis**
- **Growth Projections**
- **General Church Criteria**
- **Building Plan Schedule and Expenditures**
- **Long-Range Financial Plan**

STEP 7 *Get on the Trail*

- Monthly Planning Worksheet

LOOK OVER THE NEXT HILL

For many churches, a comprehensive and visionary one-year plan is a remarkable achievement. It comes from the heart of God, and its fulfillment depends on the wisdom and strength of God. This plan is a constant reminder of the pastor's vision and desires for that year. It provides clear direction for every program to accomplish that vision. In addition, every ministry leader and every person who serves in any capacity in the church has a clear sense of direction. That is, indeed, a wonderful blessing that comes from this planning process!

After you establish your annual plan, I encourage you to take a look over the next hill and determine a long-range plan for your church. As you continue to pray and listen to the Lord, He will give you direction for the expansion of existing ministries and the creation of new ones. Perhaps your demographic research has shown you that you need to give more attention to a particular age group or a growing ethnic group in your community. As you anticipate the success of God's Word never returning void, develop your growth projections for the next five to ten years.

Each ministry leader should be involved in developing the vision and plan for his segment of ministry. Your dialog with these leaders will clarify your common purposes so the projections will be a composite of your vision and theirs. The projections will include both numerical and qualitative goals. Focus more on increasing quality than just adding numbers.

At the end of this chapter, you will find a worksheet to help you develop these growth projections.

As you establish your long-range plans, you will see the need for a specialized team to oversee these plans. The people you choose for this group need to have the same personal and spiritual qualifications as the team you have already assembled to produce your annual plan, but those selected

As you continue to pray and listen to the Lord, He will give you direction for the expansion of existing ministries and the creation of new ones.

BUILDING A TEAM FOR THE FUTURE

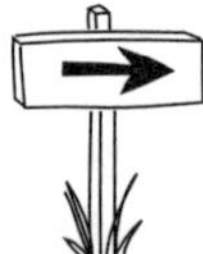

This team needs to include people who are mature in the Spirit and gifted in service.

for the long-range planning team need to have exceptional foresight and experience. They need to understand how the church is presently positioned in the community, as well as how to position it in the future so your outreach can be as effective as possible. This team needs to include people who are mature in the Spirit and gifted in service. In addition, it is helpful if their professions relate to engineering, construction, or finance. All the members, and particularly the chairman, should be well-respected by the church body. In the selection process, consider the specific assignment each person will undertake. God will provide just the right team with the right backgrounds. Their hearts are more important than their specific abilities.

The chairman of the stewardship committee and the chairman of (what might become) the new building committee will be selected from among the members of this long-range leadership team. This primary team, then, will be the network of leadership for every aspect of the planning and implementation of the long-range plan. The selection of the members of this team will be the key to the development and the implementation of the pastor's vision.

Long-range planning is immensely useful for developing, defining, and deploying the pastor's and church's vision. A long-range growth plan needs to be developed for every church, regardless of its size. An annual plan is the threshold of the vision for the future. The prayer, study, and analysis required in the annual planning process establishes the criteria for a multi-year facility plan, growth plan, and an all-encompassing financial plan. The necessity for this kind of planning is as vital as the vision for the church. In fact, if the pastor's vision cannot be expressed in such terms, it is usually doomed for failure because people can't get their arms around a poorly formed dream. They need crisp, clear, visionary direction.

THE LONG-RANGE MINISTRY PLAN

For the span of the next five to ten years, plot your projected program needs based on your vision, the assessments of the needs of your people, unique opportunities, your leadership, and the goals you have set for each segment of your ministry. Anticipate changes in demographics and your programs.

Most of your existing programs will stay in place throughout those years, and you can expect the expansion of those ministries to encourage and build more people in their faith. At this point, focus your attention on the possibility of establishing new, specialized ministries to meet the needs you have discovered from your research. Perhaps you want to start a ministry to the homeless, an outreach to an ethnic group that is growing in your community, a pre-school, or a satellite church. Ask the Lord, your team, and yourself: "What needs are surfacing that aren't being met? What doors for service is God opening?" Developing your Long-Range Ministry Plan is an exciting and faith-stretching exercise!

Ask the Lord, your team, and yourself: "What needs are surfacing that aren't being met? What doors for service is God opening?"

PROJECT STRATEGIC GROWTH

As you look at the growth history of the church (compiled in Step 3), especially during the past several years, you have a basis to begin projecting what might be God's vision for the next five to ten years. Several criteria can be used to put your finger on the quantitative pulse of the church. Membership and attendance at worship on Sunday mornings indicate the broad picture of involvement. Bible study attendance, however, gives a more realistic appraisal of those who are faithful to the mainstream activities of the church. From this group, leaders are raised up and stewardship thrives. The number of baptisms is an indicator of the way God is using our message of the gospel to change lives. New additions may also show how that message is being received, though new members may come in response to many different programs sponsored by the church. Various financial measurements indicate the faithfulness of people in giving, and this assessment provides a strong indication of how they will support a new, visionary plan. These statistics form a clear picture of the health and direction of a body of believers, but any and all of these criteria can change dramatically if God moves with power in the life of a church. Still, these indications of the past are solid and reasonable criteria for projections of the future.

Projecting numbers into the future, though, doesn't automatically make them happen. These figures anticipate what has to happen for the plan to work. They then become a statement of faith, and more appropriately, they are a list of prayer requests which guide our hearts toward the purposes of God.

They then become a statement of faith, and more appropriately, they are a list of prayer requests which guide our hearts toward the purposes of God.

PROJECT SPACE REQUIREMENTS

As we have seen, one of the most important criteria for estimating future growth is Bible study attendance. Different age groups have specific requirements of square footage per person (these are listed on the Growth and Capacity Analysis form in this Step), so the spaces required for each age group must follow these guidelines and requirements. Your long-range planning team will need to review the growth history of

Then plan ahead to be sure momentum isn't lost because space wasn't available for growth.

each age group as projections are made for the future. Capacity will be reached in some areas, such as pre-school or youth, before it is reached in others. Actually, it is not uncommon for churches to experience continual upheaval and rearrangement of rooms in attempts to balance those needs. Carefully forecast the growth in each of these areas, and calculate the respective space requirements in order to anticipate when capacity will be reached. Then plan ahead to be sure momentum isn't lost because space wasn't available for growth. People don't like being crammed into a room, so consider a room to be full when it is at or near 85 percent of capacity.

An even more important criteria for long-range planning is the size of the worship center. The failure to anticipate growth forces many churches into multiple services at times not necessarily convenient to church members, and therefore, attendance is negatively affected.

NEW CONSTRUCTION

One of the primary reasons for projecting attendance growth in worship and Bible study is to calculate their respective spaces in order to plan additional facilities on a timely basis. As we have noted, undesirable service times and crammed rooms can choke enthusiasm and cripple attendance. Certainly, it is good stewardship to consider multiple worship times and multiple uses of space, but these decisions need to be made in light of what meets the needs of the people. When building a new facility is the only or the most desired choice, advance notice to the congregation is very important, particularly when a major building program requires three-and-a-half to four years. This may seem like a protracted amount of time, but traditionally, churches follow a pattern for building:

— one year: committee selection, initial planning, and some work on the concept,
— six months to one year: concept definition and stewardship promotion, and
— two years: architectural drawings and construction completed.

Yes, some church buildings have been fast-tracked and completed sooner— often with disastrous results.

Yes, some church buildings have been fast-tracked and completed sooner—often with disastrous results. The size of the building is a determining factor in the amount of time required, but many churches don't schedule adequately. Make sure your plans are realistic and comprehensive.

The Long-Range Financial Plan is the crown jewel of the planning process, not because it is more important than the vision and ministry plan, but because it reduces all the planning to a common denominator understood by key church leadership. Most of the conflict that arises in churches occurs because of disagreements over money or disputes about control. This plan addresses and clarifies both of these issues. The Long-Range Financial Plan is a one-page document that brings the future into the present. Vision is communicated in incremental stages of implementation, time is allotted for anticipated expenditures, buildings are projected in a timely manner, staff are added as ministry demands increase, and anticipated growth rates are clearly presented for analysis and confirmation. Projected growth in attendance leads to related increases in budget receipts and budget requirements. All financial factors are displayed in the years they are anticipated.

Financial planners appreciate the fact that the available cash, as well as the bottom line debt, is forecast for each year. Any financial variable can be introduced into the spreadsheet to measure its impact on the total plan. Every leader and leadership team that has financial responsibility will function from funds anticipated in the annual plan. The Long-Range Financial Plan is simply the progressive compilation of annual plans that extend into the future to enable a visionary to look at the direction of the church.

The presentation of the long-range plan can be one of the most rewarding events the church family will experience. It gives them the opportunity to embrace a great vision that will affect them and their families for years to come. The plan will challenge their hearts and their wallets, and it will demonstrate that the pastor is a man of vision who trusts God for great things.

When you present this plan to your church, you will be painting a picture of the direction of the church and the blessings God will bring as you take steps along the way. Of course, the purpose of the plan is to reach people for Christ and edify the saints, not just to construct buildings. With enthusiasm, describe the blessings you believe God will bestow on individuals and families as your church trusts Him to accomplish this vision.

Your team will have plenty of details and figures from their research, but don't use all those in your presentation!

THE LONG-RANGE FINANCIAL PLAN

Most of the conflict that arises in churches occurs because of disagreements over money or disputes about control. This plan addresses and clarifies both of these issues.

PRESENTING THE LONG-RANGE PLAN TO THE CHURCH

The plan will challenge their hearts and their wallets, and it will demonstrate that the pastor is a man of vision who trusts God for great things.

Provide summaries, but don't get bogged down in the specifics. Your vision of the church's long-range plan needs to be full of enthusiasm, not numbing numbers; of anticipation, not boring details. Use colorful graphics to show them what the vision will look like when it is fulfilled, both for new building and for new programs.

The Lord, of course, may want to change your plans in order to meet specific needs. When we developed our long-range plans for Bellevue, the first phase was the worship center and auxiliary educational space. The second phase was the recreational building, the third phase was a multi-purpose building, and the fourth phase was a pre-school facility. By the time the second phase was completed, we realized that our people were having more babies than we had projected, so we needed to build our pre-school facility before the multi-purpose building. We praised God for all that He was doing, and our people gladly endorsed the revised plan. When your people grasp a vision for the future, they will feel more comfortable with growth and change as the plan is fulfilled. Change is part of growth and needs to be presented as healthy and desirable.

Like the annual ministry plan, a long-range plan allows the pastor to focus more fully on God's vision. With good plans, many crises are averted and time can be devoted to more productive ministry activities. When direction is sure and interruptions are minimized, the pastor and the other leaders experience much less stress. Long-range planning is, in effect, crisis prevention, and that has a tremendously positive impact on the attitudes of those in leadership because they can relax and focus on accomplishing the plan God has given them.

Long-range planning is, in effect, crisis prevention, and that has a tremendously positive impact on the attitudes of those in leadership because they can relax and focus on accomplishing the plan God has given them.

TAKE A STEP

The exercises at the end of this step are designed to help you and your planning team develop a comprehensive long-range plan for your church. All of the exercises in this section are core assessments and worksheets. They include:

— Long-Range Ministry Plan,
— Growth and Capacity Analysis,

— Growth Projections—General Church Criteria,
— Building Plan Schedule and Expenditures, and
— Long-Range Financial Plan.

LONG-RANGE MINISTRY PLAN

— *Who?:* The long-range planning team.

— *Why?:* To determine God's plan for meeting the needs of your church and your community during the next five to ten years, and to anticipate the specialized ministries that can meet these needs.

— *How?:* Analyze the demographics for your community and identify the unmet needs which have surfaced during the planning process. Brainstorm solutions (possible programs) to meet those needs, then prioritize them and finalize your plan.

— ***Then what?:*** Your Long-Range Ministry Plan gives you clear direction to plan for additional growth, facility needs, and budget projections, not only for the expansion of existing ministries but also to establish new, specialized ministries.

LONG-RANGE MINISTRY PLAN

As you look at the next five to ten years, plan your programs to meet the needs and take advantage of the opportunities that arise during your planning process. Consider these questions:

1.   What needs have surfaced that aren't being met or aren't being addressed adequately?

2.   In your demographic study of your community, what segments of the city are growing disproportionately? Look at age, ethnicity, economic status, etc.

3.   Brainstorming: What are some ways God may want your church to meet those needs and capture those opportunities?

4. Consider:

— Expanding or altering an existing ministry:

— Adding new services to meet the worship needs of a segment of the community:

— Adding specialized ministries:

5. As each of these ministries and services is scheduled to be implemented, develop a plan that includes:

    — The purpose and scope
    — Selecting and developing leadership
    — Finding resources (finances, training, facilities, etc.)
    — Elements in the stages of development of this ministry (planning, leadership, resources, test cases, communication to the congregation, full roll out, etc.)
    — Establish a schedule, a budget, and an organizational chart

    On the Long-Range Financial Plan, record each item or event in the left-hand column with corresponding expenditures in the years that it will be initiated and implemented. The costs of many (if not most) programs extend beyond the first year of implementation, so be sure to account for these expenses in subsequent years of your plan.

GROWTH AND CAPACITY ANALYSIS

— *Who?:* The long-range planning team.

— *Why?:* To project the facility needs you will have in each of the next few years based on your growth projections.

— *How?:* Examine the Space Utilization from Step 3 and factor in the growth projections. This will tell you when and how your facilities will need to be expanded.

The Growth and Capacity Analysis is a critical assessment of the anticipated growth and the space required to accommodate that growth. The percentage of increase (or decrease) is estimated for each year for Bible study age groups and for those attending worship services.

The square footage is calculated for each age group by multiplying the average attendance by the age-group factor, that is, the square footage required per person in that particular age group. The sum of all the age groups each year will be the total Bible study space required. The space required for the worship center will be the projected attendance multiplied by eleven (11) square feet per person. For a full choir area, an additional eight to ten percent of the worship center space should be allocated. In this analysis, no attempt will be made to estimate other ministry or auxiliary areas because of the infinitely varied types of programs that exist in churches. However, a church should work with an architect to custom design the building plan for the church's specific needs.

The Growth and Capacity Analysis is a forecast that will help you determine when and how you will need to creatively use *existing* facilities to meet the needs of your growing church, or it will help you determine the size of *new* buildings you will need when you outgrow your existing facilities.

This analysis must be completed in conjunction with Growth Projections—General Church Criteria in this Step. Both documents assume growth will result from the addition of space for worship or Bible Study. You will note in the example that space requirements (and correspondingly, increases in growth) anticipate a building program being completed in year 7. Realistically, growth will diminish as space is over-utilized, but it should increase as additional space becomes available. The timing of any new facility and its cost become an integral part of all the long-range planning tools in this Step. Accordingly, while each document builds upon another, they are all interrelated.

— *Then what?:* This assessment of the need for additional facilities will then be the basis for your building plan.

Growth and Capacity Analysis

	Present Yr.	Yr. +1	Yr. +2	Yr. +3	Yr. +4	Yr. +5	Yr. +6	Yr. +7	Yr. +8	Yr. +9	Yr. +10
Age Division Avg. Attendance											
(assumes Sunday a.m. on campus)											
Preschool (Average Attendance)											
Percentage increase/decrease											
Space requirements at 35 sq. ft. each											
*100% capacity											
**85% capacity											
Children (Average Attendance)											
Percentage increase/decrease											
*Space requirements at 25 sq. ft. each											
*100% capacity											
**85% capacity											
Youth (Average Attendance)											
Percentage increase/decrease											
*Space requirements at 15 sq. ft. each											
*100% capacity											
**85% capacity											
Adults (Average Attendance)											
Percentage increase/decrease											
*Space requirements at 10 sq. ft. each											
*100% capacity											
**85% capacity											
***Total Bible Study (Avg. Attd.)											
Percentage increase/decrease											
*100% capacity											
**85% capacity											
Worship (Average Attendance)											
Percentage increase/decrease											
Space requirements at 11 sq. ft. each											
*100% capacity											
**85% capacity											

*Multiply projected attendance for each year by the age division factor (sq. ft. per person) to determine 100% capacity.
**Multiply the 100% capacity number by 1.15 to determine the space required for the same number of people at 85% capacity.
***Add each age division for yearly total. **Note: Auxilliary spaces for circulation and other ministry functions to be determined by ministry need and architect.**

Growth and Capacity Analysis

	Present Yr.	Yr. +1	Yr. +2	Yr. +3	Yr. +4	Yr. +5	Yr. +6	Yr. +7	Yr. +8	Yr. +9	Yr. +10
	2001	2002	2003	2004	2005	2006	2007	2008	2009	2010	2011
Age Division Avg. Attendance											
(assumes Sunday a.m. on campus)											
Preschool (Average Attendance)	54	57	61	68	74	78	80	88	95	103	110
Percentage increase/decrease		5.56%	7.02%	11.48%	8.82%	5.41%	2.56%	10.00%	7.95%	8.42%	6.80%
Space requirements at 35 sq. ft. each											
*100% capacity	1890	1995	2135	2380	2590	2730	2800	3080	3325	3605	3850
**85% capacity	2174	2294	2455	2737	2979	3140	3220	3542	3824	4146	4428
Children (Average Attendance)	54	57	61	68	74	78	80	88	95	103	110
Percentage increase/decrease		5.56%	7.02%	11.48%	8.82%	5.41%	2.56%	10.00%	7.95%	8.42%	6.80%
Space requirements at 25 sq. ft. each											
*100% capacity	1350	1425	1525	1700	1850	1950	2000	2200	2375	2575	2750
**85% capacity	1553	1639	1754	1955	2128	2243	2300	2530	2731	2961	3163
Youth (Average Attendance)	43	45	48	53	58	61	63	69	75	81	86
Percentage increase/decrease		4.65%	6.67%	10.42%	9.43%	5.17%	3.28%	9.52%	8.70%	8.00%	6.17%
Space requirements at 15 sq. ft. each											
*100% capacity	645	675	720	795	870	915	945	1035	1125	1215	1290
**85% capacity	742	776	828	914	1001	1052	1087	1190	1294	1397	1484
Adults (Average Attendance)	237	247	265	295	320	341	348	382	414	450	479
Percentage increase/decrease		4.22%	7.29%	11.32%	8.47%	6.56%	2.05%	9.77%	8.38%	8.70%	6.44%
Space requirements at 10 sq. ft. each											
*100% capacity	2370	2470	2650	2950	3200	3410	3480	3820	4140	4500	4790
**85% capacity	2726	2841	3048	3393	3680	3922	4002	4393	4761	5175	5509
***Total Bible Study (Avg. Attd.)	389	406	435	484	525	559	571	627	679	738	785
Percentage increase/decrease		4.3%	7.2%	11.2%	8.6%	6.4%	2.1%	9.8%	8.3%	8.7%	6.4%
*100% capacity	6255	6565	7030	7825	8510	9005	9225	10135	10965	11895	12680
**85% capacity	7193	7550	8085	8999	9787	10356	10609	11655	12610	13679	14582
Worship (Average Attendance)	511	536	590	664	722	761	793	906	997	1100	1188
Percentage increase/decrease		4.9%	10.1%	12.5%	8.7%	5.4%	4.2%	14.2%	10.0%	10.3%	8.0%
Space requirements at 11 sq. ft. each											
*100% capacity	5621	5896	6490	7304	7942	8371	8723	9966	10967	12100	13068
**85% capacity	6464	6780	7464	8400	9133	9627	10031	11461	12612	13915	15028

*Multiply projected attendance for each year by the age division factor (sq. ft. per person) to determine 100% capacity.
**Multiply the 100% capacity number by 1.15 to determine the space required for the same number of people at 85% capacity.
Example: Preschool: (Yr. +6 avg. attd.) 80 x 35 (sq. ft. per person) = 2800 sq. ft. required at 100%. 2800 x 1.15 = 3200 sq. ft. required at 85% capacity.
***Add each age division for yearly total. **Note: Auxilliary spaces for circulation and other ministry functions to be determined by ministry need and architect.**

GROWTH PROJECTIONS— GENERAL CHURCH CRITERIA

— *Who?:* The long-range planning team.

— *Why?:* To anticipate growth for the next five to ten years in order to prepare adequate facilities, staffing, and other resources to meet those needs.

— *How?:* Review the history of the last few years from the Historical Growth Statistics—General Church Criteria in Step 3, then in light of the current state of your ministry and the trends you see for the future, project a reasonable rate of growth for the future. You will find that this form in Step 6 is structured exactly like the one in Step 3. The previous form looked back several years while this one looks forward several years.

Total Bible Study and worship projections are brought forward from the Growth and Capacity Analysis and summarized with church membership, baptisms, and finances. Just as increases in attendance for Bible study and worship were estimated in the last form, corresponding increases are forecast for the major categories on this one. Some of the same line items are carried forward here and to the Long-Range Financial Plan because they are relevant to both. Increases in attendance determine the space needed, and those same figures are related to the increases in budget receipts and requirements.

My experience has revealed that increases in receipts generally exceed the percentage increases in attendance. As growth is forecast, good administrative practices should keep increases in budget requirements below that of receipts. This may seem to be a complicated process, but if it is taken a step at at time, it is quite logical and easily understood.

— *Then what?:* The growth projections will determine your assessments in each of the remaining exercises in this Step.

Growth Projections
General Church Criteria

	Present Yr.	Yr. +1	Yr. +2	Yr. +3	Yr. +4	Yr. +5	Yr. +6	Yr. +7	Yr. +8	Yr. +9	Yr. +10
Church Membership											
Percentage increase/decrease*											
Bible Study (Average Attendance)											
Percentage increase/decrease											
Worship (Average Attendance)											
Percentage increase/decrease											
Baptisms											
Finances											
Budget Receipts											
Percentage increase/decrease											
Designated Gifts											
Building Fund											
Total Gifts											
Percentage increase/decrease											
Operational Budget											
Percentage increase/decrease											

*Calculate the amount for desired year by multiplying previous year by 100% plus the % estimated.
Note: Calculating growth by percentage increase in each area is derived from historical data and visionary goals.

Growth Projections
General Church Criteria

	Present Yr. 2001	Yr. +1 2002	Yr. +2 2003	Yr. +3 2004	Yr. +4 2005	Yr. +5 2006	Yr. +6 2007	Yr. +7 2008	Yr. +8 2009	Yr. +9 2010	Yr. +10 2011
Church Membership	1548	1639	1810	2031	2242	2392	2571	2993	3355	3755	4138
Percentage increase/decrease*		5.9%	10.40%	12.20%	10.40%	6.70%	7.50%	16.40%	12.10%	11.90%	10.20%
Bible Study (Average Attendance)	389	406	435	484	525	559	571	627	679	738	785
Percentage increase/decrease		4.3%	7.2%	11.2%	8.6%	6.4%	2.1%	9.8%	8.3%	8.7%	6.4%
Worship (Average Attendance)	511	536	590	664	722	761	793	906	997	1100	1188
Percentage increase/decrease		4.8%	10.10%	12.70%	8.60%	5.40%	4.30%	14.20%	10.10%	10.30%	8.00%
Baptisms	28	29	32	37	44	51	59	66	73	80	88
Finances											
Budget Receipts	$802,183	$872,775	$967,035	$1,129,497	$1,275,202	$1,397,621	$1,442,345	$1,654,370	$1,869,438	$2,121,812	$2,325,506
Percentage increase/decrease		8.8%	10.8%	16.8%	12.9%	9.6%	3.2%	14.7%	13.0%	13.5%	9.6%
Designated Gifts	$30,000	$35,000	$35,000	$35,000	$40,000	$40,000	$40,000	$45,000	$45,000	$45,000	$50,000
Building Fund	New facilities anticipated for growth purposes. Refer to Long-Range Financial Plan for cost details.										
Total Gifts	$839,683	$907,775	$1,002,035	$1,164,497	$1,315,202	$1,437,621	$1,482,345	$1,699,370	$1,914,438	$2,166,812	$2,375,506
Percentage increase/decrease		8.1%	10.4%	17.7%	12.9%	9.3%	3.1%	14.6%	4.9%	13.2%	9.6%
Operational Budget	$658,796	$698,324	$741,969	$790,197	$841,560	$892,053	$941,116	$1,019,229	$1,093,123	$1,164,176	$1,234,027
Percentage increase/decrease		6.0%	6.3%	6.5%	6.5%	6.0%	5.5%	8.3%	7.3%	6.5%	6.0%

*Calculate the amount for desired year by multiplying previous year by 100% plus the % estimated.

Example: (Church Membership Year +1) 1548 X 1.059 = 1639

Example: (Operating Budget Year +1) 658,796 X 1.06 = 698.324

Note: Calculating growth by percentage increase in each area is derived from historical data and visionary goals.

BUILDING PLAN SCHEDULE AND EXPENDITURES

— *Who?:* The long-range planning team, with the addition of an architect or builder at some point to assist in planning.

— *Why?:* To determine a clear plan for expanding or building new facilities.

— *How?:* With the projections and the facility needs just assessed, your planning team will determine exactly what buildings need to be built to serve the needs of the church. In some cases, an expansion of existing facilities will suffice; in others, new buildings will be needed. And in a few cases, the church will have reached the limit of its growth at the current site, so you need to consider relocation or launching satellite churches. When you have an idea of what you need, consult an architect or builder to get a ballpark assessment of the cost and schedule.

A typical building schedule and estimated costs are shown on the sample form to demonstrate the need for early planning for any new construction your church will need. Be sure to allow plenty of time for planning and construction in order to prevent rushed decisions and change orders, which almost always prove to be very costly. On the sample form, the "x's" indicate the year in which the specified activities take place. The lower part of the form is for projections of the estimated costs for those activities.

— *Then what?:* With a preliminary building plan in place, you will be ready to look at the revenues needed to pay for the new facilities.

Building Plan and Expenditure Schedule

FACILITY: ___________________	PRESENT YEAR ACTUAL	Yr. + 1	Yr. + 2	Yr. + 3	Yr. + 4	Yr. + 5	Yr. + 6	Yr. + 7	Yr. + 8	Yr. + 9	Yr. + 10
ILLUSTRATION:											
Indicate Year of Use											
Calculate Length of Building Program											
Indicate Building Program Ground Breaking To complete building for desired move in											
Estimate concept development design time											
Indicate Year											
Determine Fund Raising Program and Time Required											
CONSTRUCTION COSTS:											
Fund Raising											
Development Design											
Construction											
TOTAL ANNUAL COST											

Building Plan and Expenditure Schedule

FACILITY: __Worship Center__

	PRESENT YEAR ACTUAL	Yr.+1	Yr.+2	Yr.+3	Yr.+4	Yr.+5	Yr.+6	Yr.+7	Yr.+8	Yr.+9	Yr.+10
ILLUSTRATION:											
Indicate Year of Use (Example: Year 7)								X			
Calculate Length of Building Program (Example: 2 Years - Years 5-6)						X	X				
Indicate Building Program Ground Breaking To complete building for desired move in (Example: Year 5)						X					
Estimate concept development design time (Example: 1 year) Indicate Year (Example: Year 4)					X						
Determine Fund Raising Program and Time Required (Example: Year 3)				X							
CONSTRUCTION COSTS EXAMPLE:											
Fund Raising				$50,000	$26,000	$25,000	$20,000				
Development Design					$295,000						
Construction						$1,025,000	$1,680,000				
TOTAL ANNUAL COST				$50,000	$321,000	$1,050,000	$1,700,000				

Note: Anticipated $3,000,000 building program with $121,000 allowed for stewardship program.

LONG-RANGE FINANCIAL PLAN

— *Who?:* The long-range planning team.
— *Why?:* To show the cash flow each year for the next ten years.
— *How?:* Use the Long-Range Financial Plan to complete your planning for the future. Follow the instructions below for each of the sub-divisions (A-G). Begin with your current year, which comes from your annual plan, and project your vision for the next ten years. (An example is included.)

A. Growth Variables

Line A.1: Estimate the percentage of growth each year for the general "Budget Receipts" (income).

Line A.2: Estimate the percentage of growth each year for the "Operating Budget Requirements" (expenses).

B. Income

Line B.1: "Budget Receipts" are calculated by multiplying the budget amount of the previous year by the percent of change forecasted for the year in question, then adding to (or subtracting from) the previous year's amount.

Example: Year 1 projected Budget Receipts are calculated this way: Current year ($802,183) x Year 1 % Change (8.80%) = $70592; + $802,183 = $872,775.

Line B.2: "Other Sources/Designated Gifts" is a line item for gifts and contributions other than those for the general budget but not for major projects such as the building fund. (For example, a special missions fund.)

Line B.3: "Loan to Operations" is the line item used to record a loan or a partially executed line of credit from a lending institution for needs, such as a building program. On the example form, note a $3,000,000 loan has been shown in Year 4 for a proposed building program.

Line B.4: "Total Income" represents the sum of all income to the church. (Lines B.1 + B.2 + B.3)

C. Expenditures

Line C.1: "Operating Budget" is the anticipated expenditures estimated to carry on the business of the church on a day-to-day basis throughout the year. For each successive year, it is calculated by multiplying the amount of the previous year by the forecasted percent of change for the next year (from A.2) and adding to the previous year's amount.

Example: Year 1 Projected Operating Budget is calculated this way: Current year ($658,796) x Year 1 % of change (6.00%) = $39,528; + 658,796 = $698,324.

Line C.2: "Capital Improvements" is a category reserved for large, one-time expenditures such as roof repair, paving parking lots, replacing air conditioners, etc.

Line C.3: "Interest" is the expense line item for the cost of borrowing money for such large projects as building improvements or new facilities. In the example, note the Year 5 interest amount of $278,089 and the succeeding interest through Year 9 resulting from the $3,000,000 loan.

Line C.4: "Principal" is the repayment line item for the base amount of the loan. In the example, note Year 5 through Year 9, indicating the time and amounts required to liquidate the debt.

Line C.5: "Construction" is the category of actual construction costs estimated each year throughout the building program. Note that expenditures were recorded in Year 4 ($295,000), Year 5 ($1,025,000) and Year 6 ($1,680,000).

Line C.6: "Other" is a line for any other expenses that might be incurred or that you might want to highlight for monitoring purposes.

Line C.7: "Total Expenditures" is the sum of all annualized expenses of the church, Line C.1 though Line C. 6.

D. Operating Cash
Line D.1: "Change in Net Operating Cash" is the line that indicates the result of that year's cash performance. It is calculated by subtracting Total Expenditures (Line C.7) from Total Income (Line B.4). Hopefully this will be a positive number such as the one represented in the current year of the example; $832,183 - $695,796= $136,387.

Line D.2: "Cumulative Operating Cash" is the sum of Operating Cash, or carryover from the previous year, plus that cash realized for the year in question. In the example, note Year 1, the commutative operating cash of $384,451 is obtained by carrying forward the $200,000 from the current year and adding it to the Year 1 performance of $184,451. This is a critical line item because it denotes the projected cash position of the church in succeeding years through normal times, as well as through the building years. Notice in years five through seven that each year shows negative balances, but the cash build-up (or cumulative position) was able to keep the church in the black. This was no accident. The plan allowed for the selection of a building program to meet the growing needs of the church, but within financial restraints to avoid a crisis.

E. Building Program Stewardship

The cost of the loan for construction was projected under Item C. This category (Item E) allows for the documentation of the stewardship program and its costs.

Line E.1: "Special Offering Receipts" is the line item that records the annual giving anticipated for the Building Fund. For years three through seven in the example, a total of $2,460,000 was received toward the $3,000,000 building program.

Line E.2: "Special Offering Expenditures" is the category of expenses necessary for promotion, dinners, correspondence, and possibly for consulting services related to the fund-raising program.

Line E.3: "Net Available Special Offering" is the difference between Line E.1 and E.2.

F. *"Cumulative Operating Cash and Special Offering"* is obtained by the addition of Lines D.2 and E.3. This amount is of great importance since it shows the cash position of the church during a building program and while the debt is being repaid.

G. *"Debt Balance at End of Year"* indicates the amount of remaining debt each year until it is totally liquidated. In the example, note its calculation for the years 5 and 6. The debt remaining at the end of Year 5 is $2,573,196. Subtract the principal amount (Line C.4) for Year 6, $537,779 to obtain the debt balance for Year 6 of $1,975,417. The financial model permits the calculation and tracking of the debt, with all other church expenses anticipated and included, until the debt is paid back in Year 9.

— *Then what?:* This long-range plan will give you a benchmark for financial decision-making in the future. It should be updated each year and adjusted according to changes in plans.

Long Range Financial Plan

	PRESENT YEAR ACTUAL	Yr. + 1	Yr. + 2	Yr. + 3	Yr. + 4	Yr. + 5	Yr. + 6	Yr. + 7	Yr. + 8	Yr. + 9	Yr. + 10
A. Growth Variables											
A.1 Budget receipts percent of change											
A.2 Operating budget percent of change											
B. Income											
B.1 Budget receipts											
B.2 Other sources/designated gifts											
B.3 Loan to operations											
B.4 TOTAL INCOME											
C. Expenditures											
C.1 Operating budget											
C.2 Capital improvements											
C.3 Interest											
C.4 Principal											
C.5 Construction											
C.6 Other											
C.7 TOTAL EXPENDITURES											
D. Operating Cash											
D.1 Change in net operating cash											
D.2 Cumulative operating cash											
E. Building Program (Stewardship Plan)											
E.1 Special offering receipts											
E.2 Special offering expenditures											
E.3 NET AVAILABLE SPECIAL OFFERING											
F. Cumulative Operating Cash and Special Offering											
G. Debt Balance at End of Year											

Long Range Financial Plan

	PRESENT YEAR ACTUAL	Yr. + 1	Yr. + 2	Yr. + 3	Yr. + 4	Yr. + 5	Yr. + 6	Yr. + 7	Yr. + 8	Yr. + 9	Yr. + 10
A. Growth Variables											
A.1 Budget receipts percent of change	0.00%	8.80%	10.80%	16.80%	12.90%	9.60%	3.20%	14.70%	13.00%	13.50%	9.60%
A.2 Operating budget percent of change	0.00%	6.00%	6.30%	6.50%	6.50%	6.00%	5.50%	8.30%	7.30%	6.50%	11.00%
B. Income											
B.1 Budget receipts	$802,183	$872,775	$967,035	$1,129,497	$1,275,202	$1,397,621	$1,442,345	$1,654,370	$1,869,438	$2,121,812	$2,325,506
B.2 Other sources/designated gifts	$30,000	$35,000	$35,000	$35,000	$40,000	$40,000	$40,000	$45,000	$45,000	$45,000	$50,000
B.3 Loan to operations					$3,000,000						
B.4 TOTAL INCOME	$832,183	$907,775	$1,002,035	$1,164,497	$4,315,202	$1,437,621	$1,482,345	$1,654,370	$1,914,438	$2,166,812	$2,375,506
C. Expenditures											
C.1 Operating budget	$658,796	$698,324	$742,318	$790,569	$841,956	$892,473	$941,559	$1,019,709	$1,094,147	$1,165,267	$1,357,847
C.2 Capital improvements	$37,000	$25,000	$45,000	$62,000	$55,000	$53,000	$41,000	$10,000	$10,000	$15,000	$45,000
C.3 Interest						$278,089	$227,114	$170,801	$108,593	$39,870	
C.4 Principal						$486,804	$537,779	$594,092	$656,301	$725,024	
C.5 Construction	$0	$0	$0	$0	$295,000	$1,025,000	$1,680,000	$0	$0	$0	$0
C.6 Other	$0	$0	$0	$0	$0	$0	$0	$0	$0	$0	$0
C.7 TOTAL EXPENDITURES	$695,796	$723,324	$787,318	$852,569	$1,191,956	$2,735,366	$3,427,452	$1,794,602	$1,869,041	$1,945,161	$1,402,847
D. Operating Cash	$136,387	$184,451	$214,717	$311,928	$3,123,246	($1,297,745)	($1,945,107)	($140,232)	$45,396	$221,651	$972,659
D.1 Change in net operating cash	$200,000	$384,451	$599,168	$911,096	$4,034,342	$2,736,597	$791,489	$651,258	$696,654	$918,305	$1,890,964
D.2 Cumulative operating cash											
E. Building Program (Stewardship Plan)											
E.1 Special offering receipts				$50,000	$1,050,000	$780,000	$580,000	$0	$0	$0	
E.2 Special offering expenditures				$50,000	$26,000	$25,000	$20,000				
E.3 NET AVAILABLE SPECIAL OFFERING	$0	$0	$0	$0	$1,024,000	$755,000	$600,000	$0	$0	$0	$0
F. Cumulative Operating Cash and Special Offering	$200,000	$384,451	$599,168	$911,096	$5,058,342	$3,491,597	$1,391,489	$651,258	$696,654	$918,305	$1,890,964
G. Debt Balance at End of Year					$3,000,000	$2,513,196	$1,975,417	$1,381,325	$725,024	$0	$0

STEP 1 *The Captain's Compass*

- Your Personal Vision
- Your Ministry Vision

STEP 2 *Look at the Map*

- Your Plan for Planning
- Ministry Review
- Planning Team Evaluation

STEP 3 *Watch for Obstacles and Opportunities*

- Task Summaries
- Job Descriptions
- Historical Growth Statistics—Bible Study
- Historical Growth Statistics—General Church Criteria
- Community Demographics
- Obstacles and Opportunities
- Space Utilization

STEP 4 *Get Your Equipment Ready*

- Ministry Flow Chart
- Organizational Chart
- Communication System

STEP 5 *Plot Your Course*

- Ministry Leader Planning Worksheet
- The Ministry Plan
- The Master Calendar
- The Financial Plan
- Communication Plan

STEP 6 *Look Over the Next Hill*

- Long-Range Ministry Plan
- Growth and Capacity Analysis
- Growth Projections
- General Church Criteria
- Building Plan Schedule and Expenditures
- Long-Range Financial Plan

STEP 7 *Get on the Trail*

- **Monthly Planning Worksheet**

GET ON THE TRAIL

Writing a God-focused, visionary, comprehensive plan (either annual or long-range) is challenging, but when it is presented to the congregation, the real work begins. Now the concepts need to be turned into action; ideas turned into prayers; and charts translated into genuine leadership to accomplish God's gracious purposes. Change, as we said in the book's introduction, is stimulating to some of us, but it is threatening to others.

Some pastors are as bold as lions. They trust God for great things, and they share their visions with great enthusiasm. They call others to join them in the great adventure of building God's Kingdom. Other pastors are more cautious. They want to be sure all the details are addressed and all the people feel heard before proceeding. Neither way is right; neither way is wrong. Both have their positive as well as negative aspects. As you begin to implement your plan, understand your personality and your "bent" in communicating in order to maximize your effectiveness and minimize misunderstandings. For example:

— Bold risk-takers paint an exciting vision and call people to follow, but they are often impatient with those who are more cautious, who ask questions, and who need to process information more slowly.

— Inspirational leaders are excited and paint a big picture of how God will impact people, but often neglect to include details of how they will accomplish their goals.

— Sensitive leaders tell how God will redeem individuals and families, but they may not challenge or excite followers with a bold plan.

THE LEADER'S PERSONALITY AND THE PROCESS OF CHANGE

As you begin to implement your plan, understand your personality and your "bent" in communicating in order to maximize your effectiveness and minimize misunderstandings.

— Cautious and thorough leaders think through their plans in minute detail, but they are sometimes unable to convey the big picture with enthusiasm. They become frustrated when people don't grasp their logic or when they fail to show support for their plans.

Know yourself, and adjust your communication to meet the needs of all types of people in your congregation. Some want more details than others, and most want to know that the plan demonstrates genuine care for people. But *everybody* wants to know that your plan comes from the heart of God and you are excited about it!

COMMON RESPONSES TO CHANGE

Some people get on board very quickly, but some take longer to "own" the vision and the plan.

I've watched churches respond to change, and I've seen a clear pattern of responses within those congregations. Some people get on board very quickly, but some take longer to "own" the vision and the plan. If you clearly and enthusiastically communicate the process of how God gave you the vision and how the vision has inspired the plan, you can expect support from most people. But don't expect everyone—even among your leadership—to instantly become zealous supporters. Allow them time to ask questions and consider how the changes will affect them. If you anticipate their responses, you won't be caught off guard, and you'll be able to address some of their concerns before they even ask.

You probably already know some of the people in your church who are likely to challenge your vision and plan. An assertive strategy is to go to these people during the planning process and ask for their input. Thank them for their perspectives, and if possible, incorporate their ideas in some way. Then, tell your leaders and others that these people have helped shape the direction of the plan. That will put them squarely on your side and make them allies instead of adversaries. I'm not suggesting duplicity, just diplomacy. Ask God for wisdom, and trust Him to give you creative ways of overcoming adversity before it gets started, but don't mistake honest questions from the vast majority of people as opposition. As members of your local body of believers, they have the right and the responsibility to ask questions and make suggestions. If you appear to feel threatened by their questions, it will diminish your credibility and limit open communication. Appreciate them for their willingness to challenge suppositions and plans. Maintain a positive, affirming, patient attitude that communicates: "Thank you for asking that question. I appreciate your thorough analysis. Let me see if I can explain that point."

The corporate process of change in a congregation parallels the types of individual responses. We often find initial enthusiasm verbalized by those who grasp the vision immediately, with more time necessary for the rest of the congregation to understand, own the vision, and take action. Here are the common stages of change:

Initial Excitement

When a vision is first expressed at a church, quite often there is great initial excitement. We can envision new buildings, hundreds or thousands coming to Christ, marriages reconciled, families encouraged, and countries reached. This stage is thrilling, but it may last only a short time before people begin asking questions like, "How much will that cost?" "How will that change our worship service?" "Who am I going to report to now?" "What does this mean for me?" Dozens of personal and pertinent questions will be raised. As these questions are answered, people make decisions to support the plan . . . or not.

Decisions to Buy In

As the questions are asked and answered (for the 974th time!), we find out where people stand in their willingness to change. Many people will delay their support until they get answers to their questions and see if their friends are on board. You will begin to hear rumors of people who think you've lost your mind, and a few might tell you to your face that you're nuts. Watch for the responses of your leaders. They may be dragging their feet now, even though they were excited when the plan was first unveiled. (A whiner or two may have asked a question they couldn't answer, or doubts may have crept into their minds.) Notice the condition of your sheep, and take the initiative to ask if they are struggling with any element of the vision.

Opposition

If certain segments of the church family believe they have been overlooked or if a small group of deacons opposes the plan, they may mount genuine opposition. Even if the questions are fully and patiently answered, and time is given for prayer and reflection, there may still be a few people who genuinely and actively oppose you. Careful planning and good communication will minimize this opposition, but unfortunately, it is sometimes difficult to eliminate it completely.

Adjustments

Good planners know there are always midcourse corrections and adjustments to refine the plan and keep on track. Don't rush to change things too quickly just because someone objects to something. Look for patterns and take some time before making changes. Your planning process was patient and thorough, and your consideration of any adjustments needs to be handled in the same way. Thank people who make suggestions, even if those suggestions are from out in left field! Take the valid comments to the planning team, staff, or ministry leaders, and carefully consider them.

Your planning process was patient and thorough, and your consideration of any adjustments needs to be handled in the same way.

STAY ON TRACK: THE HABIT OF PLANNING

Planning can become a habit that is an integral part of your life and the life of the church. If individuals or organizations have never been taught to plan effectively, the learning curve is often long and steep at first. After a cycle or two, however, the process of gathering information, communicating, and setting goals becomes second nature. The wheels of planning and progress are greased with experience and success, and it becomes easier with each passing year.

I encourage pastors and churches to develop a planning process that involves weekly, monthly, and yearly planning. Each week, the pastor and his top leadership meet to discuss the current status of the ministry and plan for the next week. And each week they also need to take some time to look ahead to the next month and the next quarter to be sure they are prepared for the upcoming events.

Monthly plans look forward to trends and events for the next month, and maybe for two or three months. Many churches incorporate their monthly planning into regular staff and leadership meetings. You may only need an hour or two with your staff or ministry leaders to be sure you stay on track. And in fact, I encourage every staff member and every ministry leader to spend a little time in monthly planning.

Yearly plans involve the planning process that is outlined in this book. After the first year, it requires from two weeks to two months to update information and gather new insights from the leadership, the church body, and the community. The yearly planning process leads into a five-year or ten-year plan and draws vision and direction from the larger perspective.

At this point, please allow me to insert a very important facet of pastoral leadership pertaining to the planning

I encourage pastors and churches to develop a planning process that involves weekly, monthly, and yearly planning.

process. The purpose of the myriad of principles, suggestions, and techniques in this book is not to create an administrative monster. Our goal is to provide orderly and concerted plans in a clearly focused ministry, and this focus for a pastor includes building a strong team. The planning process provides an excellent opportunity for the pastor's vision to strengthen his leaders, and routine meetings need to be seen as times to sharpen vision and spiritually enrich each staff member and lay leader. If a pastor makes a priority of educating, discipling, mentoring, and inspiring his leaders, vision and wisdom will be the rewards. The great demands of the pastorate should not negate his responsibility to multiply himself in the lives of other leaders. Ironically, the administrative process, which is so often neglected, affords many wonderful opportunities for pastors to shape the minds and hearts of those on his leadership team.

Pastors benefit greatly from the cross-pollination of hearing and seeing new ideas from other pastors who are testing their plans in the trenches of real ministry. Read books that stimulate your vision and creativity. Listen to tapes that encourage you to trust God for more and to train your people effectively, and take at least one trip each year to see first-hand what God is doing at another church. Invest a little time and money in your dreams.

The planning process provides an excellent opportunity for the pastor's vision to strengthen his leaders, and routine meetings need to be seen as times to sharpen vision and spiritually enrich each staff member and lay leader.

Leading any organization requires wisdom and courage. Even the best leaders encounter difficulties and opposition, so don't be surprised when people criticize your plans, even though you've prayed and talked to so many people that you're sure you're doing what God wants you to do. To stay on track, we need to anticipate some common problems. Some of the questions may be answered quickly, but others require more research, time, and discipline to find the answer.

ISSUES AND ANSWERS

What Do You Do If . . . ?

What do you do if God calls a key staff member (or you) away?

If the vision is truly from God for that church, leadership transition need not kill the vision. Careful planning and communication can help smooth that time of change. I've seen churches devastated by a pastor's leaving, and I've seen some very smooth transitions. There are two key questions: Why did the person leave, and how is the change communicated? If a pastor is asked to resign or is fired, confusion, anger, and suspicion are often the immediate by-products.

Far too often, this decision is made in the context of a power struggle between warring factions in the church. Very little good can happen under those circumstances.

Far too often, this decision is made in the context of a power struggle between warring factions in the church. Very little good can happen under those circumstances. In such cases, the issue is not usually the pastor at all, but the pride and stubbornness of a few who demand their own way. Jesus told His followers, "A new commandment I give to you, that you love one another; as I have loved you, that you also love one another. By this all will know that you are My disciples, if you have love for one another" (John 13:34-35). Take the focus off the person and put it on the Lord. If people are truly seeking Him, their lives and their attitudes will be marked by both grace and truth. If a pastor genuinely is in sin and should be removed, trust God for wisdom, and take appropriate steps that bring healing to all those involved.

If a pastor is called to another church, he needs to take time to clearly communicate his new calling, as well as his love for the people in his present church and his desire for God to continue to bless them. Of course, the new pastor will have his own vision, so there will be some adjustments. An orderly and positive time of transition is important for the one leaving, the one coming, and for all those who stay and bring stability to the church's vision and plan.

What do you do if staff or lay leaders are hesitant to follow?

Change is threatening to many people, yet many pastors are impatient with those who aren't as excited as they are. Most of the time, an unwillingness to follow is rooted in fear. Take time to listen, to empathize, and to explain. Affirm your vision for each person. Your patience and encouragement may well win them over.

Involve reluctant people in the process of gathering information and planning. As they see the plan unfold, the vast majority of them will become proponents of the plan. If, however, their areas of ministry face significant change, anxiety might prevent them from being excited about the plan. Understand their personalities and their fears. Assure them of their important roles, and offer to answer any questions they may have.

Perhaps the most threatening part of this entire planning process to some of our leaders is the philosophy that the pastor primarily determines the vision and direction of the church while the rest of the leaders complement and support him. They are afraid this relegates them to roles as "yes men," without validation of their own calling and without giving them the freedom of seeing God fulfill their own visions. They fear being dominated by a pastor, and they are afraid they will experience little satisfaction in guiding their individual ministries. To relieve these fears, they must understand that spiritual authority and divine calling are complementary. They can experience great fulfillment (and indeed, I believe the greatest possible sense of fulfillment) if they see themselves as fully functioning members of a team under the leadership of the pastor.

Change, however, is inherently threatening, so take time to assure each person that you will lead with grace as well as with strength.

What do you do if some key deacons are against you?

We despise church politics, but they're a reality. Take time early in the planning process to communicate openly with key deacons to let them know their hopes and fears are important to you. As much as possible, involve them in meaningful ministry opportunities. The war with deacons is often lost over the administrative battle of who is going to "run" the church. Let me offer two suggestions: First, select wisely to prevent many of these kinds of leadership problems. Choose people who are committed to the lordship of Christ and to the welfare of the church. Outline the biblical requirements of servant-leadership, and expect them to grow in their faith as they serve in their ministry responsibilities. Second, gain their respect through your personal integrity, and as their pastor, maintain a balance between service and authority. As a pastor serves selflessly, he teaches that authority is not a position from which he demands compliance.

The planning process can cultivate ownership and enthusiasm among deacons and other leaders. Try to include them and utilize their gifts and experience in order to maximize the effectiveness of the body's ministry. After you involve them, encourage them, and reason with them, if some still oppose you, consider a personal conference with them, possibly including some of the loyal deacons.

What do you do if seniors don't want change?

Seniors are often the segment of the body most resistant to change, but they can be one of your greatest allies if you enlist them as a vital part of planning. Seniors in your church want to be understood, so take time to talk, to listen, to allay their fears. Let them know that you value the traditions of the church as well as their prayers and support.

They can experience great fulfillment (and indeed, I believe the greatest possible sense of fulfillment) if they see themselves as fully functioning members of a team under the leadership of the pastor.

Try to include them and utilize their gifts and experience in order to maximize the effectiveness of the body's ministry.

Let them know that you value the traditions of the church as well as their prayers and support.

I also advise you to take your leaders on retreats to build a team spirit and a common vision. Jesus did that, and you can, too.

Many of them want assurance that the senior pastor is *their* pastor. They have invested their lives in the church, and they expect (and sometimes demand) attention and time from the senior pastor. During the planning process, make a special effort to ask their opinions about programs and events they care about. Listen patiently, and answer their questions as fully as possible. Some of them may be very cranky, but don't take their criticism personally. Be positive and enthusiastic, and be sure to thank them for asking questions and being a significant part of the church's life.

What do you do if the demands of pastoring distract you from God's vision?

This is a problem for all of us. We need to prioritize and not allow the urgent to overwhelm the important. Carve out time each week to think, to reflect, and to dream God's dreams. That isn't time wasted! I also advise you to take your leaders on retreats to build a team spirit and a common vision. Jesus did that, and you can, too.

Balance is a difficult commodity, and frankly, it doesn't look the same for all of us. Still, be sure you are feeding your own soul and keeping your family life strong. Some people will expect you to be everywhere there is a need and meet with everyone who wants your time, in addition to preaching a great sermon week after week. Remember, you are accountable first to God, not to people. If you find yourself squeezed between the numerous demands (as all pastors are), the solution is not just to work harder. A better solution is to make leadership development more of a priority so there are more people involved in caring for the needs of the body.

What do you do if the money dries up?

Fluctuations in giving occur during each year, so let your projections reflect those changing conditions. Your vision should be expressed in both anticipated and actual giving. People generally give to projects and missions that grab their hearts, so be sure to share your enthusiasm often about the vision God has given you. Proper planning should always allow for mid-course corrections, most of which deal, in large measure, with finances.

I encourage you to do two things: teach the principles of good stewardship as an integral part of walking with God, and share special needs and successes with the congregation. Many churches preach about the need to give only when the finances are low. That, I believe, is a big mistake. It is much more effective to teach the principles of stewardship (time, talent, and treasure) in many different ways and in many different settings, as a part of the lordship of Christ over our lives. Bible study classes, seminars and workshops, small groups, and the worship service are all places where people can learn that all we have is the Lord's. Secondly, I believe people get excited to give when they are gripped with the need and they see God use their money to change lives. When you talk about giving, share the specific needs different ministries have, how God is meeting those needs, and how God is using those ministries to effect real change in people. People give when they have a vision, so enflame their vision!

What do you do if a staff or lay leader doesn't have the skills or heart to fulfill the vision?

After communicating your vision, listening carefully, and affirming various roles, if one of your leaders still isn't on board, it is time to sit down with that person to have an honest talk. You need to find out if the problem is rooted in the heart or the head.

I've known some staff and lay leaders who genuinely wanted to serve in a certain capacity, but they lacked the skills. In that case, we can either get them the training they need or reassign them to more suitable roles. The other problem, one of the heart, is much more difficult. Try to get below the surface problem of job performance and talk about the person's calling, his fears, and his hopes. Ask him to describe times when he has felt motivated and creative in his ministry, and try to determine what is different now. In most cases, unresolved bitterness and fears of failure cloud the person's thinking and leave him apathetic and obstinate. Affirm your love for him, support him in his struggle, and chart a course of encouragement and counseling that will help him with his core difficulties. In many cases, the pastor of an unmotivated ministry leader assumes the person is angry with him, but that is usually not the case. The problem often resides in past experiences that rear their ugly heads in his current role.

What do you do if growth projections are questioned?

This is not a matter of *if*, but *when*. You can be sure that some people will wonder if you are on target with your assumptions. Bring influential leaders into the process at each point to give input, as well as to validate the projections. Make sure you are patient with others' questions and confident of

I encourage you to do two things: teach the principles of good stewardship as an integral part of walking with God, and share special needs and successes with the congregation.

You need to find out if the problem is rooted in the heart or the head.

God's leading, then explain how you arrived at your conclusions. Let God do the rest.

Bold, confident, visionary leaders are often annoyed when others question them. More detailed, precise, cautious leaders feel threatened and wonder if they failed to think things through enough. Know yourself, complete your preparation, and anticipate tough questions.

What do you do if your assumptions don't prove true?

Sometimes we simply make mistakes. (Hopefully, the mistakes we make are not in direction but in the details.) We may have misunderstood God's leading, or we may have failed to anticipate change in the demographics of the community. Maybe a crisis in church leadership thwarts growth. Be honest about the facts, and make appropriate changes if you see patterns emerging. Plan B may be from God, and indeed, it may be better than Plan A.

What do you do if God works miracles?

Change, even positive change, creates problems and opportunities for personal growth. As we see God work to fulfill our vision, we will need to be flexible in regard to our leadership styles. We may need to find more time to pray and spend more time in leadership development than ever before. The normal schedule of personally doing a lot of the ministry activities may need to be altered to create more time to oversee others doing those activities.

The church members and leaders, too, will have to make some adjustments. Talk to pastors of other churches which are growing, and become a student of how God worked in their situations. Learn from others, and keep listening to God. Don't let success by-pass your heart and go to your head!

As we see God work to fulfill our vision, we will need to be flexible in regard to our leadership styles.

AFFIRMATION AND CELEBRATION

One of the most endearing and powerful leadership traits is the ability to give credit to others. Genuine encouragement and appreciation is the lubricant of families, churches, and any other organization, so make a habit of pointing out jobs well done and character qualities like integrity and honesty. Many high-profile leaders have the ability to motivate the masses, but they fail in personal relationships. You might find that the law of sowing and reaping takes place here, too. Affirming others eventually yields kindness in return.

Sagemont Church in Houston regularly schedules appreciation dinners for ministries in the church. They cater a wonderful meal for every person involved in that ministry, complete with table cloths and waiters. The pastors share their heart-felt thanks for each person. Stories of God's work in and through that ministry honor the Lord and encourage every person there. And they have a blast!

Most churches, and indeed, most pastors, don't do a very good job of showing appreciation. Perhaps we feel so much pressure ourselves that we focus on failures and needs instead of successes and joys. Make it a point to be a leader who is known for affirming others.

As you watch God work in individuals' lives and in the congregation at large, celebrate often God's grace and power. Learn to look for God's hand in the small things as well as the visionary plans and events. Be quick to give Him credit for His gracious work. Grumbling is contagious, but so are thanksgiving and praise. Let your life and your church be known for affirmation and celebration.

As you watch God work in individuals' lives and in the congregation at large, celebrate often God's grace and power.

At the end of this chapter, you will find this exercise:

— Monthly Planning Worksheet.

TAKE A STEP

MONTHLY PLANNING WORKSHEET

— *Who?:* The pastor, the staff, and the ministry leaders.

— *Why?:* To stay on track with the vision.

— *How?:* Each month the pastor, his staff, and the ministry leaders can do a brief analysis of their programs and leaders to be sure everybody is working together toward the common vision.

— ***Then what?:*** The monthly plans will keep your team sharp and consistently assessing how to be more effective in advancing the Kingdom of God. This habit will make yearly and long-range planning much easier to accomplish.

MONTHLY PLANNING WORKSHEET

1. Review your overall purpose and vision. How are these being accomplished in your church? How do you see God at work in your church (leadership, evangelism, events, missions, youth, etc.)?

    — How can you celebrate these blessings and show appreciation to those involved?

2. What setbacks, blockages or delays have you encountered?

    — What do you need to do about them?

3. Look at your yearly calendar. What seasonal plans need to be addressed this month?

4. Review your goals from last month in each area of ministry. How well did you accomplish the specific action plans?

    — Which goals will be carried over to this month?

5. Review the ministries of the church, and evaluate their effectiveness.

6. How are you doing personally? How is your family? What is your motivation/burn-out level? What do you need in order to experience more of God's grace and strength?

7. Whom do you need to contact to make adjustments, give encouragement, get information, etc.? When? How?

RESOURCES FROM THE ASSOCIATE, INC.

The Associate, Inc. was established to equip pastors in practical leadership skills. Today there is little, if any, training available which is designed to address the very demanding day-to-day activities of pastoral leadership. The Associate provides products and services to complement the pastor's Bible School and seminary education and to refine his vision into strategic steps of implementation. Biblical principles and procedures maximize the potential of the pastor and church through God-directed planning and organizational development. The resulting annual and long-range plans become tools for effective decision-making, leadership development, and communication.

Our products and services include books, workshops, and consulting services. To find out more about these, call (901) 482-3324 or go to www.theassociate.org.

The Associate has a partnership with Next Level Leadership Network, the leadership development arm of the North American Mission Board of the Southern Baptist Convention, to certify trainers in *Mastering the Mystery of Visionary Leadership* and *The Next Step.* To learn about becoming a trainer or scheduling a workshop in your area, call (770) 410-6597 or go to www.nextlevelleadership.com.

Find Us at www.TheAssociate.org

Our web site is designed to provide a vast array of resources to help you fulfill the vision God has given you. Go to our site and you will find:
— regularly updated articles about vision and planning
— an archive of past articles
— resources you can purchase
— forms you can download
— a community forum where you can ask pertinent questions
   and get answers from those who have seen success
— a schedule of events on vision and planning
— information about The Associate's consulting services

For More Copies of **The Next Step**
You can purchase more copies of this book so each person on your planning team, and perhaps, every ministry leader can have one.

Price: $25 each
Quantity discount:
    5 to 10 copies, $22 each
    11 to 20 copies, $19 each
To order, call (901) 482-3324 or go to our website.

To order the DISC Personal Profile System
Many individuals and groups benefit from using the DISC Personal Profile System. For information about how you can order this tool for personal encouragement, strengthening communication skills, or team building, go to this web address:
    http://www.personalizedsuccessstrategies.com

Consulting Services
Many pastors want practical answers to their specific questions pertaining to staff development, planning, growth, new construction, and a host of other topics. The Associate's consultants are skilled in helping pastors and their churches find solutions to help them grow. Objective analysis, genuine encouragement, and godly wisdom are the essential elements of our consulting services.

Here's what some pastors have said about Bob Sorrell and The Associate's consulting services:

"Bob Sorrell presents a big-picture look for your church, all in the context of a deep spiritual relationship full of faith and grace. The result is that he can lead you and your church into a ministry that will pursue the impossible!"

— *Dr. Ronnie W. Floyd*
    First Baptist Church
    Springdale, Arkansas

"Thanks for your ministry to our churches and pastors in Nicaragua. Your seminars on church administration helped us lead our ministries more effectively. For many years we have prayed for this kind of teaching."

— *Rev. Walt E. Morgan*
Executive Director
Baptist Convention
Managua, Nicaragua

"Rare indeed is the church that can find a man with a Pastor's heart, a Servant's hands, and an Administrator's head, but that is exactly what you find in Bob Sorrell. He is a gifted man who loves shepherds greatly and the Chief Shepherd more. Currently Bob is consulting with us in the reorganization of our Staff and in the administration of a $50 million phase one building project. It is without reservation that I wholeheartedly recommend him to you."

— *Ken Whitten*
Senior Pastor
Idlewild Baptist Church
Tampa, Florida

"We had purchased land, sold our facility, and relocated. Our ministries and attendance had doubled but we were struggling getting through the 1000 barrier. Bob Sorrell helped me look at self, staff, and total situation. We have, together, developed a ministry organization plan that really streamlines our ministries and should allow us to break through the difficult barrier we face. The Associate is committed to personalized master planning. Bob provided the leadership, encouragement and guidance I needed and I totally recommend the ministry of this experienced and gifted brother."

— *Gary Watkins*
First Baptist Church
Collierville, Tennessee

ABOUT THE AUTHOR

Bob Sorrell has spent the last 40 years defining and developing values in the workplace and virtues in relationships. For 21 years as Associate Pastor for the 27,000 member Bellevue Baptist Church, pastored by Adrian Rogers, his ministerial and administrative responsibility was the direction of the entire program and staff. During this time he also counseled scores of pastors, consulted with numerous churches, and conducted many church leadership retreats. His service outside his church included various denominational committee assignments, including the Executive Committee of the Southern Baptist Convention.

Prior to his call into the ministry, Bob served in engineering, manufacturing, and corporate management for 21 years as a Christian layman. At the same time, he served three churches, from the very small to the very large, as a lay leader including Chairman of Deacons for each. The combination of these experiences has provided Bob with a unique ability to apply biblical truth and spiritually sensitive, but clearly focused, administrative practices for the full range of churches, from the new church plant to the mega-church. The practical "how-to's" have been the trademark of his ministry and are captured in this book. Bob's previous work, *Mastering the Mystery of Visionary Leadership*, is being used to certify men to conduct pastor's conferences across the nation. He is currently the president of The Associate, Inc., which assists pastors and churches in vision and planning.

Bob and his wife, Buna have enjoyed 41 years of marriage. Their family includes one daughter, LeAnn, her husband, Mark, and two grandsons, Joshua and Joseph.